WAKE UP, AMERICA!

WORLD WAR I
AND
THE AMERICAN POSTER

WAKE UP, AMERICA !

CIVILIZATION CALLS
EVERY MAN WOMAN AND CHILD !

MAYOR'S COMMITTEE 50 EAST 42ND ST

WAKE UP, AMERICA!

WORLD WAR I
AND
THE AMERICAN POSTER

BY WALTON RAWLS

FOREWORD BY MAURICE RICKARDS

ABBEVILLE PRESS PUBLISHERS · NEW YORK

FRONTISPIECE:
JAMES MONTGOMERY FLAGG
Wake Up, America!, 1917
27 × 42 inches
Susan E. Meyer

EDITOR: **Alan Axelrod**
DESIGNER: **Nai Chang**
COPY CHIEF: **Robin James**
PRODUCTION SUPERVISOR: **Hope Koturo**

Library of Congress Cataloging-in-Publication Data
Rawls, Walton H.
  Wake up, America!

  Bibliography: p.
  Includes index.
  1. World War, 1914–1918—Posters. 2. Political
posters, American. I. Title.
D522.25.R38 1988   940.3'022'2   88-14638
ISBN 0-89659-888-8

CONTENTS

WAKE UP, AMERICA!

FOREWORD

As we move toward the turn of the century, the First World War recedes—ever more rapidly, it seems—into the haze of history. Our personal links with the war, embodied in the thinning ranks of its survivors, grow daily more tenuous. For the true flavor of the period we turn increasingly to other forms of record, to the diaries and papers of the rank and file, the memoirs of generals and public figures, and the printed ephemera of the time.

It is in ephemera—the "transient minor documents of everyday life"—that society leaves a special record, a record often more revealing than its formal histories. And among the whole range of printed ephemera, the most graphic and commanding is the poster.

With its unique capacity to express much in little, the poster has an important place in visual history. It is not for nothing that the social historian has latched on to it as an evidential document; not for nothing that the literature of the poster continues to grow. Nor is it surprising that a predominantly picture-oriented readership should find the poster's image as powerful as the written page.

Thus, in the last few decades, we have seen a plethora of poster books, gatherings of posters on the theme of this, that, and the other—war, revolution, the *Belle Epoque,* the circus, whatever you wish—each presented as a succession of self-explanatory visual knock-outs.

It has taken Walton Rawls, however, to realize that they are not all necessarily self-explanatory—in the matter of those of World War I, not by any means. As 1914–18 fades, together with its background detail, each individual message gets more difficult to read; in some cases it actually may be unintelligible.

Rawls reminds us that, as with every other category of ephemera, the item itself is not enough; from somewhere must come informed interpretation. It is on interpretation that this book sets its sights.

As every connoisseur knows, the poster is not a decoration. It is an instrument of persuasion—a fine-tuned means to a specific end. Its merit is to be appraised in the long run only on performance. Does it effectively carry out the mission assigned to it? Is it geared to its chosen audience, to the climate of its time, to the conditions in which it will be seen—to the challenge of competitors?

The poster cannot be assessed as just a design, a pleasing display of mass and color, an aesthetic experience. It must be viewed as a mechanism.

Too often we hear opinions *in vacuo,* in which the poster's graphic technique is seen to take precedence over its message. ("I don't know what it actually *means,*" says an enthusiast confronted by a foreign-language specimen, "but it's a *marvelous* poster. . . .")

Clearly this monoptic view of the poster is untenable, and Rawls has done much to correct it. Rejecting the temptation to analyze its graphics, its aesthetics, and its "gallery value," he sets the whole thing in sociohistorical perspective.

The study of the posters of the First World War is no idle matter. The war was our first serious exercise in mechanized mass destruction. Few were aware of it at the time, but we now see that it marked a new and terrifying phase in human affairs. The years that have followed have merely built on that beginning.

In 1914 most of the rank and file went into it starry-eyed. For the Europeans on both sides of the line, it was seen as part of the natural order of things—just another war to add to the dates in the history books. But it was not that. It was a world-size all-time trap. And we are not out of it yet.

By the time the United States joined in, Europe's innocence had been shot to pieces. America's was more or less fresh. In the posters of the period we see the apparent simplicity of it all: the New World turnaround from innocent neutrality to innocent all-out war—the mechanism of mass conversion. *Wake Up, America!*—Flagg's poster and Rawls's title piece—epitomizes a key historic process.

It has been said that history teaches that history teaches nothing. In this book, in this particular historical context, Rawls gives us a chance to take a second, deeper look.

JOSEPH CHRISTIAN LEYENDECKER
Order Coal Now, ca. 1918
20 × 29½ inches
Walton Rawls

MAURICE RICKARDS
London, May 1988

Save the products of the Land

Eat more fish —
they feed themselves.

UNITED STATES FOOD ADMINISTRATION

INTRODUCTION

What is one to make of a poster that shows a plump, happy child (naked except for socks and new sandals) perched on air beside Liberty's torch and beneath the rubric "Save your Child from Autocracy and Poverty"; or, a lovely young lady in nightdress, a baby in her arms, floating lifeless at the bottom of the sea next to the lone word "Enlist"; or, beautifully rendered fish swimming languidly among underwater growth, with the not-intentionally funny legend "Eat more fish—they feed themselves"? Like many another poster of World War I, done by the period's best-known illustrators, they are instantly fascinating and obviously praiseworthy for artistic merit, but their full intent (both in word and image) can sometimes baffle a late-twentieth-century viewer.

The purpose of these government-sponsored works of art was to communicate essential information rapidly and efficiently (in an era that preceded radio broadcasting); and from all accounts these posters succeeded admirably in conveying the right message to their intended audience; however, to us, decades later, the entire significance of some of the posters may no longer come through so clearly. To aid our understanding of America's World War I posters, this volume is designed not simply to collect and illustrate some of the best examples from all aspects of the war effort but to provide guidance into the social, political, and historical context in which these posters commendably performed their patriotic duty.

For many World War I posters to speak to us now requires an effort on our part to be more responsive to the spirit of that period—which one congressman characterized as a dominant faith in America as God's "chosen nation to finally lead in the regeneration of the world." A noble mission, that, but certainly far remote from current thinking on American foreign policy. It now seems that, in many ways, citizens of the World War I era are about as distant intellectually from post-Vietnam Americans as are the knights of King Arthur's Round Table. Indeed, it was to these very knights that the young men who went off to fly

HERBERT ANDREW PAUS
Save Your Child from Autocracy and Poverty, 1918
20 × 29¾ inches
Museum of the City of New York

CHARLES LIVINGSTON BULL
Save the Products of the Land, ca. 1918
20 × 29½ inches
Museum of the City of New York

for France (long before America entered the war) often compared themselves—observing in aerial combat a code of chivalry that Sir Lancelot might not have found wanting.

Initially, we will be concerned with examining the great dilemma faced by peace-loving, traditionally xenophobic Americans when the very survival of freedom and democracy in faraway Europe was threatened by sinister forces of autocratic militarism. Subsequently—once the dilemma was resolved in a declaration of war on Germany—we will investigate some of this country's more interesting domestic pursuits related to her rapid national mobilization. Our special focus will be on the poster's role in this mobilization, for it was on the main streets of Home Front America that these posters did their job so effectively.

It is necessary to begin this story in prewar Europe—the Old (and outmoded) World in America's eyes—to understand what this country thought it was fighting against "to make the world safe for democracy." Periodically the narrative will travel to the Western Front to examine the exploits of representative Americans in the "war to end all wars": those who ventured to Europe while their country was still a neutral nation—driving ambulances on the battlefield to save endangered lives, enlisting in the Foreign Legion to preserve French culture, flying in the Lafayette Escadrille to stop the barbarous Hun—as well as those who later fought "over there" under Black Jack Pershing and Billy Mitchell when their homeland could no longer keep out of the European conflict. Nonetheless, our underlying concern is to survey the American poster as a dramatic and representative icon of its period: to examine the various patriotic and informational chores it undertook in the war effort, to tell how its creation and production were developed into a fine art, who many of the artists were, and also to give some background information on the several masters the poster served—from enlistment to Liberty Bonds to food conservation to appeals for aid to war-devastated European communities.

A POSTER'S FUNCTION

America printed more than twenty million copies of perhaps twenty-five hundred posters in support of the war effort, more posters than all the other belligerents combined. As artist Joseph Pennell noted in a small book telling how he created a very famous Liberty Loan poster: "When the United States wished to make public its wants, whether of men or money, it found that art—as the European countries had found—was the best medium." Indeed, there were European prototypes for several American posters, including the most famous one of all: James Montgomery Flagg's self-portrait as Uncle Sam *pointedly* saying, "I Want You." Earlier, in 1914, British illustrator Alfred Leete had produced a design for the Parliamentary Recruiting Committee showing Lord Kitchener, secretary of state for war, pointing a finger at the viewer and saying, "Your Country Needs YOU." The concept was simple and direct, the way a poster must be to function effectively, and it was copied by other countries as well. No less an authority than Adolf Hitler, a corporal in the First World War and a sometime artist, admired the simplicity of British and American posters and found them more popularly compelling than the sophisticated variety produced in Germany. Later he wrote in *Mein Kampf*: "All effective propaganda must be confined to a few bare essentials, and those must be expressed as far as possible in stereotyped formulas."

These stereotyped formulas—since posters were intended to sway a mass audience—were aimed at eliciting, among other emotions, patriotism, sacrifice, outrage, and hatred. To be effective, to be believed, a poster's message had to play upon broad ideas and feelings already current. After what the newspapers described as the "Rape of Little Belgium" in 1914, the German soldier was routinely pictured by the Allies as his savage ancestor the Hun, and sometimes as a more remote forebear, the subhuman ape—two ravaging creatures (at least in popular mythology) easy to hate. As Sir Arthur Conan Doyle reminded readers of the London *Times*, "Hate has its uses in war. . . . It steels the mind and sets the resolution as no other emotion can do. The bestiality of the German nation has given us driving power. . . . We have to win and we can only win by

ALFRED LEETE
Your Country Needs You, 1914
19⅞ × 29½ inches
Imperial War Museum
The original painting.

JAMES MONTGOMERY FLAGG
First Call, ca. 1917
21 × 11 inches
Miscellaneous Man

JAMES MONTGOMERY FLAGG
I Want You, 1917
30 × 40 inches
Museum of the City of New York

ANONYMOUS
Buy Your Victory Bonds, 1917
39 × 55 inches
George M. Dembo
A Canadian variant.

keeping up the spirit and resolution of our own people.''

Harry A. Garfield, head of the wartime United States Fuel Administration, said, ''I can get authority to write a column or a page about fuel—but I cannot make everybody or even anybody read it. But if I can get a striking drawing with or without a legend of a few lines, everyone who runs by must see it.'' In commenting on this, Joseph Pennell wrote: ''That is the whole secret of the appeal of the poster—and by the poster the governments of the world have appealed to the people, who need not know how to read in order to understand, if the design is effective and explanatory.'' He went on to say, ''Again artists are working with and for the government of their country, again they are at work for the people, at work which the people can understand, for if they cannot it is worthless.''

THE DESIGN AND PRINTING OF POSTERS

The posters illustrated in this book all date from a period of less than five years, 1914 to 1919, and the majority of American posters fall within an even shorter time span—the twenty months that the United States was in the war. Although we would have to call the genre propaganda art (one artist said, ''The poster should be to the eye what a command is to the ear''), these works fall more comfortably into the tradition of commercial advertising, which goes back to the fifteenth or sixteenth century in Europe, when attractive printed handbills were posted where they could be seen in passing.

Many of the posters of World War I are authentic lithographs, in the grand tradition of the poster's turn-of-the-century golden age. Although the technology existed then, most of these posters were not printed in the more modern four-color process, where combinations of color in the original design are first photographically ''separated,'' using filters, into four primary inking colors. To print lithographs, many colors are applied to the paper one at a time from inked printing ''stones,'' in solids and patterns planned by the artist or lithographer to bring about a desired artistic effect through overlay and blending. In lithography the ink adheres only to marks on a wet stone made by a greasy crayon, a printing technique discovered in the late eighteenth century. Through most of the nineteenth century, lithography had been used as a way of *reproducing* works of art—or menus, labels, and letterheads—rather than as an artist's medium for original creations. There were exceptions, of course: notably in the monochromatic prints of such artists as Goya and Daumier earlier in the century, and in the book illustrations of Grandville and Gavarni.

In the first decades of lithography, when color was desired, it was applied by hand (or stencil) to the black-ink print pulled directly from the lithography stone. Gradually the lithographer determined that by adding colored ink to just certain parts of the same stone he could fill in broad areas of the print with a second color—for example, a blue sky, in which cloud effects could be achieved by leaving areas of the stone free of the litho grease. Eventually, additional stones were prepared for all the other hues needed for a full-color effect. This process came to be known as chromolithography, and in some cases as many as twenty or so different stones were used to create one print. Again, this was a process essentially devoted to *reproducing* works of art. The result, even when it was used as an advertisement, was generally no larger than a print.

To be sure, there already were—from the middle of the nineteenth century on—large, colorful advertisements and posters. One has only to look to the American circus tradition for these—and, in terms of techniques for catching the public's eye, that is probably where the modern advertising poster had its beginnings. But the early circus posters were primarily woodblock prints, pieced together from smaller sections, or sheets, to create huge, colorful displays often overloaded (by today's standards) with images and words.

For a more direct antecedent of the World War I poster (at least in terms of concept), one has to look to France, to the beginnings of the so-called art poster—and particularly to the work of one man: Jules Chéret. Chéret was a commercial lithographer and also a trained artist, so when he had a poster to make he was able to draw directly onto the printing stone, as other artists were doing for book illustrations or original prints. Unlike other printers, who translated someone else's work onto the stone, Chéret used lithography as a creative medium. During the time he served his apprenticeship as a lithographer, he also studied painting at the Paris École des Beaux-Arts. Influenced both by book illustration and mural painting, Chéret introduced to commercial advertising the colors and designs of the fine arts—but on a fresh, new scale for lithographed posters, that of the mural. In the 1860s he had gone to London to study advancements in color lithography and had first encountered the spectacular woodblock posters of touring American circuses. He also traveled to Venice where he discovered the ceilings and murals of his ''god,'' Tiepolo. Upon his return to Paris, Chéret secured his first poster commissions from owners of theaters and cabarets. In the last quarter of the nineteenth century he created more than a thousand exuberant and colorful posters, which revolutionized the very look of weathered Paris boulevards (Manet called Chéret ''the Watteau of the streets'').

In 1889 Chéret was awarded the Legion of Honor

JULES CHÉRET
Festival of Flowers, 1890
33 × 48¼ inches
Posters Please, Inc., New York

for "creating a new branch of art"; by then his dramatic influence on postermaking already had spread through Europe's ateliers and printshops. This burst of vitality in the commercial arts did not go unnoticed by other artists or the general public. Posters were mounted side by side with oils at exhibitions, and the first great boom in poster collecting was well under way. In the streets, the most spectacular posters were so quickly stolen that printers were obliged to issue special editions for these eager collectors—to reassure advertisers that posters paid for would definitely be seen by the public.

In the final decade of the nineteenth century, two French painters entering the poster scene were to epitomize the major directions in Europe of this commercial "branch of art" right up to the beginnings of World War I. Eugène Grasset was the first artist to introduce to advertising the languorous female beauty with free-flowing hair provocatively posed with a product amidst stylized and intertwined flora. His beautifully drawn work launched an Art Nouveau trend in poster art that reached a climax in the complex and convoluted renderings of Alphonse Mucha, perhaps best known for advertising the ap-

EUGÈNE GRASSET
Abricotine, ca. 1905
40 × 29 inches
Posters Please, Inc., New York

ALPHONSE MUCHA
Salon des Cent, 1896
17 × 25¼ inches
Posters Please, Inc., New York

HENRI DE TOULOUSE-LAUTREC
Reine de Joie, 1892
37 × 53½ inches
Posters Please, Inc., New York

pearances of actress Sarah Bernhardt. Another direction was suggested by the work of Henri de Toulouse-Lautrec, who, inspired by Pierre Bonnard's poster for France-Champagne, offered to draw one for the Moulin Rouge, a popular cabaret he frequented on boulevard de Clichy. Although this was perhaps the first oversize lithograph Lautrec worked on, it pointed a new way for the poster—that of simplified large forms bereft of detail and presented in the flat colors of the Japanese print, then in high fashion among European artists.

Americans saw these two styles directly (Grasset and Lautrec created covers and posters for *Harper's* and *The Century*) and indirectly through the work of others, including British artist Aubrey Beardsley, who combined elements of both in a highly individualized fashion. His illustrations for books, such as Oscar Wilde's *Salomé*, and for literary quarterlies, such as *The Yellow Book* and *The Savoy*, quickly caught the eye of some Americans and influenced (among others) Will Bradley and Edward Penfield, two of the country's most promising poster artists. This influence showed itself less in subject matter than in its call for simplification, where narrative content was subsumed in bold forms shown without distractions or nonessentials, and where shapes were

AUBREY BEARDSLEY
The Yellow Book, April 1894
6⅛ × 9½ inches
Victoria and Albert Museum

LUDWIG HOHLWEIN
Café Odeon, 1908
35⅝ × 47⅜ inches
Posters Please, Inc., New York

THE BEGGARSTAFFS
Harper's, 1895
78¼ × 86⅜ inches
Victoria and Albert Museum

LUCIAN BERNHARD
Manoli, 1915
37¾ × 27¾ inches
Merrill C. Berman

created as flat colors (with or without outlines) or by patterns unaffected by hints of a third dimension. The ideal came to be a single dominant image that took on the resonance of a symbol, something intended to be quickly perceived rather than pondered. (Wilde himself had pointed out that "art is at once surface and symbol.") This idea, best seen in the work of Ludwig Hohlwein and Lucian Bernhard in Germany and that of the Beggarstaffs in England, was without precedent in American advertising posters (which long had essayed verisimilitude) and did not by any means sway all advertisers or artists.

THE ARTIST AND ILLUSTRATOR IN AMERICA

In the first decade of the twentieth century, the finest in American art and literature was popularly thought to be found in the many illustrated magazines that had blossomed in step with advances in printing technology (more than fifty magazines had a circulation in excess of one hundred thousand). And posters of a new kind in America, by Bradley, Penfield, and Maxfield Parrish, began to appear at newsstands and in bookshop windows in support of such hightone literary periodicals as *Scribner's*, *Harper's*, *Lippincott's*, *The Century*, and *The Chap-Book*. These posters did not fail to attract the literate public, or others taken with their graphics, and one critic quipped that "editions of posters surpass in number and in demand editions of the reviews themselves." However, the larger-circulation magazines depended less on posters. *Collier's*, for instance, was featuring the more traditional work of illustrators Frederic Remington, Charles Dana Gibson, and John Sloan (as well as Penfield and Parrish); and J. C. Leyendecker had begun his long series of distinctive covers for *Saturday Evening Post*, which by 1913 was boasting "more than two million a week"—a world record circulation. This was also a great period for the illustrated book. Remington had done detailed western scenes for the works of Owen Wister, Francis Parkman, and Theodore Roosevelt, among others; and Howard Pyle, Edwin Austin Abbey, Arthur Bur-

EDWARD PENFIELD
Harper's, May 1896
11⅞ × 17¾ inches
Posters Please, Inc., New York

WILL H. BRADLEY
Bradley His Book, 1896
27 × 39⅞ inches
Posters Please, Inc., New York

COLES PHILLIPS
Light Consumes Coal, ca. 1918
20½ × 28 inches
George M. Dembo

PETER BEHRENS
General Electric Company, 1907
20¾ × 26⅝ inches
Merrill C. Berman

dett Frost, N. C. Wyeth, Maxfield Parrish, and Jessie Willcox Smith were creating wonderfully evocative images for children's classics that would forever capture in youthful minds the look of many an imaginary hero and villain.

While for many critics the first decades of this century may not have been quite a golden age for the poster in America, the period was certainly the golden age of the illustrator. Gibson, Flagg, the Leyendecker brothers, and Howard Chandler Christy were not only among the best paid of all Americans but among the best known and most admired. Their work was instantly recognizable from regular association in books and magazines with the country's most popular writers (Flagg, for instance, illustrated the stories of P. G. Wodehouse, Sinclair Lewis, and Booth Tarkington for *Cosmopolitan*, and the Gibson Girl and Leyendecker's Arrow Collar Man were such icons of popular culture that they attracted love letters by the hundreds.

In the work of the majority of American artists who contributed posters to the war effort, there is little evidence of direct inspiration from European precedents; Americans were more responsive to a home-grown tradition. However, Adolph Treidler can be seen to echo the German master Hohlwein in his *Collier's* covers, where flat-patterned coat fabrics shape the outlines of figures without reflecting the forms they cover; and Coles Phillips seems to have been aware of the work of the Beggarstaffs in his development of the ''Fadeaway Girl,'' where the background so exactly matches the color or texture of the girl's costume that only certain of her attractive features stand out. In his poster ''Light Consumes Coal,'' Phillips sets a flat bulb shape against a stylized pattern of vines within a circle, a treatment similar to one conceived by Peter Behrens in 1907 for A.E.G., the German General Electric Company. For J. C. Leyendecker, European posters were definitely first-hand encounters when he studied in Paris at Académie Julian. In August, 1896, a cover he did for *The Century* (''First Prize, Century Poster Contest'') was almost pure Art Nouveau: a voluptuous lady is shown in a diaphanous gown with poppies at her temples and in her hair at the ends of locks fanned out around her head. In another few years this alien influence was far behind Leyendecker; his own inimitable style had been formed for the rest of his career.

For other poster artists of World War I, who were mostly trained in America, exposure to (or interest in) foreign influences was relatively rare and indirect in the first decade of this century. New European movements such as Cubism, Fauvism, Expressionism, Dadaism, and abstract art were practically unheard of on Main Street America. The country's better-known painters, such as William Merritt Chase, Childe Hassam, J. Alden Weir, John Twachtman, and Maurice Prendergast, were still under the sway of their earlier exposure to French Impressionism. Book

JOSEPH CHRISTIAN LEYENDECKER
The Century, August 1896
16 × 21½ inches
Illustration House

and in 1913 the famous Armory Show had caused a stir among sophisticated Americans both pro and con modernist art. Theodore Roosevelt, who later seemed in many ways to have characterized the age, reviewed the Armory Show for *The Outlook* and concluded that "the lunatic fringe was fully in evidence, especially in the rooms devoted to the Cubists and the Futurists, or near-Impressionists." America, in general, had little respect for the Old World's autocratic institutions or any inclination to ape the alien fads of Europe's bohemian, anarchistic artists. Royal Cortissoz, the prominent art critic of the *New York Herald* put it this way: "The United States is invaded by aliens, thousands of whom constitute so many perils to the health of the body politic. Modernism is of precisely the same heterogeneous alien origin and is imperiling the republic of art in the same way."

Given the country's outright suspicion of foreign ideas, her attitude toward the avant-garde, and the background and character of the artists enlisted to produce most of the government's "pictorial publicity" in World War I, it would have seemed un-American if all of these posters had been seen to follow the lead of Europe's art posters. Perhaps because mostly they did not, very few of these dramatic works have been included in histories of the poster—and usually it is the same three or four examples. No doubt other reasons may be responsible for the disregard of many spectacular World War I posters (commerce may seem less distasteful to some critics than patriotism), but there has been little effort, except among collectors, to explore this genre in breadth or depth. In an essay on the history of posters in the Museum of Modern Art's catalog *Word and Image*, one writer dismisses them by saying that the "use of styles thought to be popular with the general public and the temptation to say too much and show too little killed the majority of war posters." Well, if for some art historians the majority of American World War I posters seem to have been "killed" by such misjudgments of their creators, they certainly did not meet their deaths without first handsomely accomplishing their primary mission. Admittedly this is not the first criterion for inclusion in a history, but many a beautiful poster from this genre lies unknown and unappreciated in collections all across the country.

and magazine illustrators, however, were more likely to have felt akin to slightly older countrymen like Thomas Eakins and Winslow Homer, who had focused on the American experience in a naturalistic, narrative way that corresponded to an illustrator's need to make a printed story come to life visually. Painters like William Glackens, John Sloan, George Luks, and Everett Shinn (all trained newspaper illustrators) would carry on the slice-of-life narrative genre, but in so realistic a vein that they would be called "Ashcan" painters.

From 1908 on, Alfred Stieglitz had shown European modernists and American independents to New Yorkers in his fifth-floor gallery at 291 Fifth Avenue,

THE POSTER ARTISTS

Except for artists like Penfield, J. C. Leyendecker, Treidler, and Louis Fancher, the majority of contributors to the war effort were not themselves experienced poster designers. Gibson, Flagg, Christy, and numerous others received the training of fine artists but chose to go into illustration—possibly because of financial reasons or so that their talents

would be showcased before a far larger audience. The distinction between artist and illustrator had not then become so rigid, and Flagg went so far as to say that "the only difference between a fine artist and an illustrator is that the latter can draw, eats three square meals a day, and can afford to pay for them." However, Christy was actually obliged to

WE CAN DO NO OTHERWISE

PAINTED BY KENYON COX, N.A.

"THE SWORD IS DRAWN THE NAVY UPHOLDS IT!"

U.S. NAVY RECRUITING STATION

drop out of the painting class of William Merritt Chase when it was learned that he sold work for magazine publication.

There were, to be sure, recognized fine artists among those who produced posters for the war effort—men like Kenyon Cox, Arthur G. Dove, Henry Reuterdahl, Robert J. Wildhack, Edwin H. Blashfield, Joseph Pennell, William Glackens, George Bellows, and Frank E. Schoonover—but most participants were indeed from the ranks of popular magazine and book illustrators. An illustrator's job, according to Flagg, was to ''enter into the spirit of the story and actually know each character'' before picturing a scene. With aims different from those of successful poster designers such as Bradley and Penfield, the illustrator was trained not to simplify and eliminate but to be realistic, detailed, and, above all, evocative. Remington, for instance, was a stickler for accuracy in the details of his work for *Harper's* and *Collier's*; he traveled west regularly to record the variety in dress and weapons of various Indian tribes and the equipment and escapades of the U.S. Cavalry in the field. Along with Christy, Glackens, Reuterdahl, and George Luks, Remington went to Cuba as an artist/

correspondent in the Spanish-American War. Had he not died following an operation in 1909, Remington would certainly have contributed posters to this later war.

Flagg, Christy, and Harrison Fisher, among other illustrators, were also much sought-after portraitists. Their work evoked the sumptuous bravura painting style of the nineteenth century, particularly that of John Singer Sargent, where bold brushwork and build-up of forms through the juxtaposition of rich colors constituted the ideal. Because of their popular success as artists, these men had little reason or inclination to adjust their well-known styles to what others thought more appropriate for poster work. Who is to say that posters of a different sort would have been more effective? At any rate, the simplification of forms and flat patterning so valued by some poster historians is hard to come by in the output of the government's Division of Pictorial Publicity. Except in the case of those who had done this kind of work before, like Penfield, Phillips, and Fred G. Cooper (who seems to have contributed the lone woodcut to the war effort), the artwork in these posters derives mostly from an American tradition

KENYON COX
The Sword Is Drawn,
ca. 1917
28 × 42½ inches
Guernsey's

FRED G. COOPER
America's Tribute to Britain,
ca. 1918
20 × 30 inches
Meehan Military Posters

EVERY GIRL PULLING FOR VICTORY

VICTORY

VICTORY GIRLS
UNITED WAR WORK CAMPAIGN

A leading poster artist supports the war effort.

EDWARD PENFIELD

Every Girl Pulling for Victory, ca. 1918
22½ × 28 inches
Museum of the City of New York

Will You Help the Women of France?, ca. 1917
54 × 36 inches
Museum of the City of New York

Join the United States School Garden Army, ca. 1918
20 × 30 inches
Museum of the City of New York

Yes Sir—I Am Here!, ca. 1918
27 × 40 inches
Museum of the City of New York

Will you help the Women of France?

SAVE WHEAT

They are struggling against starvation and trying to feed not only themselves
and children: but their husbands and sons who are fighting in the trenches.

of narrative, documentary, and historical genre painting. In numerous ways these posters, as posters, are more akin to the spirit and intention of Chéret than to poster designers who came after. Many World War I graphics have Chéret's exuberance and color, and most share his vision of posters as murals. Not content with simply delivering a pitch, these works take on the resonance of paintings begging to be hung. Arguably the most beautiful of them all is J. C. Leyendecker's ''Order Coal Now.'' One could not easily pass this by without making a note to check the coal bin well before winter sets in.

The neglect of these often extraordinary posters in art-historical circles may well stem in part from their not building upon European precedents; there is, however, little doubt that they succeeded in their primary purpose of exhorting the intended strong response from Americans of their period. Making dramatic use of emotion-laden symbols such as the American flag, the Statue of Liberty, and Uncle Sam, these posters served as a call to action when democracy was in peril and reinforced an American's pride in his country, his readiness for sacrifice in her defense, and his innate patriotism.

ANONYMOUS
To the Recruiting Office, ca. 1915
39½ × 15 inches
Maurice Rickards

268 270 KENNINGTON ROAD, LONDON, S.E.

THE

IG OFFICE

I. A PROVENANCE OF CALAMITY

"God has given us on our flank the French, who are the most warlike and turbulent nation that exists, and He has permitted the development in Russia of warlike propensities that until lately did not manifest themselves to the same extent." Thus spoke Chancellor Otto von Bismarck before the Reichstag on February 6, 1888. He went on to express concern that Germany might find herself surrounded by hostile neighbors should another European war break out and that a military alliance between France and Russia would leave the fatherland vulnerable to simultaneous attack on two separate fronts. Partly to counter the putative threat of Russia's belligerency, Germany had earlier formed the Austro-German Alliance of 1879, which pledged, in part: "Should, contrary to the hope and sincere desire of the two high contracting parties, one of the two Empires be attacked by Russia, the high contracting parties bind themselves to come to the assistance of each other with the whole military strength of their empire." If Russia were to attack, Germany would not be forced to fight alone on her eastern flank. In addition, Austria, a country Germany had defeated in the Seven Week War of 1866, would provide a strategic buffer to the southeast, along with Hungary, Austria's partner in the Dual Monarchy. Opposite Germany's North Sea coast was the only other major power—besides France—from whom she might have anything to fear. However, it seemed unlikely that Britain would join Germany's age-old enemy against her in any future conflict, since the kaiser was a grandson of England's Queen Victoria, and France was a republic and not a monarchy. Britain was, as Bismarck later told the Reichstag, "the old traditional ally with whom we have no conflicting interests."

ELLSWORTH YOUNG
Remember Belgium, 1918
20 × 30 inches
Museum of the City of New York

ANONYMOUS
Have You Taken Part in the War Loan?, ca. 1915
39 × 26 inches
Miscellaneous Man

In 1881 Germany and Austria had found it expedient to mollify Russia by secretly reviving with her the League of the Three Emperors, signing an agreement in language similar to the alliance between the first two: "In case one of the high contracting parties should find itself at war with a fourth great power. . . ." Germany then brought Italy into her orbit in May of 1882 through the Triple Alliance, a treaty that further committed the Germans and Austrians to potential military adventure: "If one, or two, of the high contracting parties, without direct provocation on their part, should chance to be attacked and to be engaged in a war with two or more great powers nonsignatory to the present treaty, the 'casus foederis' will arise simultaneously for all the high contracting parties." Naturally, French leaders were disturbed to see a country with whom they shared a border align itself with their old enemy, for France

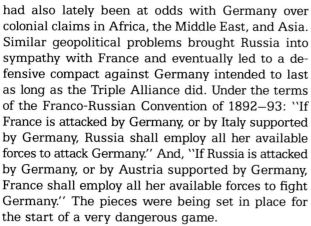

G. CAPRANESI
Subscribe to the Loan, ca. 1917
27 × 41 inches
Miscellaneous Man

A. S.
Subscribe to the 5th Austrian War Loan, 1917
34½ × 47 inches
Miscellaneous Man

had also lately been at odds with Germany over colonial claims in Africa, the Middle East, and Asia. Similar geopolitical problems brought Russia into sympathy with France and eventually led to a defensive compact against Germany intended to last as long as the Triple Alliance did. Under the terms of the Franco-Russian Convention of 1892–93: "If France is attacked by Germany, or by Italy supported by Germany, Russia shall employ all her available forces to attack Germany." And, "If Russia is attacked by Germany, or by Austria supported by Germany, France shall employ all her available forces to fight Germany." The pieces were being set in place for the start of a very dangerous game.

Isolated by the English Channel from direct involvement in Europe's territorial squabbles, Great Britain had been content to remain aloof from political entanglements on the Continent. She had not fielded an army in Europe since the Battle of Waterloo in 1815, and as the world's mightiest seapower her interests stretched far beyond the nearby shores of Europe. "Sea power," according to Sir Eyre Crowe

of Britain's Foreign Office, "is more potent than land power, because it is as pervading as the element in which it moves and has its being. Its formidable character makes itself felt the more directly that a maritime state is, in the literal sense of the word, the neighbour of every country accessible by sea." Britain, however, now looked with dismay at the continuing series of alignments among European nations that left her without committed allies of her own. France was a traditional enemy, so it was not there that she turned first for alliance but to giant Russia, whose fleet was third largest in the world, and whose czar was also one of the English queen's grandsons. Russia was not amenable to an alliance in 1898, so Britain turned to Germany—but with some reluctance since the kaiser supported the Boers' resistance against Britain in South Africa. Colonial Secretary Joseph Chamberlain (father of the future prime minister) reassured his countrymen in a speech in Leicester on November 30, 1898: "I cannot conceive any point which can arise in the immediate future which would bring ourselves and the Germans into

THINK!

ARE YOU CONTENT FOR
HIM TO FIGHT FOR **YOU**?

WON'T YOU DO YOUR BIT?

WE SHALL WIN
BUT **YOU** MUST HELP

JOIN TO-DAY

H. OAKLEY
Think!, ca. 1915
20 × 25 inches
Maurice Rickards

ANONYMOUS
Grand Tour, ca. 1915
20 × 30 inches
Maurice Rickards

GRAND TOUR.

The Allies are now arranging a Trip
for Sportsmen (Aged 19—38)

TO BERLIN

All hotel expenses & railway fares paid

Good Shooting and Hunting.

Rifles & Ammunition

SUPPLIED FREE

Also Cheap Trips up the Rhine.

APPLY AT ONCE TO:
The Recruiting Officer, Chester Castle,
or any Recruiting Office.

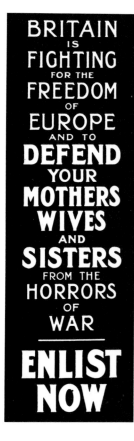

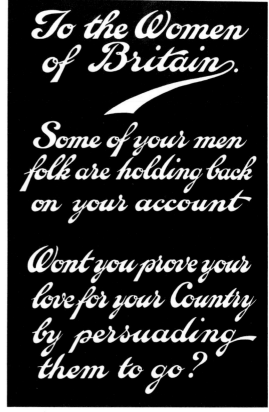

Daddy, what did YOU do in the Great War?

ANONYMOUS
Britain Is Fighting for..., ca. 1915
8 × 22 inches
Maurice Rickards

E. KEALY
Women of Britain Say—Go!, ca. 1915
20 × 30½ inches
George M. Dembo

ANONYMOUS
To the Women of Britain, ca. 1915
20 × 30 inches
Maurice Rickards

SAVILE LUMLEY
Daddy, What Did You Do in the Great War?, ca. 1915
20 × 30 inches
Imperial War Museum

W. A. FRY
There's Room for You, ca. 1915
20 × 30 inches
Maurice Rickards

THERE'S ROOM FOR YOU

ENLIST TO-DAY

PUBLIC WARNING

The public are advised to familiarise themselves with the appearance of British and German Airships and Aeroplanes, so that they may not be alarmed by British aircraft, and may take shelter if German aircraft appear. **Should hostile aircraft be seen,** take shelter **immediately** in the nearest available house, preferably in the basement, and remain there until the aircraft have left the vicinity: do not stand about in crowds **and do not touch unexploded bombs.**

In the event of **HOSTILE** aircraft being seen in country districts, the nearest Naval, Military or Police Authorities should, if possible, be advised immediately by Telephone of the TIME OF APPEARANCE, the DIRECTION OF FLIGHT, **and whether the aircraft is an Airship or an Aeroplane.**

GERMAN
AIRSHIPS

BRITISH
AIRSHIPS

Note specially the shape of the Airships and the position of the passenger cars

Note specially the sloped-back wings of the German Aeroplanes

AEROPLANES

AEROPLANES

PRICE TWOPENCE

ANONYMOUS
Public Warning, 1915
19½ × 30 inches
Imperial War Museum

ANONYMOUS
Silence, ca. 1916
20 × 30 inches
Miscellaneous Man

34

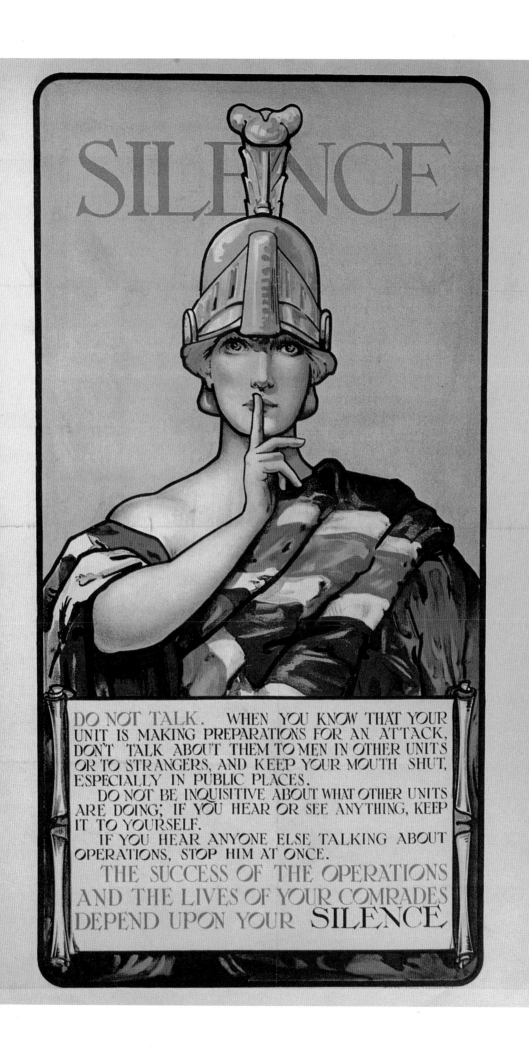

antagonism of interests." Negotiations for an alliance with Germany nonetheless failed, and so Britain next sought the friendship of newly emerging Japan, a move to protect her interests in the Pacific that ultimately resulted in the Anglo-Japanese Alliance of January, 1902. This unlikely affiliation greatly alarmed Russia, which already was experiencing problems that would lead to the Russo-Japanese War in 1904, and so Russia turned again to France for even closer ties. This prompted Britain to seriously investigate an improvement of relations with her old antagonist France, and thus in April, 1904, the Anglo-French Entente Cordiale was signed.

This alliance, of course, reawakened Germany's not-so-latent fear of encirclement, which was further heightened when Britain approached Russia again, this time with better results (since Russia in the meanwhile had been defeated by the Japanese and in 1905 had suffered a revolution). The result was the Anglo-Russian Entente of August, 1907. At this point, the eventuality most feared by Germany had fully come to pass: she was virtually surrounded by potential enemies. The Triple Alliance formed by Germany, Austria, and Italy was now fully countered by the new Triple Entente of Britain, France, and Russia.

A PROLONGED PEACE—AND PLANS FOR WAR

At the turn of the century, Europe had been at peace since the Franco-Prussian War, which ended in 1871. After that, Europeans did not see armed conflict on the Continent for more than a generation. However, Russia and Turkey clashed in the Balkans in 1877–78, Germany quarreled with France in 1907 over control of Morocco, and in 1908 Austria-Hungary aroused the impotent anger of Russia by annexing Bosnia-Herzegovina, which her client state Serbia regarded as the center of Serb national feelings. Only in the Balkans, "the powderkeg of Europe," where Serbia, Greece, Bulgaria, and Montenegro fought among themselves in 1911 and again in 1913, did actual fighting erupt in the new century.

Even though Europe was at peace in the early years of the twentieth century, it was an armed and tense peace; for a new nationalism had become the dominant political fact, and it found overt expression in the parading of military might and in preparations for a future war. Following the Franco-Prussian War, all European countries had instituted universal military service for a two- or three-year hitch, and almost all able young men were obligated to learn the rudiments of soldiering. England, alone, retained the traditional small, long-term professional army. Because she controlled the seas, Britain found no pressing need to garrison a large conscript army for the defense of her island kingdom.

The Industrial Revolution had lately provided Europe with the means for mass production, and by the turn of the century Germany had overtaken England as the greatest industrial power in Europe. Now military planners could be certain of sufficient weaponry, and, with universal conscription, no shortage of adequately trained men for grand offensives. In 1870 the Prussian warlords had ably demonstrated the devastating effect (on the French) of the attack that became the theoretical tactic of choice among European strategists: a rapid strike by massive forces. However, since that war, the effectiveness of defensive artillery had been appreciably enhanced

through the development of high-explosive shells, the introduction of breechloaders that boosted the rate of fire, and improvements in bore rifling that increased a gun's accuracy. The Anglo-Boer War and the Russo-Japanese War had clearly illustrated the effects of modern firepower on massive frontal assaults, but it was a lesson apparently lost on German and French strategists.

In 1903 French General Ferdinand Foch published *The Principles of War*, in which he relied heavily on the precepts of German theorist Karl von Clausewitz, author of the influential three-volume work *On War* (1833): "Blood is the price of victory. You must either resort to it or give up waging war." Foch believed that "of all faults, only one is degrading, namely inaction." His battle strategy called for "striking one supreme stroke on one point . . . an intentional, resolute, sudden, and violent action of the masses on a selected point." His theoretical counter to the threat of defensive firepower was "a quarter of an hour's quick fire by a mass of artillery on a clearly determined objective"—a tactic that would prove sadly ineffective in practice; for even after suffering seven straight days of bombardment, the Germans still managed to kill or wound nearly half the sixty-six thousand men who charged them in the Battle of the Somme's first hour. Unfortunately for her soldiers, France's grand strategy for conducting war was clearly based on Foch's guiding principle: "Whatever the circumstances, it is the . . . intention to advance, with all forces, to the attack."

The massed offensive had become the primary hypothetical tactic among all the rapidly expanding armies of Europe, with victory necessarily going to the army that attacked first and hit hardest. Germany accepted this in principle but developed her own specific war plans. General Alfred von Schlieffen, chief of the General Staff at the turn of the century, confronted the same basic problem that earlier had troubled Bismarck: how to fight a war on two fronts should France and Russia, now allies, jointly attack.

JULIUS GIPKENS
German Exhibition of Captured Aircraft, 1917
18¼ × 17½ inches
Imperial War Museum

KARL SIGRIST
Subscribe to the War Loan, ca. 1917
17¾ × 27½ inches
Meehan Military Posters

He strongly maintained that in the opening days of a war "the whole of Germany must hurl itself against one opponent." Schlieffen's defense strategy was to dispose quickly of one foe before devoting Germany's full resources to battling the other. Since there seemed little chance of rapidly overcoming so vast a country as Russia, France would necessarily be the first target of what came to be known as the Schlieffen Plan.

France had long anticipated the hostile aims of German war plans and had built a chain of elaborate fortifications facing Germany, from Nancy to Verdun, to protect the approaches to Paris. Schlieffen was, of course, aware of this line of fortresses and was dubious about the effectiveness of massed frontal assaults against it. His grand strategy would hinge on outflanking the French fortifications by pushing south through Switzerland or north through Belgium (or both) and invading France behind her fortifications. By 1905 Schlieffen had concentrated his planning on the Belgian invasion route, as would his successor, General Helmuth von Moltke (nephew of the field marshal of the same name who had led the

Prussians to victory in 1871). For Moltke, the proper conduct of war was "an element in God's national order." He ultimately regarded the Schlieffen Plan as so flawless that it was inalterable, even when the kaiser, at the last moment in August, 1914, sought to redesignate Russia as Germany's first target: "The deployment of an army of a million men was not a matter of improvisation. . . . and, once worked out, could not be changed. . . . our concentration of strong forces against France and light defensive forces against Russia must be carried out as planned."

Both France and Germany were supremely confident that their own separate strategic plans would enable them to win the long-expected war quickly and decisively—within a matter of weeks—and they prepared for it with all deliberateness. In 1911 General Friedrich von Bernhardi published a book called *Germany and the Next War*, and some of its chapter titles give an indication of the contents: "The Right to Make War"; "The Duty to Make War"; "World Power or Downfall"; "Germany's Historic Mission."

Great Britain continued to remain somewhat detached from Europe's arms race as long as she pre-

LUCIAN BERNHARD
This Is the Way to Peace, ca. 1918
18¼ × 25½ inches
Meehan Military Posters

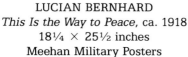

FRITZ ERLER
Help Us Win!, 1917
16¼ × 22¼ inches
Meehan Military Posters

served a clear superiority at sea; however, at the beginning of the twentieth century Germany had begun a serious naval program under Admiral Alfred von Tirpitz. In 1905 Germany laid the keel for her first dreadnought, arming it with ten twelve-inch guns rather than the customary four. By 1908 Germany had announced a program to launch four of these leviathans a year, and Britain began to be disturbed. In 1912, First Lord of the Admiralty Winston Churchill commented on the need to meet this challenge: "The British Navy is to us a necessity and, from some points of view, the German Navy is to them more in the nature of a luxury. Our naval power involves British existence. It is existence to us; it is expansion to them."

This rapid expansion of the kaiser's fleets was provoked by recommendations in a book by an American naval theorist published in 1890: *The Influence of Sea Power upon History, 1660–1783* by Captain Alfred Thayer Mahan. Kaiser Wilhelm wrote that he was "trying to learn it by heart. . . . It is on board all my ships and constantly quoted by my captains and officers." In January of 1914, Winston Churchill warned: "The world is arming as it never armed before. Every suggestion of arrest or limitation has been brushed aside."

A SUNDAY IN SARAJEVO

In the fifteenth century, the Ottoman Turks, after conquering the Byzantine Empire, established an outpost at a Slavic crossroads settlement maintained by the Romans in the first century. The Turks proceeded to operate a marketplace there and to build the finest mosque in all of the Balkans, turning Sarajevo (a name derived from the Turkish word for palace) into a prosperous provincial capital. Over the years, as the power of the Turks went into decline (Czar Nicholas I memorably characterized the Ottoman government as "the sick man of Europe"), Sarajevo and environs increasingly attracted the attention of Austria to the north, which, in 1878, as a result of the partitioning of Bulgaria by the Congress of Berlin, received the provinces of Bosnia and Herzegovina to administer. In 1908 the Austro-Hungarian Empire, a dual monarchy since 1867, took a further step and annexed the area, much to the anguish of neighboring Serbia, which still regarded Bosnia as central to Serb nationalism. The foreign minister of Serbia warned that "Austria-Hungary, the implacable enemy of Serbia and the Serb race, was preparing to destroy every symptom of resistance in a people who wanted to live independent." The Serbs looked in vain for aid from their fellow Slavs in a demoralized Russia, which earlier had supported Serbia as a buffer against Austro-Hungarian expansion. In May, 1911, a group of Serbian army officers formed a secret society, called The Black Hand, to arm and train resistance forces.

In June of 1914, Archduke Franz Ferdinand, nephew of Emperor Franz Josef and heir to the Hapsburg throne, decided to make a state visit to the capital of the empire's newest acquisition. On June 28, his fourteenth wedding anniversary, fifty-one-year-old Franz Ferdinand arrived in Sarajevo, Bosnia, with his wife Sophie. Seven young Serbs (five of them under twenty) were there awaiting his visit, each armed with a bomb, a pistol, and a vial of cyanide in case of capture. Nineteen-year-old Gavrilo Princip had been stationed on Appel Quay near the Latin Bridge over the shallow Miljacka River, past which the archduke and his wife were scheduled to proceed on their way to the town hall. His would be the third chance at assassinating the archduke, if confederates posted nearer the beginning of the procession's route should fail. An explosion just up the quay led Princip to assume that his comrades had accomplished their mission, so he was completely surprised when the archduke's car sped right past him undamaged— the bomb had missed its target! Princip was disconsolate at his own failure to attack and drifted away into the crowds.

When the archduke, in plumed headdress and bemedaled tunic, left Sarajevo's town hall, his four-car procession was sent along an unscheduled route as a security measure. The lead vehicle took a wrong turn, and the imperial motorcade was stopped while

BOARDMAN ROBINSON
Left Behind in Serbia, ca. 1917
21 × 29 inches
Museum of the City of New York

THÉOPHILE ALEXANDRE STEINLEN
Save Serbia Our Ally, 1916 (1917 in English)
24 × 36 inches
Museum of the City of New York

LEST WE PERISH

CAMPAIGN *for* $30,000,000.

AMERICAN COMMITTEE
FOR RELIEF IN THE NEAR EAST

ARMENIA — GREECE — SYRIA — PERSIA

ONE MADISON AVE., NEW YORK.

CLEVELAND H. DODGE, TREASURER

RUOTOLO
American Women's Hospitals, ca. 1917
14 × 23 inches
Miscellaneous Man

ALBERT EDWARD STERNER
America's Gift to France, 1920
20 × 30 inches
Miscellaneous Man

the machine was backed up out of an alley. As fate would have it, the archduke's open car came to a halt right in front of schoolboy Princip, who pulled out the gun given him by The Black Hand and fired it twice. One shot hit Franz Ferdinand in the neck, piercing his jugular vein, and the other struck his wife Sophie in the abdomen. As the archduke's blood spurted everywhere, he reached out for his fatally struck wife and cried: "Soferl, Soferl! Don't die. Live for my children!" Neither lived longer than a few minutes. Princip was captured, survived his cyanide, and discovered that as a minor he could not be executed. He was sentenced to twenty years in prison; in 1918 he died of tuberculosis.

THE AFTERMATH OF MURDER

Austria's leaders saw the archduke's murder and the complicity of the Serbs as a good opportunity to teach Serbia a lesson—and possibly to extend the empire farther into the Balkans. Accordingly, after consultation with Germany, Austria drew up a harsh ultimatum in highly provocative language and delivered it to Serbia on July 23. Of the ten humiliating demands made of that small country, most were

ETHEL FRANKLIN BETTS BAINS
Lest We Perish, ca. 1917
20 × 28 inches
Museum of the City of New York

reluctantly accepted. But it was not Austria's intention to let Serbia off lightly, so that country's reply was summarily rejected and Austria's army was ordered into partial mobilization. In view of the potential threat to her client state, Russia had already gone into partial mobilization on July 20, expecting that such a move would moderate any rash action by Austria. However, on July 28 Austria declared war on Serbia, and by the thirty-first Russia had taken the next step toward full mobilization. With Austria and Russia fully mobilized, Germany found herself obligated by treaty to support the consequences of her ally's intemperate venture. General von Moltke expressed hope that hostilities could be contained.

41

LUDWIG HOHLWEIN
People's Charity for German Prisoners of War, ca. 1917
11¾ × 16¼ inches
Imperial War Museum

PÁL SUJÁN
National Exhibition for War Relief, 1917
24½ × 47½ inches
Imperial War Museum

He knew that if Austria actually attacked Serbia, Russia would be obliged to come to her aid, which would, in turn, compel her ally France to mobilize. With Russia in readiness for war, Germany felt threatened; therefore, on July 31 she sent Russia an ultimatum, demanding that her military alert be downgraded. When Russia refused to demobilize, Germany, on August 1, was bound by national honor to declare a state of war with Russia. This politically inevitable move against Russia did not fully conform to Germany's operational plans for her next war: if the elaborately worked-out Schlieffen plan were to be followed, Germany would not go into action against Russia without first eliminating the threat of attack from the west by invading France. Moving her armies through Belgium would risk bringing England, Belgium's protector, into the conflict, but it was a chance Germany was willing to take in the belief that Britain was preoccupied with unrest in Ireland.

By July 27 Winston Churchill had already telegraphed the British fleets: "European political situation makes war between Triple Entente and Triple Alliance powers by no means impossible. Be prepared to shadow hostile men-of-war and consider disposition of H.M. ships under your command from this point of view. Measure is purely precautionary." Earlier, Foreign Secretary Sir Edward Grey had reassured the French ambassador that Britain would not stand aside if France were attacked. Grey had told the German ambassador that Britain's attitude toward the impending situation might hinge on the question of Belgium, "which appeals very strongly to public opinion here." On August 2 Germany sent Belgium an ultimatum, demanding free passage of her armies across Belgian soil should she respond to a threatened invasion from France. This was refused. On August 1, in response to Germany's movement into Luxembourg, France had gone into full mobilization, and on August 3 Germany declared war on France, giving as justification the build-up of French forces along the German border. Fearing the worst, Belgium's King Albert appealed to the French and British for aid on August 3.

On the afternoon of August 4, the German Empire

LUDWIG HOHLWEIN
Ludendorff Donation for the War Disabled, 1917
23 × 34½ inches
Miscellaneous Man

HORRMEYER
And Your Duty?, 1918
8¾ × 13 inches
Meehan Military Posters

ANONYMOUS
European War, ca. 1915
20 × 30 inches
Maurice Rickards

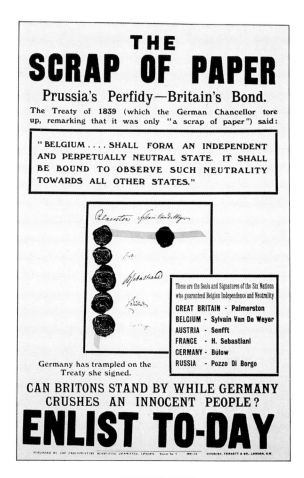

ANONYMOUS
The Scrap of Paper, ca. 1915
20 × 30 inches
Meehan Military Posters

massed sixty thousand combat troops in front of Belgium's forts at Liège, and by that evening General Karl von Bülow's Second Army had crossed the border into Belgium. Britain, a guarantor of the neutrality of Belgium since 1831, immediately sent Germany a stern ultimatum with a midnight deadline to withdraw the invasion or face a declaration of war. Early on the afternoon of the fourth, the British fleets were sent the following message: "The British ultimatum to Germany will expire at midnight Greenwich Mean Time, 4 August. No act of war should be committed before that hour." This was followed later with a general message: "The war telegram will be issued at midnight authorizing you to commence hostilities against Germany, but in view of our ultimatum they may decide to open fire at any moment. You must be ready for this." As statesman Sir Edward Grey so prophetically put it: "The lamps are going out all over Europe; we shall not see them lit again in our lifetime."

RELIEF FOR BELGIUM AND FRANCE

When war broke out that August, nearly two hundred thousand Americans vacationing in Europe were stranded, including thirty thousand school teachers who, in the words of Herbert Clark Hoover, "had pinched, saved and planned for this one trip to Europe all their lives." A successful American engineer with major projects worldwide, Hoover had maintained his headquarters in London since 1902. Born in Iowa in 1874 of Quaker descent, he was to celebrate his fortieth birthday just a week after Germany declared war on France. The next day, Hoover received a desperate call for help from the American Embassy, which was swamped with citizens demanding their rights to be looked after and returned out of this chaos to their safe homeland. Having fled from Germany, France, and Belgium, these Americans were to find that Britain's banks were unwilling to exchange pounds sterling for their travel funds in marks and francs. To aid his countrymen in distress, Hoover quickly established a committee of volunteers from among his prominent friends, who immediately set about pooling an emergency fund, providing clothes to replace those abandoned or lost, finding shelter for those without any, and arranging passage home for the unfortunate strandees. By the time Congress addressed the unforeseen plight of America's citizens in Europe, the job already had been done. Hoover's committee had expended $1.5 million in loans and expenses and had cared for 120,000 people. Walter Hines Page, the American ambassador, informed President Wilson of the success of this endeavor and thanked heaven for the Atlantic Ocean: "Now, when all this half of the world will suffer the unspeakable brutalization of war, we shall preserve our moral strength, our political powers, and our ideals."

Hoover had planned to return to America that fall, but while making final preparations he was approached by a series of emissaries from Belgium, all aware of the extraordinary work he had done for his fellow citizens in Europe. Germany had overrun Belgium and northern France in a matter of weeks, making prisoners of ten million people, and three quarters of them were Belgian. Britain's naval blockade of Germany had also cut off all exports to Belgium, which brought in most of its cereals and flour and half of its other foodstuffs. In addition, German occupation forces were confiscating all of

LOU MAYER
Jewish War Sufferers, ca. 1917
21 × 28 inches
George M. Dembo

F. LUIS MORA
Free Milk for France, ca. 1917
23 × 33 inches
George M. Dembo

that country's local stockpiles for their own use. Hoover was begged to intervene with the British on behalf of the starving Belgians, and he succeeded, through the help of Ambassador Page, in getting one final shipment of food through to Belgium. But that would be the last of it, the British government informed him, for fear that Germany would seize further shipments to feed their own people—defeating the effect of the blockade. The problem presented to Hoover, he recorded in his *Memoirs*, "was not 'relief' in any known sense. It was the feeding of a nation. . . . There was no former human experience to turn to for guidance." As he analyzed the job confronting him, it meant finding the money to buy food for ten million, shipping it across the ocean, and delivering it to the Belgians through double lines of belligerent nations.

Hoover asked for two days to weigh the situation; then in the last week of October he accepted full responsibility for feeding the desperate peoples of Belgium and northern France—on the conditions that he receive no remuneration and have complete charge. Immediately he set up the Commission for Relief in Belgium, and his first act was to order ten million bushels of Chicago wheat on his own account. Like everyone else, Hoover expected the war to end in a matter of months; so, tremendous as this un-

DON'T LET THEM DIE
YOU CAN SAVE THEM

SEND CONTRIBUTIONS TO THE
WOMEN'S APPAREL ASSOCIATION
132 West 42nd Street   New York City
J. Wise, *TREASURER*

WOMEN'S APPAREL UNIT
of
Women's Oversea Hospitals, U.S.A.

dertaking seemed, he first considered it a matter of seeing Belgium safely through a temporary crisis. As he wrote later, "The knowledge that we would have to go on for four years, to find a billion dollars, to transport five million tons of concentrated food, to administer rationing, price controls, agricultural production, to contend with combatant governments and with world shortages of food and ships, was mercifully hidden from us."

Hoover was not only required to feed a nation but to build a fund-raising network all over the world and to locate abundant supplies of food staples wherever they could be found, even in such remote parts as Manchuria, Burma, and Argentina. Also, because of the mutual distrust among the belligerents, he discovered that he would need to take over all local distribution in the occupied areas. The cost to the Commission quickly rose from $12 million a month to $25 million, and proceeds from charity drives definitely were not adequate to the task. Hoover, therefore, went directly to the belligerents for their support, but he discovered, to his disbelief, that in this war hunger had become a tactical weapon. The British government opposed aiding the Belgian people because it was sure that the food shipments would ultimately end up in Germany. But also, it suited England's purposes to have the Germans clearly responsible in world opinion for starving Belgium. The German government, on the other hand, argued that the British blockade was the cause of widespread deprivation among its own people and that it was preposterous to take part in feeding the French and Belgians while German women and children did without.

In the end, Hoover skillfully played America's role as an uncommitted, resource-laden neutral to the hilt, convincing Britain that further blocking of relief to Belgium would surely turn American public opinion against continued aid to Britain. And if Germany permitted Belgium to starve, America would certainly be moved to enter the war on the side of the Allies. Eventually Berlin agreed to guarantee the Commission's food loans to the sum of $100 million. Britain then pledged to Belgian relief £1 million per month (the equivalent of almost $5 million), and France provided $3 million a month to feed her citizens in captivity. America contributed nearly a third of the

L. C. CLINKER and M. J. DWYER
Don't Waste Food While Others Starve!, ca. 1917
20 × 30 inches
State Historical Society of Iowa

Commission's expenses, and because many Commission executives worked without remuneration the overhead of the operation amounted to less than one-half percent of the total cost. Under its own charter and flag, the Commission directed a fleet of sixty cargo ships, and it ultimately succeeded in saving ten million subjugated peoples from starvation. "In time," Hoover later wrote, "we won the confidence of both belligerent sides and became a sort of neutral state of our own."

M. LEONE BRACKER
Don't Let Them Die, 1918
21 × 30 inches
Museum of the City of New York

II. "THE IMPOSSIBLE WAR"

Main Street Americans followed the news of events in Europe that summer with considerable shock and bewilderment. "This was most strikingly registered in the newspaper cartoons and comments which expressed astonishment that such an archaic institution [as war] should be revived in modern Europe," wrote social reformer Jane Addams, who would share a Nobel Peace Prize in 1931. The shock was coupled in some minds with a bittersweet satisfaction that decadent and autocratic Old World empires were finally bringing upon themselves a well-deserved Armageddon. From the smoking ruins of their leaders' folly, the good and decent European peoples would surely call upon America's aid, both to save them from further excesses of militaristic autocracy and to guide them in remaking the Old World in her democratic image. It was Indiana Senator Albert J. Beveridge who assured his colleagues that "God has marked the American people as his chosen nation to finally lead in the regeneration of the world."

On the day Kaiser Wilhelm II declared war on his cousin Czar Nicholas II, an editorial in the *New York Times* revealed something of American distaste for the militaristic pretentiousness of totalitarian Europe: "The threat of war on this unprecedented scale, its very nearness, the overwhelming fear that it may not be averted are proofs of the backwardness of Europe. By permitting themselves to be brought so near to war they prove that their civilization is half a sham. They have reverted to the condition of savage tribes roaming the forests and falling upon each other in a fury of blood and carnage to achieve the ambitious designs of chieftains clad in skins and drunk with mead."

To many thinkers of the era, especially those in the numerous and influential peace movements, war was a brutal anachronism for resolving differences between modern nations. Since 1909, a widely circulated book by Norman Angell had argued persua-sively that war was no longer possible in the twentieth century; it had become an unprofitable option for any country. Translated into a dozen languages, *The Great Illusion* had something of a cult following, including men as influential as Reginald Brett, second Viscount Esher and adviser to King George V, who lectured that "commercial disaster, financial ruin, and individual suffering" would be on such a scale that each day war becomes "more difficult and improbable." David Starr Jordan, newly retired president of Stanford University and a crusader for international

ANONYMOUS
An American Triumph!, 1898
30 × 40 inches
Maurice Rickards

HARRY TOWNSEND
War Rages in France, ca. 1917
20 × 30 inches
Illustration House

peace, had written in 1913 that the "Great War of Europe, ever threatening, ever impending," should really be called "The Impossible War." The major nations of the world were now so economically interdependent that a devastating modern war would yield no winners and certainly no profit; furthermore, out of self-preservation, international bankers would soon put an end to financing the armaments race. In fact, credit already had been tightened, leading to a worldwide depression in the fall of 1913, for fear that troubles in the Balkans might spark a general war.

Woodrow Wilson, the son and grandson of Presbyterian ministers, took office in 1913 as president of the United States—a scant three years out of academia and the presidency of Princeton University—following two years as governor of New Jersey. Raised in the Old South, Wilson as a boy had witnessed the devastation and deprivations brought on by the Civil War, and this experience had marked him indelibly with an abhorrence of even the idea of war. A confirmed pacifist, he had served as a vice president of the American Peace Society, as had his secretary of state, William Jennings Bryan. Both men were determined that peace-loving, democratic America would become the shining example for misguided, militaristic autocracies in the Old World. Later, Bryan was to say that his most notable achievement in office had been the almost thirty treaties he negotiated between hostile nations who agreed to eschew fighting while their problems were arbitrated. These were for Bryan indisputable proofs of the triumph of reason, and, guided by the words of the prophet Isaiah, he awarded the ambassador of each country in arbitration a plowshare paperweight beaten out of an old sword.

In early August, 1914, after proclaiming that America must remain neutral in the European conflict ("Every reform we have won will be lost if we go into this war"), President Wilson confidently informed the belligerents that he would make himself available to act as mediator in resolving their differences. In 1899 (for the first time ever in peace) and again in 1907, the nations of the world had met in The Hague to deal with limitations on armaments and the problems of preserving the uncommonly long peace in Europe. They also codified the rules of "civilized" warfare and initiated a framework for rational settlement of international disputes—under the provisions of which Wilson offered to arbitrate. The belligerents declined Wilson's offer; each pleaded self-defense and that their national honor required a traditional fight to the finish (which all confidently expected was no longer than a few weeks away).

Wilson was led to believe that the time simply was not ripe for his services as a peacemaker, so he would have to "watch and wait," as he said, until his offer was welcomed by the belligerents. Again, as he did ten times between August and November, 1914, he reaffirmed America's neutrality, both on the basis of hastening world peace by her example and of maintaining a disinterestedness that gave her unquestioned moral force as the potential mediator of the belligerents' differences. Nevertheless, in the spring of 1914 Wilson already had sent his chief deputy Colonel Edward M. House to Europe in hopes of lessening tensions between England and Germany and of slowing the rapid build-up of armaments. House spent almost three months conferring with European statesmen, but he garnered no conciliatory agreements. He wrote to Wilson from Berlin, "The whole of Germany is charged with electricity. Everybody's nerves are tense. It only requires a spark to set the whole thing off."

THE MONROE DOCTRINE AND MANIFEST DESTINY

During her Gilded Age, from the end of the Civil War to the beginning of the Spanish-American War, America had paid little attention to the problems or concerns of the rest of the world. As Senator Henry Cabot Lodge accurately remarked, "Our relations with foreign nations today excite generally only a languid interest." Just as long as Europe exported a steady supply of cheap labor and was prevented by tariffs from introducing competitive goods, America was hellbent on fulfilling the 1845 prophecy of John L. O'Sullivan that it was "our manifest destiny to overspread the continent allotted by Providence." Awash in profits from Civil War business, the North directed the cash toward expanding basic industries, extending the railroad network, exploiting the natural resources and markets of the Middle and Far West, and aggrandizing municipal structures and services in major cities. America had been launched into a period of widespread speculation and currency inflation—a booming economy that, even with periodic setbacks like the panics of 1873 and 1893, led to spectacular growth and the accumulation of great wealth in relatively few hands.

One of these men of great wealth, steel magnate Andrew Carnegie, retired in 1901 after selling his company for $250 million to J. P. Morgan, who, in turn, merged it with seven other steel companies to form U.S. Steel. Carnegie then undertook a program of "redistributing" his fortune. In his article "Wealth," published in the *North American Review* in 1889, Carnegie expressed his belief that it was

---

LLOYD MYERS
Britishers You're Needed, ca. 1916
28 × 40½ inches
Museum of the City of New York

BRITISHERS
-YOU'RE-
NEEDED
GREAT BRITAIN
FRANCE
COME
ACROSS
NOW
UNITED
STATES
LLOYD MYERS

FRANCIS ADAMS HALSTEAD and V. ADERANTE
Columbia Calls, 1916
30 × 40 inches
Museum of the City of New York

the rich man's responsibility to distribute his surplus wealth "for the improvement of mankind," for he "who dies thus rich, dies disgraced." A self-educated immigrant from Scotland, Carnegie devoted more than $60 million to building 2,811 free public libraries around the world. Included in the $350 million he "distributed" (still leaving him with more than a billion dollars in 1914), $6 million went to provide organs for 7,689 churches.

In the years just prior to World War I, Carnegie turned his philanthropic attention to preserving peace and preventing war, funding a vast Peace Palace in The Hague where nations could settle disputes before a permanent world court without resorting once again to barbaric war. To further this work, he gave $10 million to found the Endowment for International Peace. Significantly, he centered his efforts on militaristic Europe, for in 1911 he expressed sentiments concerning his adopted homeland that were widely shared by Americans of all backgrounds: "She has not an enemy in the world, nor need she have. The rulers have no cause of complaint against her. The masses of people in all civilized lands see in her the standard to which they fondly hope to attain and they love her. Hence an army and navy, maintained at present standard, are ample and more than ample. We have no enemies, all nations are our friends, and we are friends of all."

Despite Carnegie's rosy perceptions of his new homeland, it should be noted that America had also spent the decades since the Civil War in subduing and confining the last free-roaming Indian tribes, removing vestiges of Spanish colonialism in the Caribbean, challenging British and German intervention in Venezuela, squabbling with Mexico in the Southwest, maneuvering Colombia out of sovereignty over the Isthmus of Panama, annexing the Hawaiian Islands, installing American military governments in Haiti and Santo Domingo, shelling and capturing the Mexican port of Vera Cruz, and persuading Denmark to relinquish the Virgin Islands. However, most of this aggressive activity was firmly in line with long-established tenets of United States foreign policy.

Up to the beginnings of World War I, America's relations with other countries could be said to have been governed by three major principles: freedom of the seas, which went back to the country's independence in 1776 and was again fought for in 1812; no permanent or entangling foreign alliances, a policy formulated by Washington in his Farewell Address of 1796 and reiterated by Jefferson in his 1801 Inaugural; and elimination and prohibition of European hegemony in the New World, which was laid down in the Monroe Doctrine of 1823. In a word, the traditional foreign policy of the United States was widely characterized as isolationism; in return for not interfering with America's Manifest Destiny to dominate the fortunes of the New World, European powers could be certain that America would refrain from taking sides in Old World struggles or intrigue—

so long as her rights to ply the seas in pursuit of foreign trade were not infringed upon. Therefore, when war first broke out in Europe it was almost axiomatic for America to have no intention of getting involved.

The situation had been somewhat different when America became involved with Spain in 1898, the last war she had fought against a European power. In 1895 native insurgents rebelled against Spanish colonial rule in Cuba, which, along with Puerto Rico, was all that remained of Spain's once-extensive empire in the New World. In attempting to smother the uprising before Americans pressed the Monroe Doctrine, Spain sent General Valeriano Weyler to Cuba, where he earned his nickname, "The Butcher," by imprisoning entire populations of some rebellious areas. The insurrection wreaked havoc not only on the Cubans, who died by the thousands in primitive concentration camps, but on American investments in Cuban agriculture. As sugar and tobacco crops were destroyed in three years of fighting, American businessmen saw a profitable trade dwindle to practically nothing. American military intervention was demanded by some to eliminate Spain's unwelcome presence in the Caribbean, and the idea was especially appealing to the newly emerging sensationalist press, which delighted in attracting readers with stories of Spain's cruel and decadent ways. In September, 1895, William Randolph Hearst bought the New York Journal and immediately launched a circulation war with the New York World, owned by Joseph Pulitzer. Among other tactics, Hearst lured away well-known cartoonist Richard F. Outcault of the World and began featuring his popular comic strip "The Yellow Kid." Not to be outdone, Pulitzer hired Philadelphia newspaper illustrator George B. Luks to do his own version of the strip for the World, and soon New Yorkers faced a hard choice each Sunday morning between rival adventures of the Yellow Kid—a development that brought the term "yellow journalism" into the language.

In January, 1897, Hearst sent the famous correspondent Richard Harding Davis to Cuba for more firsthand details on the bloody rebellion. He was accompanied by Frederic Remington, the great illustrator of the vanishing West. After sketching a few "atrocities" for the Journal, including the public strip-search of an attractive Cuban woman by Spanish soldiers, Remington got bored and cabled Hearst: "Everything is quiet. There is no trouble. There will be no war. I wish to return." Hearst is said to have mysteriously replied: "Please remain. You furnish the pictures and I'll furnish the war." Early in 1898, Davis published Cuba in War, a book whose reports of inhuman behavior and atrocious conditions helped support a growing sentiment that it was America's duty under the Monroe Doctrine to intervene and end the slaughter of innocents by a corrupt and autocratic Old World power.

Nevertheless, even though there was sympathy

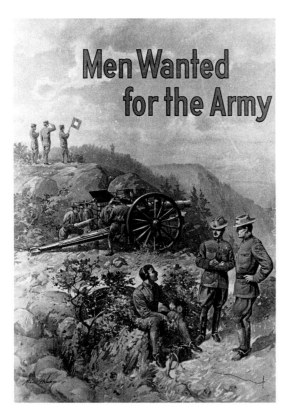

MICHAEL P. WHALEN
Men Wanted for the Army, ca. 1910
30 × 40 inches
George M. Dembo

I. B. HAZELTON
Men Wanted for the Army, 1914
30 × 40 inches
George M. Dembo

E. CAMMILLI
The Call to Duty, 1917
30 × 40 inches
George M. Dembo

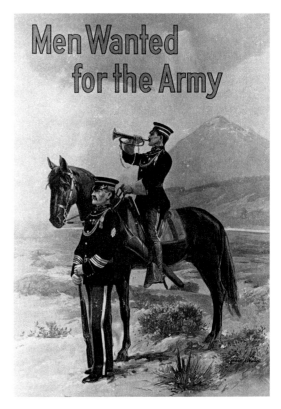

MICHAEL P. WHALEN
Men Wanted for the Army, ca. 1910
30 × 40 inches
Miscellaneous Man

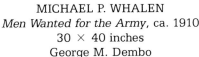

MICHAEL P. WHALEN
Men Wanted for the Army, ca. 1910
30 × 40 inches
George M. Dembo

H. DEVITT WELSH
U.S. Army Signal Corps, ca. 1916
27 × 39 inches
Miscellaneous Man

for Cuba's prolonged efforts at independence, most Americans maintained a reluctance to become entangled in the problems of a European country—even in *our* hemisphere. Both President Grover Cleveland and his successor William McKinley were able to resist the pressures to intervene—until, on February 15, 1898, the U.S. battleship *Maine*, on a friendly visit, mysteriously exploded and sank in Havana Harbor, with the loss of two officers and 258 men. Spanish investigators claimed the explosion had been internal, while their American counterparts blamed an external blast for detonating the warship's forward powder magazine—a mystery never solved. Although a new political ministry in Spain already had begun to make concessions and offered Cuba limited autonomy—raising hopes of peaceful settlement—exhortations in the yellow press to ''Remember the *Maine*!'' aroused widespread anti-Spanish feeling in the United States. On April 19, 1898, Congress passed resolutions that recognized Cuba's independence, demanded Spain's withdrawal, and authorized the president to use force in effecting these aims. Spain promptly severed diplomatic relations with

the United States, and on April 25 a state of war was declared.

A few days earlier, Spain's Atlantic Fleet had steamed into the harbor of Santiago, Cuba, where it subsequently was blockaded by the steam-powered steel ships of America's ''New Navy,'' now the sixth largest in the world. On the other side of the globe, the U.S. Asiatic Squadron, under Commodore George Dewey, sailed into Manila Bay on May 1 and promptly destroyed the Spanish fleet defending the Philippine capital. Before the end of June, an American force of regulars and briefly trained volunteers was landed in Cuba (including Lieutenant Colonel Theodore Roosevelt, who had resigned the post of assistant secretary of the Navy to help organize the First U.S. Cavalry Volunteers, better known as the Rough Riders). In a small-scale preview of endemic shortcomings in coordination and organization that would plague the War Department well into World War I, Roosevelt's cavalry regiment embarked for the war zone minus its horses and half its men. On July 1, by taking San Juan Hill on foot, they gained the high ground commanding Santiago Harbor. On July

3, the Spanish fleet in the harbor, vulnerable to American field artillery, attempted to run the blockade to reach open sea but fell victim to the U.S. Navy. Shortly after the surrender of Santiago, with American armies landed and victorious in both Puerto Rico and the Philippines, Spain began negotiations for peace. Hostilities were ended on August 12, less than four months after they began, and the peace treaty was signed on December 10, 1898. Under the terms of that document, America suddenly found herself with a widespread colonial empire of 120,000 square miles, which included Cuba, Puerto Rico, and, unexpectedly, the Philippines and Guam.

In just a few months at the end of the nineteenth century, the United States of America had become a world power, with far-flung outposts to man in the Caribbean and the Pacific, a conviction that it was her responsibility to oversee New World interests, and a renewed determination to avoid European entanglements. Along with her new status came a deep-seated confidence that the Old World powers—corrupt, outmoded, and autocratic—would be no match against America's democracy, vigor, and decency.

INNOCENCE ABROAD

Another American of great wealth who, like Andrew Carnegie, came to see himself as a benefactor of mankind was the auto manufacturer Henry Ford. After two business failures, Ford finally got a company going successfully in 1903; his aim was to "build a motor car for the great multitude." By 1910 he was operating the largest and most efficient automobile plant in the world, producing nothing but his Model T, the "tin lizzie" that in 1912 accounted for ninety-six percent of the low-cost car market. By 1914, the Ford Motor Company was doing $120 million in business and had a cash surplus of almost $49 million. Having achieved his goal to make a car even his own workers could afford—the Model T cost $550 in 1914, $345 in 1916—Ford decided to do even more for his employees—"aid the man who sweats," he always advised. More than doubling his company's daily wage for unskilled labor to $5, he also reduced the workshift to eight hours. These innovations earned Ford worldwide recognition as a man of social conscience and won him the "right" to be heard on any subject. In an interview with the *New York Times* published on April 11, 1915, Ford said that there would have been no war if Europe had spent its money on tractors instead of armaments and that moneylenders and munitions-makers were the real instigators of wars. "I am opposed to war in every sense of the word. I try to be consistent. If war came here and I were offered treble prices to manufacture motor cars for military purposes I would burn down my plant before I would accept an order"— a sentiment modified when he began to manufacture tanks for the American Expeditionary Force.

On August 21, 1915, Ford was quoted further on the subject of war, this time in the Detroit *Free Press*: "I will do everything in my power to prevent murderous, wasteful war in America and in the whole world; I will devote my life to fight this spirit of militarism. . . . The preparation for war can only end in war." Under a headline that stretched across three columns, HENRY FORD TO PUSH WORLDWIDE CAMPAIGN FOR UNIVERSAL PEACE, this interview was picked up by major newspapers all over the country.

Not long afterward, Ford was called on by a Madame Schwimmer, on behalf of peace and the International Woman Suffrage Alliance.

Rosika Schwimmer was a Hungarian journalist active in the international peace movement. Shortly after the beginning of the war, she came to America to continue her efforts for peace, since her status as an enemy alien restricted travel in the Allied countries. While still in Europe she had urged the neutral countries to set up an "International Watching Committee" that would act as an intermediary in settling the differences between the belligerents. President Wilson had already offered his good offices as a neutral mediator, but, having been rebuffed, had settled back impatiently to watch and wait until the belligerents eventually recognized the value of his offer. To Schwimmer and other peaceworkers, this was not the most effective approach, for, as Wilson had discovered, no country wanted to be the first to ask for another's mediation on its behalf once hostilities had begun. Schwimmer urged that a committee of neutral nations offer mediation plans to all of the belligerents on a daily basis, making it possible for them at some point to simply accept a plan rather than be put in the position of seeking help. "This would take away the stigma of humiliation which is dreaded more than anything else by the nations. They prefer to sacrifice any further number of their people because of false pride."

Through the aid of Carrie Chapman Catt, president of the American branch of the International Woman Suffrage Alliance, Schwimmer was able to gain an interview with Wilson and present her plan, which was similar to the "continuous mediation" idea of Julia Wales that had been endorsed by the legislature of Wisconsin and forwarded on to Washington. Wilson still preferred his own plan, which was to have his

PAUL HONORÉ
The Spirit of Woman-Power, ca. 1917
30 × 40 inches
Museum of the City of New York

56

"THE SPIRIT OF WOMAN-POWER"

WOMEN
Serve Your Country Where You Can
REGISTER APRIL 27 - MAY 4
Woman's Committee of Council of National Defense Michigan Division

K. WARDLE
The Empire Needs Men, ca. 1916
20 × 29 inches
Miscellaneous Man

Five hundred miles of Germans,
Five hundred miles of French,
And English, Scotch and Irish men
All fighting for a trench.
And when the trench is taken
And many thousands slain,
The losers, with more slaughter,
Retake the trench again.

In January, 1915, a group of suffragist leaders had formed the Woman's Peace Party, with Jane Addams of Chicago's Hull House settlement as chairman. And on February 27, an Emergency Peace Federation convened in Chicago to discuss peace resolutions and to urge Wilson to take a more active role in mediation. Three hundred strong, the representatives called for a "perpetual court of mediation" that would send the belligerents continuously revised "standing proposals." As in the Schwimmer plan, warring countries finally would have the opportunity of choosing an acceptable third-party formula for ending the war with their honor intact. The plan was forwarded to President Wilson for his endorsement and possible action, but it failed to persuade him to abandon hope of ending the war through his own intervention.

In mid-April, Jane Addams and Rosika Schwimmer, as part of a forty-seven-woman American delegation, set sail on the Dutch ship *Noordam* to attend the International Congress of Women in The Hague. Detained in the English Channel by the British Royal Navy, the delegation reached the Congress only hours before it started. Official representatives from Britain never did arrive, for the English government felt that such a conference might prove harmful to the morale of Allied troops. Delegates from one German city were even put in jail upon their return for daring to meet with enemy women. The purpose of the Congress was to demonstrate women's solidarity against the war and to develop an acceptable plan for ending it. Twelve countries were represented, and in four days more than a thousand women passed resolutions that were mainly concerned with preventing a recurrence of war, since out of deference to the belligerents' delegations they had chosen not to deal with the causes or conduct of the current war. They resolved to deliver personally the recommendations of their congress—which included establishing a Conference of Neutrals for mediation—to the leaders of all European governments. Received during May and June, 1915, by twenty-one ministers and two heads of state, the delegates presented their resolutions and also determined to their satisfaction that the belligerents might indeed be willing

GUY LIPSCOMBE
Britishers Enlist To-day, ca. 1916
27 × 42 inches
Museum of the City of New York

personal envoy Edward House work behind the scenes in Europe to arrange his eventual nomination as world peacemaker. Meanwhile, Secretary of State Bryan impatiently advocated an immediate peace settlement in Europe under *any* terms, in order to save innocent lives and end the senseless destruction. House, on the other hand, in direct discussion with the belligerents, had come to feel that so much blood already had been sacrificed by all parties that it was naive to think the Allies would agree to end the war without something more to show for it than just peace. In January, 1915, Wilson once again sent House on a secret mission, to determine more accurately when the belligerents might welcome his offer of mediation. Barely six months into the war, both sides in the conflict were faced with a military stalemate, dug in as they were in a network of trenches that stretched from the North Sea all the way to Switzerland. Each side had already suffered casualties that exceeded one million. Edwin Dwight was to assess the situation succinctly in the April 8, 1915, issue of the original *Life* magazine:

BRITISHERS

ENLIST TO·DAY

280 BROADWAY

"Every Garden a Munition Plant"

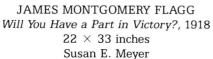

JAMES MONTGOMERY FLAGG
Will You Have a Part in Victory?, 1918
22 × 33 inches
Susan E. Meyer

JAMES MONTGOMERY FLAGG
Stage Women's War Relief, ca. 1917
22 × 30 inches
Susan E. Meyer

to begin negotiations for peace through a neutral mediation body—if the United States were a participant. Jane Addams reported that, except in France, each leader contacted said that his country "would be ready to stop the war immediately if some honorable method of securing peace were provided." She quoted one unnamed minister as saying, "What are the neutrals waiting for?"

Upon their return from the International Congress of Women, the American delegates issued a manifesto through the Woman's Peace Party, which then numbered about forty thousand members. It read in part: "The excruciating burden of responsibility for the hopeless continuance of this war no longer rests on the will of the belligerent nations alone. It rests also on the will of those neutral governments and people who have been spared its shock but cannot, if they would, absolve themselves from their full share of responsibility for the continuance of war."

Meanwhile, Colonel House had returned from his own mission to Europe and had reported to Wilson that the time still was not ripe for his offer to mediate. As House had learned earlier, the Allies were reluctant

to see the war end with nothing to show for it. British Minister for War David Lloyd George was to express this forcefully in a later *New York Times* interview: "Peace now or at any time before the final and complete elimination of this [German] menace is unthinkable. . . . The fight must be to the finish—to a knockout."

The American delegates to the International Congress of Women were extremely surprised to find, after all their efforts, that Wilson was no closer to accepting their reasonable solution to ending the war, even though they had already laid the groundwork. Wilson assured them he had read their proposals and welcomed their efforts for peace, but he could not presently follow their recommendations. It would not be possible for America to call a neutral conference without inviting everyone, including the countries of Central and South America, and with such a large and unwieldy body it would be difficult to stay in control of its actions. Also, the Allies had made it very clear that, with the Central Powers deep into their territory and commanding a military advantage, mediation would not yet be welcome.

In desperation the Woman's Peace Party considered focusing the tremendous pressure of public opinion on the president, but since they could not rely on newspapers, which were only too eager to ridicule their efforts, they tried a new plan. With eight thousand dollars contributed by Mrs. Henry Ford they contacted ten thousand women's organizations, which, in turn, swamped the White House with "continuous mediation" telegrams over a three-day period. Jane Addams sadly concluded that the extra clerks hired to handle the rush "doubtless possessed the only pairs of eyes which ever saw the telegrams."

It was at this point, having despaired of gaining government aid or sanction, that Rosika Schwimmer became determined to enlist the private aid of Henry Ford, who so publicly had pledged his great fortune to the cause of peace. In concurring with Schwimmer's idea, Addams noted that "perhaps it was in character that the effort from the United States should be initiated not by the government but by a self-made business man who approached the situation from a purely human point of view, almost as a working man would have done." On November 17, 1915, Schwimmer saw Ford and explained her idea for a committee of neutrals that would carry on continuous mediation until the right formula for peace was arrived at. Ford seemed to welcome the idea of being respectfully consulted on ways to achieve a peace settlement—considering all his public pronouncements on the subject—and he quickly expressed a willingness to finance the planning of a neutral conference. In conversation, Schwimmer must have suggested how demonstrative of solidarity it would be if the American delegation set out for Europe in a body, aboard a single ship, and Ford immediately saw great publicity value in that. He promised to meet with the ladies in New York to work out details, and by November 23 he had secured an appointment with President Wilson. Ford told the president he supported the neutral conference for continuous mediation and was hiring the first available ship that "could take a large delegation to Europe." Wilson offered him few signs of support, although Ford reported that the president did assure him he was quite within his rights. In his diary, Colonel House characterized Ford as "crude, ignorant and with very little general information," but when Ford set his mind to something he went after it wholeheartedly. By midnight, November 23, he had secured a large block of passenger space on the *Oscar II*, departing

ANONYMOUS
The Salvation Army Lassie, 1918
30 × 40 inches
Walton Rawls

HOWARD CHANDLER CHRISTY
The Motor Corps of America, ca. 1918
33½ × 43 inches
Museum of the City of New York

December 4 for neutral Norway. Some of the peace-makers balked at the necessity for this group arrangement, regarding themselves as perfectly capable of reaching the conference on their own, but Ford argued that publicity for the Peace Ship would raise American awareness of their mission and enhance the importance of their conference.

With little time to spare, Ford sent out invitations by telegram to the most likely peace delegates—including his old friend Thomas A. Edison—and followed up with formal letters by November 27. As he phrased it initially, "We'll get the boys in the trenches home by Christmas." To this the *New York Tribune* responded on its front page: GREAT WAR ENDS CHRISTMAS DAY: FORD TO STOP IT; this was just a beginning to the mostly tongue-in-cheek press coverage the Peace Ship would receive. In most news articles, the projected conference of neutrals was totally ignored. Delegates who already had agreed to go suddenly dropped out, protesting that although willing to support "continuous mediation" they would not expose themselves to ridicule. Ford, however, was a great believer in advertising and publicity and maintained that even the joshing was better than no attention at all. About fifty newsmen signed

up for the voyage, representing almost all of the major newspapers, the wire services, and a few magazines.

Fifty-five citizens accepted Ford's all-expenses-paid invitation to become a peace delegate, but of them only the governor of North Dakota and the lieutenant governor of South Carolina could have been said to have any national standing. No major peace organizations publicly endorsed the trip, not even the Woman's Peace Party whose plan the delegation was ostensibly acting upon. Of course Rosika Schwimmer went, and Jane Addams was determined to go. She wrote later that although a "group of very eccentric people had attached themselves to the enterprise, so that there was every chance for a fiasco, I still felt committed to it. . . . I was inclined to consider the sensational and unfortunate journey of the American contingent as a mere incident to the undertaking, for after all the actual foundations of the conference itself would have to be laid on the other side of the Atlantic. It became clearer every day that whoever became associated with the ship would be in for much ridicule and social opprobrium, but that of course seemed a small price to pay for a protest against war." Unfortunately, when the *Oscar II* weighed anchor, Addams lay hospitalized in Chicago with "spinal disease," a recurring ailment from which she did not recover for several weeks. Part of the difficulty in recruiting notable delegates may have been the haste with which the voyage was organized, as well as public characterizations of it as misguided, but there was also increasing sympathy for the critical plight of the Allies and some apprehension about the danger of exposure to German submarines in the war zone.

According to an article in *The New Republic*, Ford belonged to "the tradition of self-made men, to that primitive Americanism which has held the theory that a successful manufacturer could turn his hand with equal success to every other occupation." In this instance, Ford was determined to become a peacemaker, to be known as the man who got the boys "out of the trenches by Christmas." Whether he was aware of it or not, his focus on Christmas echoed the appeal of Pope Benedict XV just a year earlier "to cease the clang of arms while Christendom celebrates the Feast of the World's Redemption." The pope's truce proposal was accepted immediately by Germany, on condition that the other belligerents go along, but, as the pontiff later noted, "Our Christmas initiative was not crowned with success." Now a second wartime Christmas was coming around, and there was strong sentiment for ending the bloodshed on the Western Front, where even on days with no

major action an average of three thousand men were killed. There had, indeed, been unofficial Christmas truces all along the front in 1914, when men spontaneously stopped shooting each other and met in no-man's-land to wish their enemies Merry Christmas and to sing carols with them, to take photographs and to swap souvenirs. Some of the Germans even proposed a truce for New Year's Day as well—to see how the photos came out! The *New York Times* ran a story about these incredible events in the New Year's Eve issue, under the headline, FOES IN TRENCHES SWAP PIES FOR WINE. Perhaps the wonder of these stories of common soldiers defying the deadly plans of their leaders had stuck in Ford's mind, convincing him—given his standing with the workingman—that if he could just talk directly to the boys in the trenches he could persuade them to drop their arms and call a permanent truce.

The *Detroit Free Press* described the scene as the delegates were boarding the *Oscar II*: ''As it was at the beginning of the Ford Peace Ship plan, so it was at the pier today. Nobody knew where to go, nobody knew anything except that here was a ship that Henry Ford was taking to Europe to stop the war, get the boys out of the trenches by Christmas, and lots of other things.'' Although other writers made literary references to Twain's *Innocents Abroad* and Brant's *Ship of Fools*, the newspaper poet Edgar

A. Guest was willing to give the Peace Ship delegates the benefit of the doubt:

It may be folly, it may be wrong,
and all that critics say,
And to end the strife and slaughter grim
this may not be the way,
I've shaken my head in a time of doubt,
I confess that I cannot see
Whether or not it's the thing to do,
or just what the end will be,
But just the same when the ship sets out,
I'll cheer for your splendid pluck
And wave my hand in a fond farewell
and wish you the best of luck.

After a relatively untroubled voyage through the war zone—Ford had developed a bad cold and was not often seen—the *Oscar II* reached Christiana (now Oslo) in neutral Norway, and the peace delegates disembarked on Sunday morning, December 19. Early on the following Thursday morning (two days before Christmas and nowhere near the trenches), Ford slipped out of his hotel with hardly a word and headed back home. The undaunted American peace

WLADYSLAW THEODORE BENDA
Polish Army in France, ca. 1916
27 × 26 inches
Miscellaneous Man

WLADYSLAW THEODORE BENDA
Following the Paths of Our Fathers, ca. 1916
27 × 26 inches
Meehan Military Posters

VOJTECH PRESSIG
Czechoslovaks! Join Our Free Colors!, ca. 1917
25 × 36 inches
Museum of the City of New York

party, enlisting a Norwegian delegation, moved on to Stockholm, and then to Copenhagen, where Schwimmer had arranged receptions to gather additional neutral delegations for the conference in The Hague. Their aim was to add a Dutch delegation to their group and then elect representatives to the neutral commission for continuous mediation. However, there were several obstacles in their path, the most immediate of which was the absence of a safe route from Denmark to Holland. The alternatives were to cross German territory or to risk threading the minefields of the North Sea by ship. Fortunately, the American ambassador to Denmark persuaded the German ambassador to permit the peace delegation to cross his country in a sealed train. Although not officially responsible for the multinational delegates, Ambassador Maurice F. Egan was not about to let the peacemakers navigate the treacherous North Sea, for if anything happened the American government would have "suffered the criticism that the Saracens had to endure when they intercepted the famous Children's Crusade of the Middle Ages."

Another obstacle, which no one had seemed to consider, was that in the previous April representatives of ten countries already had met in The Hague and set up the Central Organization for a Durable Peace. Even though their purpose was less to take action against the war than to protect the rights of smaller countries in whatever peace treaty eventuated, the mere existence of this body diminished the inclination among Dutch neutral peace organizations to cooperate in the American plan.

The Peace Ship delegates finally decided to reschedule for late February their conference to set up a neutral mediation commission. This time they would meet in Stockholm, giving the staff several weeks to organize the meeting properly and to attract American delegates who, for whatever reasons, were not able to join the Peace Ship mission. Eventually the Neutral Conference did get under way, with five delegates each from Norway, Sweden, Denmark, Holland, and Switzerland, and three from the United States. From the beginning, Henry Ford had guaranteed the conference an income of ten thousand dollars a month—but, in February, 1917, he announced that he was withdrawing his support after March 1. Like other antiwar activists at that time, he felt he would have to make an exception of "this war." In *Peace and Bread in Time of War*, Jane Addams speculated on the alternatives for pacifists on the eve of American intervention in the European War: there were those who would protest against war even at the cost of going to jail; those who, holding to their convictions as best they might, would perform all noncombatant service open to them through the Red Cross and other agencies; those who condemned war in the abstract but were convinced of the righteousness of this war, that it would end all wars; and those who felt that once war was declared by the United States they must surrender private judgment and abide by the decision of the majority.

Among the newspaper reporters who traveled with the Ford delegation was Elmer Davis, a young man who one day would make his mark in radio, a communications medium then several years from its public debut. In writing about the Peace Ship for the *New York Times*, he called his fellow voyagers "the largest and most heterogeneous collection of rainbow chasers that ever found a pot of gold and dipped into it for six weeks."

H. R. HOPPS
Destroy This Mad Brute, ca. 1916
28 × 41 inches
Guernsey's

ENLIST

Fred Spear

III. *LUSITANIA'S* 202nd CROSSING

Within several months of the war's beginning, Great Britain had begun an unofficial blockade of Germany's major seaports by mining the North Sea and declaring it off-limits to any but her own vessels. Britain could enforce this because she had by far the largest naval and merchant fleet in the world. Against her thirty-one capital ships, Germany, with the next largest fleet, could only oppose eighteen. By including armed merchant vessels in the blockade, England could station ships fifteen to twenty miles apart all through her home waters and intercept most incoming ships. Even before the year 1915 was well under way, Germany was forced to ration food staples it could no longer import by sea; in April, food riots broke out in several German cities when the bread ration was cut further.

On August 28, 1914, in a demonstration of her naval might, Britain had sent a squadron into German waters at Heligoland Bight and, with damage to only one of her own ships, had sunk or severely wrecked several German light cruisers. Though much of Germany's powerful fleet was effectively bottled up in port by the blockade, German cruisers managed on December 16 to cross the North Sea and bombard Scarborough and other English towns, killing seventy-eight civilians and returning without challenge. On the next attempt at a raid, in January, 1915, the Germans were intercepted at the Dogger Bank and lost one cruiser while suffering damage to two others. This halted Germany's surface adventures in British-controlled waters for a year and a half, but her Asiatic squadron continued to harass British shipping in the Pacific and South Atlantic until, within about six months, all German raiders were hunted down and sunk or captured.

When the German fleet went out again, this led to the greatest naval battle of the war, on the afternoon and evening of May 31, 1916, in waters between Denmark's Jutland Peninsula and the coast of Norway. In a running exchange of salvoes that involved nearly

250 ships of all classes, Britain's Grand Fleet under Admiral Sir John Jellicoe battled the German High Seas Fleet commanded by Admiral Reinhard Scheer. Both sides claimed the victory, but Britain's loss in tonnage was nearly twice that of Germany's. Nonetheless, the German surface fleet did not venture out again from its mine-protected harbors.

The German Navy still had one trump card left to play: the *Unterseeboot*, or submarine. If Britain were to continue to deprive innocent women and children of adequate sustenance by interdicting Germany's trade with neutrals, surely Germany had every right to resort to submarine warfare as a countermeasure. In September, 1914, a single U-boat had demonstrated its effectiveness by sinking three British cruisers in one day. Of course Britain had submarines as well, but only eighteen of her seventy-four were actually seaworthy. Of thirty-three in the German Navy, twenty-one U-boats were of advanced design and capable of long-range operation. Even the United States Navy had submarines—after all, an American had first invented the stealthy craft—but few of America's forty-nine submarines would play an active part in the war.

The kaiser decided that an all-out submarine attack on merchant ships in British waters would likewise prevent England from receiving necessary foodstuffs and munitions, and perhaps that would force Britain to relax her restrictions on neutral trade. Accordingly, on February 5, 1915, Germany issued a proclamation on shipping and commerce in British home waters, a copy of which reached the American State Department:

The waters surrounding Great Britain and Ireland including the whole English Channel to be a war zone. On and after the 18th of February 1915 every enemy merchant ship found in the said war zone will be destroyed without it being always possible to avert the dangers threatening the crews and passengers on that account. Even neutral ships are exposed to dangers in the war zone, as in view of the misuse of neutral flags ordered on January 31st by the British Government and of the accidents of naval war,

F.W.K.
War Loan for U-boats Against England, ca. 1917
22⅞ × 28⁵⁄₁₆ inches
Imperial War Museum

HANS RUDI ERDT
The U-boats Are Out!, ca. 1917
36½ × 54 inches
Imperial War Museum

mistakes will not always be avoided and they may be struck by attacks directed at enemy ships.

On February 10, the Wilson administration, doubly concerned about this threat to freedom of the seas *and* the country's burgeoning foreign trade, issued an uncommonly strong response: "In the event that German submarines should destroy on the high seas an American vessel or the lives of American citizens, it would be difficult for the government of the United States to view the action in any other light than as an indefensible violation of neutral right." The statement closed with the warning that if anything of this nature should happen the German government would be held to "a strict accountability." Immediate reactions to this note from both pacifist and pro-German factions in the United States indicated alarm that America's position was so rigid that any accident might lead her into war. The German government, expounding its legal right to trade with neutrals but recognizing the danger of inadvertently provoking America, responded that Germany's position might be modified if Britain were made to relax her blockade

and permit badly needed foodstuffs to reach German ports. If so, Germany pledged to continue abiding by the venerable "Cruiser Rules," which had governed encounters on the high seas since 1512. By this practice, a warship was entitled to fire a shot across the bows of a vessel to halt her and to conduct a search to determine whether she was armed or carrying contraband destined for a belligerent. If she proved unarmed and neutral, the ship was to be permitted to continue her voyage unmolested; otherwise, she would become a prize of war and subject to destruction. Britain, in attempting to prevent anything from reaching Germany, was challenging all ships that entered European waters—including those of American registry. Britain maintained that even though cargoes were invoiced to neutral-country merchants, she could not be sure they were not destined for transshipment to the enemy. British Foreign Minister Grey pointed out that neutral Holland in the first few months of the war had imported more than four times the tonnage of copper she ordinarily purchased in one year.

Instead of just searching ships on the high seas, Britain would sometimes divert the vessels into a nearby port, where she could sift the cargo at leisure for contraband or anything useful to her own war effort. This decidedly illegal practice of interrupting neutral commerce, with its attendant delays, loss of cargo, and spoilage of perishable goods, greatly antagonized American shipowners and exporters. Freedom of the seas was the keystone of America's foreign policy, and the liberties Britain took with American shipping led many patriots to heatedly point out to government leaders parallels with the year 1812. Britain went even further in attempting to halt trade with the enemy and published a blacklist of American and Latin American companies suspected of supplying the Central Powers. On July 23, 1916, Wilson wrote to his special envoy Colonel House, then in England, that "this blacklist business is the last straw." A strong note of protest about interference with neutral shipping was sent to Britain, but bad relations continued until the end of the year, when it dawned on England that she and her allies were almost totally dependent on American exports.

President Wilson, anxious to stem anti-British feeling in America, offered the belligerents a plan called "The Freedom of the Seas," whereby all blockades would be lifted and unarmed merchant ships would be permitted to ply the seas untroubled, with only belligerent warships subject to attack. Germany welcomed the plan, but the British Admiralty would have none of it. Winston Churchill already had secretly ordered the arming of British merchantmen, instructing them to fly neutral flags in British waters and to ram any surfaced submarine that fired the traditional shot across the bows. Obviously British merchantmen thereafter could expect little consideration under Cruiser Rules. Sometime earlier, former prime minister Arthur James Balfour (who would succeed Churchill as first lord of the Admiralty in 1915) had warned of the vulnerability of British shipping to submarine menace in the Channel, but the government had discounted the threat of underwater attack. As Churchill wrote, "I do not believe this would ever be done by a civilized power."

The British Admiralty had long felt more threatened by the dreadnought program Germany had launched in 1904 under Admiral Alfred von Tirpitz, which by 1908 was adding four heavily armed leviathans to the Imperial German Fleet every year. So, shortly

RUTTAN
A Wonderful Opportunity for You, ca. 1917
20½ × 28 inches
Museum of the City of New York

R. F. BABCOCK
Join the Navy, ca. 1917
28 × 42 inches
Museum of the City of New York

after the turn of the century, the British government had approached the Cunard Line with an offer to finance construction, under Admiralty direction, of two rather special ocean liners—which were to come under naval authority in time of war. The government

specifications for the liners, to be christened *Mauretania* and *Lusitania*, called for so much reserve horsepower that, as the Cunard designer pointed out, the engines and boilers would require an extraordinary volume of hull space—so much so that insufficient room might be left for the tons of coal needed to fuel this power plant.

The designer, Leonard Peskett, faced numerous other difficulties in planning a ship that would satisfy both Cunard and Admiralty leaders, who were de-

FRANCIS XAVIER LEYENDECKER
These Men have Come Across, ca. 1917
21 × 11 inches
Museum of the City of New York

termined to outdo Germany's *Kaiser Wilhelm II*, then the world's most powerful vessel. To compensate for the sheer weight of the giant engines, fuel, and further additions—and to maintain proper buoyancy and stability—the ships had to be designed with uncommon draft and height, the boat deck standing nearly seventy feet above the waterline. It became too difficult to build into the liners' design the usual transverse watertight compartments (which confine flooding in case of damage to the hull), so Peskett reverted to a precedent of lengthwise watertight compartments, subdivided into a few sections along the hull. In certain ships-of-the-line, compartments had been built along the sides of the hull for storing coal and as an additional buffer against direct hits by enemy gunfire. Following this lead, Peskett combined watertight compartments along the vulnerable sides of the new ship with storage space for the tons of coal required for a high-speed ocean crossing. Of course he had to design hatches from the boiler

AMERICA CALLS
ENLIST IN THE NAVY

rooms into the lengthwise watertight compartments to provide stokers efficient access to the coal supplies; in times of emergency, these hatches would be sealed.

A booklet issued by the Cunard Line states that construction of the *Lusitania* was begun in September, 1904, and that she was launched on June 7, 1906, "just fourteen months, three weeks, from the laying of her keel." Her maiden voyage, from Liverpool to New York, began on September 7, 1907, and she subsequently made "two hundred and one successful trips across the Atlantic. . . . On her second west-bound trip she averaged 24 knots, and reduced the passage between Liverpool and New York to well under 5 days (4 days, 19 hours, 52 minutes)."

According to author Colin Simpson, the *Lusitania* was taken out of transatlantic service in the summer of 1913 and fitted up with deck rings for later emplacement of twelve naval guns, eight of them six-inch caliber. Just after the war started, the ship was claimed by the Admiralty and returned to dry-dock in Liverpool, where certain other modifications were undertaken, including the enclosure of a large stretch of the shelter deck and the removal of passenger accommodations from the deck directly above the engine rooms. There is no public record of the purpose of these alterations, but one might assume that when the *Lusitania* returned to normal passenger service she was no longer as vulnerable to attack and that the Admiralty would henceforth control what she carried as cargo. At any rate, she was then listed on the Admiralty Fleet Register as an "armed auxiliary cruiser."

As a neutral, the United States was obliged to embargo shipments of American war matériel and munitions to European belligerents; nevertheless, with Britain's merchant fleet (which formerly transported most of America's international commerce) otherwise occupied, prospects of dramatically increasing America's share of world trade prompted ideas for circumventing some of the restrictions. The country had earlier felt the bad effects of a deepening recession, so Democratic party leaders (afraid that economic crisis might affect Wilson's reelection) convinced the administration that it was not to America's future advantage to unduly restrict expanding export-trade partnerships—since other neutral countries might then establish permanent footholds. Secretary of Commerce William C. Redfield wrote an article entitled "America's International Trade as Affected by the European War," in which he said "that we are saving when others are losing, that we are living when others are dying, that with us the path is upward and with them it is in large measure downward. It seems certain that one result is to be our own greater industrial independence."

JOSEPH CHRISTIAN LEYENDECKER
America Calls, 1917
28 × 41 inches
Museum of the City of New York

JAMES MONTGOMERY FLAGG
The Navy Needs You!, ca. 1917
28 × 42 inches
Susan E. Meyer

America had eyed the German merchant vessels that early in the war tied up for refuge in her neutral harbors, hoping they could be substituted for the British vessels withdrawn from American commerce for war duty. America's trade with the Allies in war supplies was fast becoming the mainstay of the nation's economy, and the government had need of these ships. However, neither Britain nor France would condone the flaunting of international conventions that forbade the transfer of belligerents' vessels to neutral registry to avoid their capture.

On September 7, 1916, under great incentive to rebuild the country's once-proud merchant fleet (while the belligerents were too busy to compete), President Wilson signed the Shipping Act into law. It made provisions for setting up a Shipping Board to purchase, charter, requisition, and operate a commercial fleet, and it established an Emergency Fleet Corporation to be responsible for new construction. Soon every coastal shipyard in America was laying keels for the new merchant fleet. The Emergency Fleet Corporation was headed by Charles M. Schwab of Bethlehem Steel, and his great contribution was the

WILLIAM DODGE STEVENS
Teamwork Builds Ships, ca. 1918
51 × 36 inches
Museum of the City of New York

JOHN E. SHERIDAN
Rivets Are Bayonets, ca. 1918
25 × 38½ inches
Museum of the City of New York

JAMES MONTGOMERY FLAGG
Together We Win, ca. 1918
29 × 39 inches
Susan E. Meyer

idea of designing a cargo ship that could be quickly fabricated from common items of bridge or structural steel. Each part of the ship was planned in such a way that it could be manufactured at any number of steelworks throughout the country. For instance, the shipyard at Port Newark, New Jersey, received prefabricated parts from fifty-six different suppliers and steel plates from twenty-seven mills around the country.

Within weeks of the American declaration of war, the Shipping Board finally seized the nearly one million tons of German shipping in American harbors. And in the summer of 1917, the Emergency Fleet Corporation took title to 163 ships being built for Britain on American ways, to clear $86 million of that country's debt to the United States. America was thereby well on her way to recovering her status as a great maritime nation. By the end of the war, the Shipping Board had amassed a cargo fleet of 2,600 vessels, sixteen percent of these new.

In 1917, Britain's merchant fleet had been eight times the size of America's. However, with severe losses to U-boats before the Armistice, the British fleet would end the war fifteen percent smaller than four years earlier. America's wartime losses totaled less than ten percent of Britain's in the same period, and by war's end America's fleet had grown to nearly half the size of Britain's, almost sixty percent larger than its prewar size.

By the summer of 1918, the Emergency Fleet Corporation had a great array of shipbuilding facilities under its direction, including the huge Hog Island shipyard near Philadelphia, which could launch seventy-eight ships at once. The country was fast approaching the goal of launching one hundred ships a day, and it reached a total of ninety-five on the Fourth of July, the subject of an especially dramatic poster. In the final half of 1918, almost three million tons of new ships slid down the ways, matching the world's total launchings of an average year before the war.

Anglophile J. P. Morgan, Jr., who formerly had spent half his time in England and had turned over his residence there for a military hospital, could not bear the idea that Britain might lack for anything in her war effort. In January, 1915, the bank his father founded became the purchasing agent in America for both the British War Office and the Admiralty, as well as financial agent for the British government. In its first year as England's purchasing

JAMES HENRY DAUGHERTY
The Ships Are Coming, ca. 1918
20 × 30 inches
State Historical Society of Iowa

JOSEPH CLEMENT COLL
The Tidal Wave, 1918
20½ × 30 inches
University of Texas at Austin

agent, the House of Morgan exported goods to the amount of $1,100,453,950—much of it officially embargoed and a good bit of it via the *Lusitania*. America's trade with Britain and France would quadruple by 1916, while dwindling by about ninety-nine percent with the Central Powers.

In the first six weeks following the kaiser's imposition of a war zone on British waters, German submarines torpedoed twenty-five merchant ships, with loss of life in only five of the sinkings. On March 28, 1915, a submarine surfaced near the British passenger liner *Falaba* and fired a shot across her bows. When the liner failed to halt, the submarine continued firing bow shots, eventually bringing the *Falaba* to a standstill. The submarine's commander then gave the ship's crew and passengers ten minutes to board and lower their lifeboats. After granting an additional ten minutes or so, the U-boat was forced to submerge when rescuers appeared but sent a parting shot into the *Falaba*. The ship almost vanished in a terrible explosion, and more than one hundred people perished, among them an American citizen. President Wilson's protest was somewhat

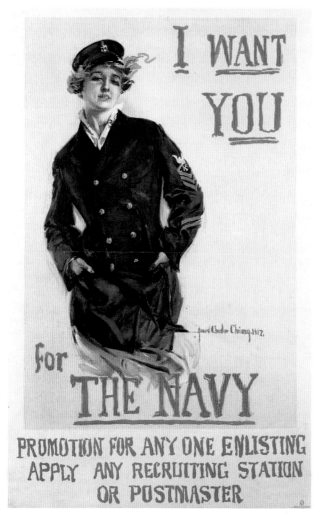

HOWARD CHANDLER CHRISTY
I Want You for the Navy, 1917
27 × 41½ inches
Museum of the City of New York

muted by a German countercharge that the United States had been caught red-handed shipping munitions to the Allies. Apparently there were thirteen tons of high explosives in the *Falaba*'s hold.

In the following month, another twenty or so merchantmen were reported sunk in British waters; that was news Americans of German descent followed with growing alarm. They feared that by accident a passenger liner with many Americans on board might be torpedoed, giving Wilson cause to make good his warning to their fatherland—with all the personal difficulties that would cause their families and businesses. The German-speaking community in New York was well established and prosperous, and some of its members decided, after consulting with the German Embassy in Washington, to warn their neighbors of the dangers of entering British waters on a British ship. Discovering that the next big liner to sail would be the *Lusitania*, they placed, just below the Cunard sailing announcements, the following advertisement in the New York papers: "Notice! Travellers intending to embark on the Atlantic voyage are reminded that a state of war exists between Germany and her allies and Great Britain and her allies; that the zone of war includes the waters adjacent to the British Isles; that in accordance with formal notice given by the Imperial German Goverment, vessels flying the flag of Great Britain, or of any of her allies, are liable to destruction in those waters and that travellers sailing in the war zone on ships of Great Britain or her allies do so at their own risk." It was signed, "Imperial German Embassy, Washington, D.C."—at the suggestion of military attaché Captain Franz von Papen, a future chancellor of Germany.

Although the warning attracted some attention, it had very little influence on the travel plans of the more than two hundred Americans who boarded the *Lusitania* before 10:00 A.M. on May 1, 1915. Among the nearly two thousand passengers and crew was Alfred Gwynne Vanderbilt, one of the country's richest men. After all, where was the risk? This ship was the largest and fastest passenger liner in Atlantic service, with more than two hundred safe crossings to her credit. And, as she neared British waters, even though her size and four-stack silhouette clearly identified her as a passenger liner, it was expected that the neutral "Stars and Stripes" would be run up her jack staff—as a precaution—even though no submarine could match her speed. However, unknown to the voyagers, in the ship's hold were forty-two hundred crates of American-made rifle ammunition, weighing 173 tons, and 51 tons of shrapnel shells, as well as numerous other less-well-identified items—all certified "nonexplosive in bulk."

On the morning of the day before the *Lusitania* would first catch sight of Ireland, U-20, a German submarine under the command of Captain Walter Schweiger, sank the *Candidate* in British home waters, and later that same day the *Centurion*. The Admiralty duly signaled Captain William T. Turner of the *Lusitania* that there were "submarines active off the south coast of Ireland." However, the captain later claimed he was not told what evasive measures to take or that the cruiser *Juno*, which was to meet and escort the *Lusitania* through the dangerous approaches to Liverpool, unaccountably had been called back by Admiralty orders.

Midday on May 7, 1915, Captain Turner, presumably having slowed his ship's speed so as not to venture into perilous waters without his cruiser escort, found himself eight to ten miles off the Old Head of Kinsale on the southwest coast of Ireland without having yet made the expected rendezvous with *Juno*. Unknown to him, the *Lusitania* had been sighted through the periscope of U-20.

Years later the log of U-20 was published in the *Journal of Modern History*, and it refutes some of the "facts" brought out in the Board of Trade inquiries concerning the *Lusitania*'s loss. Because of the unprecedented warning statement in New York newspapers—ostensibly inserted by the German Embassy—it was assumed that the sinking was premeditated. To the contrary, the captain of U-20 came upon the *Lusitania* by chance, as he was returning home to replenish supplies and torpedoes. The liner's Captain Turner was criticized for sailing so close in to land and for not taking the normal zigzag evasive action, but little was made of the failure of his armed naval escort to appear as expected. There is now some speculation that high British officials may have recalled the *Juno* in a desperate gamble—that should the *Lusitania* be sunk with a considerable loss of American lives the United States could not fail to enter the war and come to England's aid.

As fate would have it, Captain Schweiger had chanced to sight the liner and by 2:10 P.M. had decided to torpedo her. He had onboard copies of the British publications *Jane's Fighting Ships* and *The Naval Annual*, both listing the *Lusitania* as armed; hence, she was fair game. As he recorded the event in the submarine's log, U-20 made a "clean bow shot from 700 meters range," which struck the starboard side of the *Lusitania* just behind the bridge, producing what Schweiger regarded as an unusually powerful explosion. "The ship stops immediately and quickly heels to starboard, at the same time diving deeper at the bows. She has the appearance of being about to capsize. Great confusion on board. . . . Many boats crowded come down bow first or stern first in the water and immediately fill and sink." Captain Schweiger then submerged to twenty-four meters and headed out to sea. He added: "I could not have fired a second torpedo into this throng of humanity attempting to save themselves."

Many survivors of the *Lusitania* spoke of a second torpedo striking the ship—even of first seeing its wake—and a boatswain was quoted in *Lloyd's Weekly News* as reporting that "the first torpedo struck nearly amidships, another went into the bow, and just as the boats were being launched another exploded right under them." Apparently the second explosion was of the cargo in No. 1 hold, which ruptured the hull, opened up the lengthwise watertight compartments to the sea, quickly flooded the nearly emptied coal bunkers along the length of the starboard side, and spilled seawater into the engine rooms through unclosed hatches. The ship quickly took a fifteen-degree list to starboard, thrusting beneath the water portholes left open on the lower decks. Because of the severe list, the lifeboats on that side swung out on their davits eight or ten feet beyond reach—some sixty feet above the water. The port-side lifeboats now hung in over the deck or were jammed against the hull and could not be lowered; only six to ten of the ship's forty-eight lifeboats could be safely put into service. After just eighteen minutes—the similarly disabled *Titanic* had stayed afloat three and a half hours—the great ship *Lusitania* plunged headlong into the sea, leaving twelve hundred of her nearly two thousand passengers and crew to drown—among them 128 Americans.

NAVY RELIEF SOCIETY
OFFICIAL RELIEF ORGANIZATION OF THE U.S. NAVY
CARES FOR THE NAVY'S
WIDOWS AND ORPHANS
SUBSCRIPTIONS RECEIVED BY ANY BANK
The Emergency Fund Committee   280 Broadway, New York City

FRANK BRANGWYN
Look After My Folks, ca. 1917
28 × 41 inches
George M. Dembo

FRANK BRANGWYN
Help Your Country Stop This, ca. 1917
79 × 62 inches
Museum of the City of New York

HOWARD CHANDLER CHRISTY
Gee, I Wish I Were a Man, 1918
27 × 41 inches
Museum of the City of New York

ALBERT EDWARD STERNER
Over There, 1917
40 × 59 inches
Museum of the City of New York

Almost two hours passed before the first ragtag rescuers—small motorboats, tugs, and fishing vessels—were able to reach the desperate survivors. In the following days, more than two hundred bodies washed ashore in Ireland and were brought to Queenstown, where the Cunard Line had offered to pay a bounty for them.

When news of the disaster reached London, American Ambassador Walter Hines Page was giving a dinner party for Wilson's envoy House, who subsequently told the group that, in his opinion, no more than a month would pass before the United States entered the war. House cabled Wilson that "America has come to the parting of the ways." The next day, Page also wired Wilson his analysis: "The freely expressed unofficial feeling is that the United States must declare war or forfeit European respect."

Americans were shocked by this "senseless murder" on the high seas of more than one thousand noncombatants, and many patriotic citizens—remembering how Wilson had warned Germany of "strict accountability"—braced themselves for war. After all, the president had shelled the Mexican seaport Vera Cruz for far less cause than this. Anti-German feeling first stirred by stories of the rape of Belgium raged anew, but the nation was still strongly divided about getting entangled in the European War. A lack of interest in the squabbles of Europe's autocracies was deeply rooted in many areas of the United States, for it was largely to escape becoming cannon fodder for kings that many had come to America. As Henry Ford saw the situation, "New York wants war, but the United States doesn't. The peoples west of New York are too sensible for war." Still, one New Yorker, Arthur Brisbane, in an editorial in Hearst's *American*, reflected clear antiwar sentiments: "Whether the *Lusitania* was armed or not, it was properly a spoil of war, subject to attack and destruction under the accepted rules of civilized warfare. . . . The *Lusitania* incident is, of course, no cause for a declaration of war."

Wilson had dreaded the possibility that a German accident might force him to make good his earlier warning. However, he was determined not to become a belligerent at this time, thereby losing his standing as world peacemaker and leader of the most powerful disinterested neutral nation. On May 10, just three days after the *Lusitania* disaster, Wilson made a speech to newly naturalized American citizens. "The example of America must be a special example. The example of America must be the example not merely of peace because it will not fight, but of peace because peace is the healing and elevating influence of the world and strife is not. There is such a thing as a man being too proud to fight."

On May 11, Wilson met with his cabinet to draft a note of protest to Germany over the loss of so many American lives. The cabinet was badly divided over how strongly the response should be worded, with Secretary of State William Jennings Bryan especially concerned that provocative language was likely to lead to war. Nevertheless, the note sent May 13 eventually was made "deliberately abrasive"; it demanded that unrestricted submarine warfare be ended and that Germany pay compensation. The German reply expressed sympathy for America's loss and offered reparations, but it refused to acknowledge that the sinking was "an illegal act," since the *Lusitania* was armed and transporting American-made munitions destined for the Allies. Wilson labeled this response unacceptable and on June 9 sent the German ambassador another note, which Bryan found so harsh that—refusing to sign it—he resigned from the cabinet. In parting he said, "Germany has a right to prevent contraband from going to the Allies, and a ship carrying contraband should not rely upon passengers to protect her from attack."

The final American note about the *Lusitania* went out on July 21, 1915, warning Germany that any repetitions "must be regarded by the Government of the United States, when they affect American citizens, as deliberately unfriendly." On August 19, the White Star liner *Arabic* was sunk with the loss of two American lives. In response to America's strong protest over this sinking, the German government eventually agreed to make reparations and pledged that henceforth passenger liners would not be torpedoed without warning or without adequate provision for the safety of innocent noncombatants. Chancellor Theobald von Bethmann Hollweg was worried that another incident might indeed bring America, with fresh and abundant resources, into the conflict. Despite the eagerness of Germany's admirals to give free rein to their U-boat commanders, the chancellor would succeed in keeping the navy in check until January 31, 1917.

Another significant consequence of the *Lusitania* disaster—at least for the subject of this book—was a news report from Cork, Ireland, that received wide circulation in America: "On the Cunard wharf lies a mother with a three-month-old child clasped tightly in her arms. Her face wears a half smile. Her baby's head rests against her breast. No one has tried to separate them. . . ." This heartbreaking image was the inspiration for one of the very first American posters of World War I, done in Boston in 1915 by Fred Spear, who added to the picture simply the word "Enlist"—two years before America entered the war.

LAURA BREY

IV. "A RENDEZVOUS WITH DEATH"

Theodore Roosevelt, who as president had demonstrated America's new role as a world power in 1905 by helping end the Russo-Japanese War and in 1907 by sending the Great White Fleet on a globe-girdling, fourteen-month cruise, remained determined that his country never "accept a secondary position in international affairs." Disclaiming a third term as president, he had left office in 1909 expecting to continue to wield power through his hand-picked successor William Howard Taft. After it became clear that this was unworkable, Roosevelt sought to regain the presidency in the 1912 election, by challenging both incumbent Republican Taft and Democrat Woodrow Wilson as the "Bull Moose" candidate. Losing to Wilson, whom he thenceforth would detest, Roosevelt was to become, when war broke out in Europe, the country's most indefatigable foe of neutrality and pacifism. Wilson, on the other hand, was a longtime pacifist who saw great value in maintaining neutrality in the European conflict—so that America could wield unquestioned moral power in mediating the peace negotiations and guide the world to better ways of preventing wars. To Roosevelt, for whom pacifists were "flubdubs and mollycoddles," the issues at stake were "elemental": "The free peoples of the world have banded together against tyrannous militarism and government by caste. It is not too much to say that the outcome will largely determine for daring and liberty-loving souls, whether or not life is worth living." Roosevelt publicly castigated Wilson's timidity in the face of the German invasion of Belgium and France, the Turks' campaign of genocide against the Christian Armenians, and the loss of innocent American lives on the high seas. The old Rough Rider demanded immediate military intervention and even pledged to form a volunteer

---

LAURA BREY
On Which Side of the Window Are You?, 1917
26 × 38½ inches
University of Texas at Austin

force and lead it to France, just as he had done when duty called in Cuba.

Under Wilson's official proclamation of neutrality on August 3, 1914, "no person within the territory and jurisdiction of the United States shall take part, directly or indirectly, in the war, but shall maintain a strict and impartial neutrality." Yet well before the United States finally entered the war, ten thousand young Americans had volunteered to join the French as foot soldiers and fliers. And hundreds of American college boys were driving ambulances at the front to aid the Allies. Some sixteen thousand American citizens had enlisted in the Canadian and British expeditionary forces, among them Arthur Guy Empey, a boy from New Jersey who joined the British Army following the *Lusitania* disaster. Wounded in France, Empey wrote about his experiences as a "Tommy" in *"Over the Top" by an American Soldier Who Went*, ending with his hope that someday soon "the boys in the trenches would see the emblem of the 'land of the free and the home of the brave' beside them, doing its bit in this great war of civilization." The book sold more than 350,000 copies in 1917 and was made into a movie.

Paris, then cultural center of the Western world, had attracted thousands of foreign students, artists, writers, and expatriates of all sorts. When Germany invaded their adopted country, many of them felt an urgent desire to save France from the Hun—and Paris in particular. Three thousand Italian expatriates offered themselves in a body to France as the Legion of Garibaldi. And resident Germans and Austrians by the hundreds were ready to renounce their Teutonic heritage if called to defend their new motherland. After a week of fending off foreign volunteers, the French Ministry of War announced that on August 21 alien nationals would be permitted to enlist in the army for the duration of the war. Expatriate Americans also longed to unite with their French brothers to stem the German attack, but to swear allegiance to France in joining the army would have cost them their citizenship. They soon discovered

POUR LA LIBERTÉ
DU MONDE

Souscrivez à l'Emprunt National

BANQUE NATIONALE DE CRÉDIT

that the legendary French Foreign Legion asked no questions and required only an oath "to serve with faithfulness and honor." So a small band of idealistic Americans immediately began to practice their military drills in the Palais-Royal Garden, and on the appointed day forty-three enlisted in the Foreign Legion as privates, with a monthly pay of thirty cents.

Among the enlistees was a young Harvard-educated poet from New York named Alan Seeger, who for two years had lived in the Latin Quarter of Paris. He later explained in a letter written in the Aisne trenches and published in *The New Republic* why so many young Americans joined the French Foreign Legion:

> Paris—mystic, maternal, personified, to whom they owed the happiest moments of their lives— Paris was in peril. Were they not under a moral obligation, no less binding than their comrades were bound legally, to put their breasts between her and destruction? . . . Did not the benefits and blessing they had received point them a duty that heart and conscience could not deny? . . . Suddenly . . . boon companions had gone. It was unthinkable to leave the danger to them and accept only the pleasures oneself . . . in defense of which they were perhaps even then shedding their blood in the north.

Within two months of his enlistment Seeger was at the front, armed with an eight-shot, bolt-action rifle first issued in 1868 and a long, thin bayonet designed for hand-to-hand combat in the massive, all-out attacks French strategists believed would drive the Germans out of their homeland.

By August 16, 1914, Germany's huge siege guns had devastated Belgium's modern forts in front of Liège, which had guarded a twelve-mile-wide mountain pass just below the Dutch border. The Germans then poured through this defile onto the flat Belgian plain that gave access to France. They were surprised and even offended by the stoic resistance of little Belgium, particularly by civilian snipers, whom the Germans later executed by the hundreds—along with others who stood in their way. Because a German soldier was ambushed there, the ancient town of Louvain was systematically destroyed. After breaching the forts of Liège, Germany had placed five armies totaling one million men on French soil, each force assigned a wheeling swath from the north that eventually was to push the opposing armies up against the Swiss Alps. The collapse of France was expected to take no more than several

weeks; the kaiser had need of his armies for similar work against the Russians to the east.

France's grand strategy was to draw up her armies in a strong front stretching from Abbeville on the Somme River all the way south to the Swiss border. Then with indomitable spirit and superior strength in depth, the French armies were to launch a massive, unstoppable attack against the German invaders that would send the *Boches* reeling with great losses back across their border. However, all the way along an advancing line, the Germans were driving the French ahead of them—in full retreat. Under the German plan, General Alexander von Kluck was to sweep to the west of Paris, overrun it, and continue to push the French armies ahead of him to their doom in the south. But on August 20, far earlier than Germany had expected, Russia invaded East Prussia and dealt the defensive forces a punishing blow. Much ahead of schedule, German troops had to be withdrawn from the right wing in France to stem the Russian thrust. This weakened a force already overextended by the success of its drive, and the German General Staff decided to join the two armies in its right wing, Kluck's and that of

JULES ABEL FAIVRE
We Will Get Them!, 1916
30½ × 45 inches
Meehan Military Posters

SEM (SERGE GOURSAT)
For the Freedom of the World, ca. 1916
30½ × 46¼ inches
Meehan Military Posters

General Karl von Bülow. Kluck, then about twenty miles from Paris, made an abrupt turn to the southeast, taking him east of the French capital, which was thought to be but lightly defended since the government already had fled. However, the German offensive had piled up substantial French forces around Paris, which then assaulted the flanks of both Kluck and Bülow as they passed through the Marne valley, with a twenty-mile gap between them. This counterattack became known as the Miracle of the Marne, for British and French armies (reinforced from Paris by troops that came to the front in taxicabs!) stopped the German advance so successfully that by mid-September the kaiser's armies had been forced to withdraw eastward some twenty-five miles to positions behind the Aisne River. There they dug in—just temporarily, they thought. Opposite them, the French and British spaded up their own trenches, but not with the care and precision of the German engineers; for, despite earlier lessons, the French strategists still believed that attack and attack again was the formula for victory. "You can't go down and forward at the same time," said one French general.

Among those dug in on the Aisne was Foreign Legionnaire Alan Seeger, who recorded his experience this way:

We first saw fire on the tragic slopes
　Where the flood-tide of France's early
　　gain,
Big with wrecked promise and abandoned
　　hopes,
　Broke in a surf of blood along the Aisne.

The armies were to remain entrenched there far longer than anyone expected (for trench warfare figured in no country's plans); but as Seeger wrote his mother a few months after settling in on the Aisne: "The lull during the winter has allowed each side on this front to fortify itself so strongly that, in my opinion, the deadlock here is permanent." During letups in battle he wrote poems and articles reflecting one soldier's views of the war that the *New York Sun* and *The New Republic* published, gaining him something of a romantic reputation back home. Among his poems written during the long stalemate was "A Message to America," prompted by his country's failure to enter the war even after the *Lusitania* sinking. Seeger contrasts Roosevelt's pronouncements with those of Wilson and particularly reacts to the president's latest justification for American neutrality: "There is such a thing as a man being too proud to fight." He has little respect for America's current leaders.

Are these, in the world's great parliament,
The men you would choose to represent
Your honor, your manhood, and your pride,

And the virtues your fathers dignified?
Oh, bury them deeper than the sea
In universal obloquy;
Forget the ground where they lie, or write
For epitaph: "Too proud to fight."

I have been too long from my country's
　　shores
To reckon what state of mind is yours,
But as for myself I know right well
I would go through fire and shot and shell
And face new perils and make my bed
In new privations, if ROOSEVELT led. . . .

Four million men spent most of the year 1915 in muddy and vermin-infested ditches on the Western Front, periodically charging each other's entrenchments and gaining or losing ground in hardly more than hundreds of yards. In Flanders, Germans were the aggressors; in Artois and Champagne, the French and British took the initiative. By the end of 1915, the French armies found themselves in practically the same positions they had dug into as the year opened. However, the cost of these inconclusive actions had been incredible: France had lost in a year almost 1.5 million young men, out of a total population of about 40 million.

Over Christmas 1915, General Erich von Falkenhayn, chief of the German General Staff, prepared a memorandum for the kaiser outlining his analysis of the year-long stalemate. Without admitting that he despaired of ever breaking the deadlock, Falkenhayn had thought of a devilish way to turn it to German advantage. Given the mad propensity of French generals to throw wave after wave of infantry into an attack, no matter how futile, Falkenhayn proposed to launch an unusual winter assault on France, one pressed not hard enough to win but yet with sufficient force to keep the battle going indefinitely—until the French armies bled themselves to death repeatedly charging German machine gunners. The German assault was to hit a narrowly restricted target the French could not fail to defend at whatever the cost, and Falkenhayn chose historic Verdun, a heavily fortified bastion about 140 miles east of Paris. Verdun was the apex of a prominent salient into the German front, and so all through January and early February Falkenhayn secretly moved Germany's heaviest artillery and six infantry divisions into a narrow sector fronting the city's forts. At quarter past seven on the morning of February 21, he ordered a two-day bombardment with fourteen

MAURICE NEUMONT
They Shall Not Pass, 1918
31¼ × 47 inches
Miscellaneous Man

hundred guns that would throw two million explosive shells into Verdun's defenses. The German offensive continued without letup for several months; but by June the battlefront had widened and the French, under General Henri Philippe Pétain (who pledged, "They shall not pass"), had begun a counteroffensive that gradually would win back the last of Verdun's forts by December 18, 1916. In fiercely defending the no-longer strategic Verdun for ten harrowing months, France poured in seventy percent of her army, losing half a million men; Falkenhayn's scheme had cost the Germans only one hundred thousand fewer casualties.

Writing home of a soldier's life in the trenches, Seeger assured his family that death in battle held no terror for him: "It is by far the noblest form in which death can come. It is in a sense almost a privilege to be allowed to meet it in this way. The cause is worth fighting for. If one goes it is in company with the élite of the world. *Ave atque vale!*" He wrote:

I have a rendezvous with Death
At some disputed barricade,
When Spring comes back with rustling shade
And apple-blossoms fill the air—
I have a rendezvous with Death
When Spring brings back blue days and fair.

It may be he shall take my hand
And lead me into his dark land
And close my eyes and quench my breath—
It may be I shall pass him still.
I have a rendezvous with Death
On some scarred slope of battered hill,
When Spring comes round again this year
And the first meadow-flowers appear.

God knows 'twere better to be deep
Pillowed in silk and scented down,
Where Love throbs out in blissful sleep,
Pulse nigh to pulse, and breath to breath,
Where hushed awakenings are dear . . .
But I've a rendezvous with Death
At midnight in some flaming town,
When Spring trips north again this year,

And I to my pledged word am true,
I shall not fail that rendezvous.

In the early summer of 1916, about one hundred miles northwest of Verdun, British general Sir Douglas Haig was developing plans for a battle on the Somme front that would entail the greatest joint British and French assault of the war. Ostensibly the offensive was to draw German forces out of the Verdun sector so as to relieve the pressure on French armies besieged there for more than four months. On July 1, 1916, at 7:28 A.M., the Battle of the Somme opened with nearly a quarter million British and French infantrymen charging German entrenchments "softened" by a seven-day-long fusillade of over 1.5 million artillery rounds. The bombardment failed to crush the German fortifications, and sixty thousand Allied soldiers were laid waste by machine-gun fire that very first day (thirty thousand in the initial hour of the charge!). Yet Haig and the other generals continued the battle for almost five months longer, piling up more than a half million casualties for the Allies alone. Among the Allied soldiers in this campaign were the poets Robert Graves, Siegfried Sassoon, John Masefield, and Alan Seeger. In *Good-bye to All That*, his reminiscences of World War I, Graves was to characterize the almost stationary Western Front he fought on as a giant sausage machine, grinding up young men, spewing out corpses, and remaining "firmly screwed in place." Indeed, in three and a half years of stalemate, the front would move back and forth within a range of less than ten miles.

On the evening of July 23, Seeger was part of a detachment of Foreign Legionnaires ordered to neutralize German machine-gun nests in the village of Belloy-en-Santerre. In the Legionnaires' very first assault, Seeger was hit by six machine-gun bullets in the stomach and legs. He did what he could to dress his wounds and jammed his new Chauchat automatic rifle into the ground to mark his presence for the stretcher-bearers; nevertheless, when found next morning this brave Legionnaire had already kept his rendezvous with death. Alan Seeger, *poilu* and poet, was buried with hundreds of others just south of the village—only a few weeks past his twenty-eighth birthday. In his final letter home, he had written: "If you are in this thing at all, it is best to be in to the limit, and this is the supreme experience."

THE DEADLY SCENT OF NEW-MOWN HAY

On April 22, 1915, at the second battle of Ypres, a new and terrifying weapon had been introduced to warfare: poison gas. Although the French had lofted tear gas by rifle grenade into German trenches as early as August, 1914, and the Germans had loosed the same irritant on the Russians in January, 1915, the new gas used at Ypres was far more toxic than anything tried before. At sunset, German soldiers were ordered to open cylinders of greenish-yellow chlorine gas at the firing steps of their trenches, and, as it boiled out into the atmosphere, the heavy mist was driven by prevailing winds into the burrows of the unsuspecting enemy. Ten thousand Allied troops gasped in agony and immediately fled; five thousand of them died horribly within ten minutes. German strategists had intended to break the long stalemate in the trenches with this new weapon, but, unprepared for such success, the German troops failed to capitalize on it by occupying the abandoned Allied positions. The initiative was lost: once recognized, chlorine gas was easily neutralized in subsequent attacks by breathing through pads soaked in hyposulfite.

The Germans then brought forth phosgene, an even more lethal poison. The French quickly retaliated in kind when this gas was identified, launching canisters of it from trench mortars and in artillery shells. Wafting in with the smell of new-mown hay, phosgene brought little warning of its deadly effect. This pestilential agent was followed by chlorpicrin, or vomiting gas, which defied the usual neutralizers

W. G. THAYER
Learn to Adjust Your Respirator, ca. 1918
20 × 30 inches
Maurice Rickards

and eventually overwhelmed the activated charcoal filters of the soldiers' gas masks. Chlorpicrin was not so deadly in itself, but when an unfortunate trooper raised his mask to vomit, he risked inhaling other—lethal—gases that were often mixed with it.

By the summer of 1917, both sides of the conflict had developed adequate defenses against existing poison gases, through advanced respirators as well as through training in quick response to telltale signals—like the smell of new-mown hay. The war had returned once more to stalemate, but on July 17, again at Ypres, Germany let loose the blistering mustard gas. In low concentrations it was barely noticeable, with a scent like lilac in bloom. The gas lingered with full potency for weeks in shell holes and dugouts, waiting for a frightened *poilu* to dive in for protection from the machine guns. Spring and summer were thenceforth even more traumatic on the Western Front—when lilacs bloomed and hay was newly mown.

FRANK BRANGWYN
At Neuve Chapelle, ca. 1915
20 × 30 inches
Meehan Military Posters

Horrible as death was by poison gas (phosgene turned into hydrochloric acid in one's lungs), it accounted for no more than thirty thousand deaths in World War I—about the number of British soldiers killed by German machine-gunners in the very first hour of the Battle of the Somme.

HIGH ADVENTURE

For Theodore Roosevelt this war was "The Great Adventure," and, although President Wilson refused to let him lead a volunteer unit into battle, he was to see four sons in the war; one of them, Quentin, was killed as a flier. Another who saw the war as high adventure was James Norman Hall of the famous Lafayette Escadrille, who published his war diary in 1917: "I am writing a journal of high adventure . . . in which all the resources in skill and cleverness of one set of men are pitted against those of another set." Adventure, a spirit of gamesmanship, and the war's opportunities for testing one's manhood proved too irresistible for many idealistic American college boys. Historian William L. Langer, who went to France in 1917, reflected on this prevalent feeling many years later, in his preface to the reissue of *Gas and Flame in World War I*: "We . . . were simply fascinated by the prospect of adventure and heroism. Most of us, I think, had the feeling that life, if we survived, would run in the familiar, routine channel. Here was our one great chance for excitement and risk. We could not afford to pass it up." From Harvard alone twenty brave volunteers were already dead by 1916; the first American citizen to die in the war, on February 27, 1915, was Harvard graduate Edward Mandell Stone, class of 1908.

With America officially neutral, the early alternatives for action overseas with the Allies were relatively few: the Canadian or British expeditionary forces, the French Foreign Legion, the Harjes Formation of the American Red Cross, or the American Volunteer Motor Ambulance Corps organized in 1914 by Richard Norton, son of Harvard's Charles Eliot Norton (only the last two groups, which were later

H. BLYLEVEN ESSELEN
You Drive a Car Here, ca. 1916
19 × 27 inches
University of Texas at Austin

ANONYMOUS
Great War Film, ca. 1916
28 × 43¾ inches
George M. Dembo

N. NUYTTENS
American Field Service, 1917
22½ × 34½ inches
University of Texas at Austin

to be combined as the Norton-Harjes Ambulance Corps, offered the chance to serve under the American flag). Ernest Hemingway, John Dos Passos (who had been studying architecture in Spain), Malcolm Cowley, and Sidney Howard were among those who volunteered to drive ambulances at the front rather than wait for America to join the Allies. E. E. Cummings went to the Norton-Harjes Corps right out of Harvard, but in 1917 he was imprisoned by the French for several months on charges of ''treasonable correspondence,'' an episode related in *The Enormous Room*. Most of the ambulance drivers were recent college graduates, and of the approximately 1,100 who volunteered, 325 were from Harvard and 187 from Yale, followed closely by Princeton with 181.

Even a forty-one-year-old former Harvard economics professor was responsive to the highly con-

tagious spirit of adventure that infected American youth. Within a month of the war's beginning, Abram Piatt Andrew, a former assistant secretary of the treasury as well as director of the United States Mint, had contacted his friend Robert Bacon, president of the American Hospital in France, to offer his services for the duration of the war; he had been defeated in a primary bid for a seat in Congress. However, the only job at the American Hospital he qualified for was ambulance driver.

Andrew reported for duty in January, 1915, to find the American Hospital relocated to larger facilities, the former Lycée Pasteur, to better handle the great number of casualties caused by General von Kluck's drive on Paris and the intense fighting along the Marne. Most of the vehicles assigned to ambulance service had been donated by American ex-

ANONYMOUS
The New York Decorators Ambulance Fund, ca. 1916
41⅛ × 29⅛ inches
University of Texas at Austin

patriates, and whenever drivers could be found for them the ambulances were sent up to the front. This arrangement proved too unpredictable for the French Army, and further volunteer forays into the battlefields were discouraged. Nevertheless, the British Expeditionary Force was still willing to employ volunteer ambulance drivers in its sector to the north—but strictly behind the lines—to transport the wounded to hospitals in other parts of France.

Andrew's first assignment for the British was in the Dunkirk area, where he met trains from the front and drove the wounded to hospital ships at the docks or to nearby hospitals. He noted in his journal that five to eight trains arrived every day, each with four to six hundred wounded and dying from the battlefields. More than seventy thousand casualties already had reached the station since the war began, barely six months earlier, and it was estimated that twelve to fifteen thousand wounded were then in Dunkirk. "There are said to be more than six hundred thousand wounded today in the hospitals of France. All over the country, from the Channel to the Mediterranean, schools, colleges, churches, hotels, museums, town halls, and every available sort of building have been made over into hospitals."

Andrew began to feel that additional lives could be saved if severely wounded men were picked up

more quickly from the trenches and treated first at emergency dressing stations just behind the lines. Essential as his job was at Dunkirk, he thought he could be of greater service working at the front. Through the help of Bacon, who appointed him inspector general of the American Hospital ambulance service, Andrew was able to plead his case directly at French Army headquarters. Finally he received permission, as an experiment, to lead an ambulance unit serving French divisions in the south, near the Vosges Mountains.

On his way to the front he noted in his journal the number of graves alongside the road, many of them piled with articles of clothing: "here a hat, or a torn coat, or a pair of shoes, there a comb or brush, or sponge, or wallet, which might by some chance catch the eye of some wife or mother and help her to identify the whereabouts of a lost husband or son."

Although initially on trial, since French Army regulations forbade foreign civilians in the combat zone, Andrew's first frontline ambulance unit—ten vehicles manned by thirteen American volunteers— more than proved its worth to local battlefield commanders. Eventually, the French Army gratefully assigned American ambulance units directly to its fighting divisions, a formal arrangement Andrew

ANONYMOUS
This Is the Only American Ambulance Now Saving Lives in Russia, ca. 1916
20 × 30 inches
Miscellaneous Man
Message at bottom attached to a poster for a Russian literary magazine.

Pegasus at Work for the Allies

AMERICAN POETS' AMBULANCES IN ITALY

Quick Response to Immediate Need

November 24th the Poets' Committee had raised nearly $150,000 and had fifty of its cars on the fighting line with thirty more being rushed to completion. Car, costing $2000, will bear donor's name.

HELP ITALY NOW!

Checks, in large or small amounts, drawn to order of George A. Plimpton, Treasurer, should be sent to
R. U. JOHNSON, Chairman, 70 FIFTH AVENUE (Room 411), NEW YORK

ANONYMOUS
American Poets' Ambulances in Italy, ca. 1917
21 × 14 inches
University of Texas at Austin

C. LeROY BALDRIDGE
Pvt. Treptow's Pledge, 1918
20 × 30 inches
Museum of the City of New York

had worked out by the summer of 1915. Thus was created the Field Service of the American Ambulance. Still mostly dependent on the American Hospital for operating funds (even though the volunteers paid for their own upkeep), Andrew's ambulance corps was rapidly becoming an independent operation. Of necessity, Andrew made an urgent trip back to America to solicit more funds for the Field Service and to recruit volunteers from colleges all over the country. His approaches to pacifist Henry Ford for both money and dependable Model T ambulances were spurned, and so Andrew was obliged to buy vehicles from regular dealers and modify them for use at the front.

In the spring of 1916, the American Ambulance Field Service won its place in history at the Battle of Verdun, where casualties numbered nearly one million—500,000 of them French. Working night and day from February to June, Andrew's ambulance corps undertook a task so overwhelming that an estimated 150,000 of the dead—never recovered from no-man's-land—had to be left to decompose where they lay. From among those bones, in 1920, France selected her Unknown Soldier and buried him with honor beneath the Arc de Triomphe. For many years at Verdun, one could see a line of rusting bayonets protruding from the soil where a squad of

French soldiers, buried alive in their trench by a nearby shell burst, still await a signal to go over the top.

In April, 1917, when the United States entered the war, Andrew expected that his Field Service ambulance corps would become an active unit of the American Expeditionary Force—given its two long years of battlefield experience. However, the U.S. Army already had its own ambulance corps and was training some twenty thousand men for the front in Allentown, Pennsylvania. The Army's surgeon-general, William C. Gorgas, took little interest in the future of the Field Service, but, in September, 1917, it was integrated into the U.S. Army Ambulance Corps, with Abram Piatt Andrew given the rank of major.

Among the early Field Service volunteers was C. LeRoy Baldridge, who, when America entered the war, became a combat artist. His famous poster "Pvt. Treptow's Pledge" played an important role in the success of the Fourth Liberty Loan. Above Baldridge's drawing of a dead soldier there is the following message: "He had almost reached his goal when a machine gun dropped him. In a pocket of his blouse they found his pledge: 'I will fight cheerfully and do my utmost as if the whole issue of the struggle depended on me alone.'"

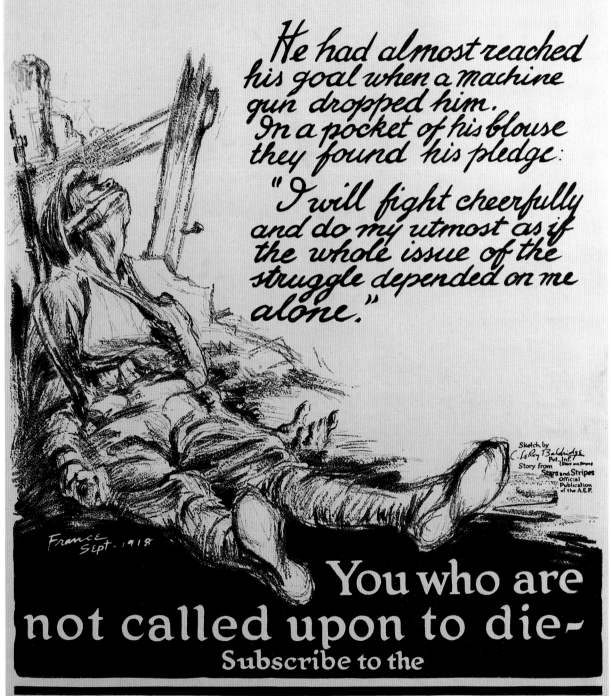

Pvt. TREPTOW'S PLEDGE

He had almost reached his goal when a machine gun dropped him.
In a pocket of his blouse they found his pledge:

"I will fight cheerfully and do my utmost as if the whole issue of the struggle depended on me alone."

Sketch by
C. LeRoy Baldridge
Pvt. Inf.
(Stars and Stripes)
Story from Stars and Stripes
Official Publication of the A.E.F.

France
Sept. 1918

You who are not called upon to die—
Subscribe to the

FOURTH LIBERTY LOAN

FLYING FOR FRANCE

Another young American who enlisted in the Foreign Legion with Alan Seeger that first August was William Thaw II. He was a cousin of the Harry K. Thaw who achieved notoriety by murdering the famous architect Stanford White—for alienating the affections of his beautiful wife, the actress Evelyn Nesbit. Twenty-one-year-old Bill Thaw, the son of a Pittsburgh industrialist, was among the first Americans to learn how to fly. In the spring of 1914, he had come to France to enter the Schneider Trophy race, bringing along his own airplane, a Curtiss pusher. When the war began, Thaw offered himself to the French Air Service as an experienced pilot, but when his offer was not taken up he joined the Foreign Legion. Eventually winning a transfer to the Service Aéronautique, he flew initially as an aerial gunner and then as a pilot. Thaw was accepted into France's advanced combat tactics school at St. Cyr and became the first American to fly in combat against the Germans.

About the time that Abram Piatt Andrew reported to the American Hospital to drive ambulances, an-

other idealistic young American, twenty-eight-year-old Norman Prince, arrived in Paris from Prides Crossing, Massachusetts. Moving into the fashionable Hotel Palais d'Orsay, he inevitably made contact with his well-connected countryman Dr. Edmund Gros of the American Hospital, who was then helping Andrew to form his ambulance corps. Besides being a licensed pilot, Prince was fluent in French, having spent his summers abroad. His greatest ambition was to fly for France against Germany and ultimately to lead *"une escadrille Américaine."* After several discouraging encounters with French bureaucracy, Prince persuaded Gros to arrange an introduction to the head of the military air service, who seemed to take his proposal for an all-American squadron to heart. Seeing the propaganda value of a counterpart to Lafayette's role in securing American freedom, the French general assured Prince that he favored the creation of an Escadrille Américaine in good time. In the meanwhile, Prince and some of his compatriots enlisted first in the Foreign Legion (so as not to lose their citizenship), with the ultimate idea of arranging a transfer into the Service Aéronautique.

By the fall of 1915 there were seventeen Americans in the French Air Service, and Prince felt the time had come to pluck them out of their separate units and organize his all-American squadron. Dr. Gros, active in recruiting Americans for both ambulance corps and air service, personally favored integrating Americans into existing French squadrons where needed; nevertheless, he agreed to aid Prince and introduced him to Mr. and Mrs. William K. Vanderbilt, leaders of the American community in France. These two were firm advocates of America's entry into the war, and they thought that an American Escadrille might greatly aid pro-intervention sentiments back in the United States. They jointly contributed twenty thousand dollars to furthering the cause, and on April 20, 1916, after Prince's unremitting effort, *L'Escadrille Américaine* was finally a reality. Known officially as N. 124 (*N* for the Nieuport fighters they were to fly), the Escadrille consisted at first of two French officers, seven American fliers (all enlisted men), seventy ground crewmen, and six airplanes. The Americans, besides Norman Prince and Bill Thaw, were Elliot Christopher Cowdin, Kiffin Yates Rockwell, Weston Bert Hall, James Rogers McConnell, and Victor Emmanuel Chapman. Stationed at Luxeuil-les-Bains as fighter escorts for French bombers, they first went up as a squadron on May 13, 1916—with no sighting of an enemy aircraft.

GEORGE DORIVAL and GEORGE CAPON
The German Eagle Will Be Defeated, 1917
31½ × 45¾ inches
Imperial War Museum

M. FALTER
For the Supreme Effort, 1918
30¾ × 47¼ inches
Meehan Military Posters

Pour le suprême Effort

EMPRUNT NATIONAL
SOCIÉTÉ GÉNÉRALE

The Escadrille Américaine first flew the 100-mile-per-hour Nieuport II biplane (nicknamed *BéBé*), the most advanced of French single-seat fighters. Powered by a nine-cylinder rotary engine, the plane weighed about eleven hundred pounds and had a wingspan of 24½ feet. The curious thing about a rotary engine is that the entire power plant, with the propeller firmly affixed to it, was designed to spin around on a shaft—partly to air-cool the cylinders. This engine ran at only one speed—full tilt—and the plane had to be held back by ground crew until all cylinders were firing smoothly and the pilot was ready to mount to the sky. The only possible speed control was the ignition switch, by which the pilot could "blip" the engine off and on as he maneuvered. The Nieuport's armament at the time was a single drum-fed .303-caliber Lewis gun, mounted above the cockpit on the top wing so that its bullets would safely clear the spinning propeller. The forty-seven rounds of ammunition in the drum could be expended in as little as five seconds, and reloading the gun was a challenging feat for a pilot during a dogfight.

On May 18, 1916, the American Escadrille claimed its first victory, a German plane shot down by Kiffin Rockwell. Two days later the squadron was transferred to an airfield in the vicinity of Verdun, to spot targets behind German lines for French artillery. As many as seventy French pilots in a single month had been killed flying this dangerous mission, and the battle had raged since February. Reeling from the slaughter at Verdun, the French appear to have changed their minds about the best propaganda value of the Escadrille; perhaps they now speculated that the shedding of American blood might bring the United States into the war a bit faster. Planes were sent up over the lines to monitor enemy troop concentrations, locate hidden gun emplacements, and record the exact map coordinates of a planned target. The pilot—if he escaped being hit by the enemy—would mark locations on a map, recross the lines, and drop the chart to his own artillery. Assigned to fly two missions a day, the cavalier airmen could then also go up singly when it suited them. Escadrille pilot James Rogers McConnell, in his book *Flying for France*, described what it was like to view the fighting from high above Verdun: "For us, the battle passes in silence, the noise of one's engine deadening all other sounds. In the green patches behind the brown belt, myriads of tiny flashes tell where the guns are hidden; and those flashes, and the smoke of bursting shells, are all we see of the fighting. It is a weird combination of stillness and havoc, this Verdun conflict viewed from the sky."

On June 23, 1916, young Victor Chapman failed to return from one of his sorties, becoming the first of the Escadrille to be killed. A graduate student in Paris at the beginning of the war, Chapman, like so many, said he enlisted in the Foreign Legion "for the cause of humanity, the most noble of all causes."

When he transferred into the air service and began to fly, he confided that it was "like being made a Knight." Chapman wrote home that "this flying is much too romantic to be real modern war with all its horrors. . . . How like a game of prisoner's base it all is!"

The Escadrille spent nearly four months in the Verdun sector, building the unit's total of aerial victories against the enemy to thirteen. However, almost two months went by without even one officially confirmed downing; the French expected independent corroboration to credit a victory, and that proved difficult when most of the aerial combat was well back of German lines. On the other hand, German pilots could drive by car to the crash sites of their victories to collect evidence for confirmation—or souvenirs. Baron Manfred von Richthofen, the Red Baron, would cut identification numbers and insignia from the wreckage of his victims' planes, but less to confirm his victories than to decorate his rooms—as if they were hunting trophies. Indeed, he thought of himself as a hunter: "When I have shot down an Englishman my hunting passion is satisfied for a quarter of an hour." He also began engraving silver cups with dates and relevant details of his victories. By the end of April, 1917, he noted that his collection had reached fifty-two, not too far short of his final total of eighty victories against Allied aviators.

By midsummer 1916, the pilot roster of the Escadrille had grown to twelve, and two dozen or more Americans were training for it in French squadrons, partly as a result of considerable publicity in the American papers. As Chapman had written his sister, "the reporters in town see their chance for news; and they will soon have us bringing down a German a day apiece, and dying gloriously weekly." Near the end of September, the Escadrille was supplied with five Nieuport 17s, a single-seater that could climb and fly faster than their original *BéBé*s. But besides that, the 17s were equipped with a belt-fed Vickers .303-caliber machine gun mounted just in front of the pilot and capable of firing through the propeller arc. A cam arrangement synchronized the firing with propeller rotation and prevented an accidental shattering of the whirling blades. The earliest such device was an inverted iron wedge on the propeller blade that simply deflected most bullets hitting it. The Germans had developed the first synchronized firing system in the spring of 1915, but the new French mechanism was a bit more reliable. The formidable German ace Max Immelmann had shot himself down more than once—but fatally on June 18, 1916.

On October 12, 1916, Gervais Raoul Lufbery, at

JOURNÉE DE L'ARMÉE D'AFRIQUE
ET DES TROUPES COLONIALES

DEVAMBEZ, PARIS

CRÉDIT LYONNA

SOVSCRIVEZ AV 4ᵉ. EMPRV

JULES ABEL FAIVRE
Subscribe to the Fourth National Loan, ca. 1917
31½ × 23½ inches
Meehan Military Posters

NATIONAL

thirty-one the oldest flier in the Escadrille, downed his fifth German and became the first American "ace" of the war. (The qualifying number of confirmed kills for this distinction would be raised by France in May, 1917, to ten. Germany had gradations of ace, with the treasured "Blue Max" awarded for twenty victories.) On the same mission with Lufbery, escorting French bombers to German rifle factories at Oberndorf-am-Neckar, Norman Prince downed his third German aircraft. On returning to base, the twenty-nine-year-old founder of the Escadrille Américaine crashed his plane and was fatally injured.

In mid-November, the Escadrille was renamed at the insistence of Robert Lansing, Bryan's successor as secretary of state, who was pressured by pro-German Americans and the kaiser's embassy because the unit's well-publicized name tended to belie America's neutrality. By then there were about sixty Americans flying for France in one squadron or another, and Prince's old unit became known briefly as *L'Escadrille des Volontaires*. In December, 1916, the group adopted another name: *L'Escadrille Lafayette*. It is said that the name was suggested by pilot Edmond Charles Clinton Genêt, great-great-grandson of the Citizen Genêt who went to America in 1793 as minister of Revolutionary France. The American government eventually demanded Genêt's recall, but since return to France could have meant the guillotine he was permitted to remain, without portfolio. Later, he married the daughter of New York's Governor George Clinton. Ironically, young Genêt would become the first American killed in France after the United States entered the war.

By the end of 1916, the Escadrille Lafayette had been transferred to an airfield at Cachy, near Amiens, and the pilots had begun to decorate the group's airplanes with a distinctive Indian head symbol, much as their famous field-mates the French *Groupe des Cigognes* had emblazoned their planes with storks. On one of their frequent binges in Paris, the Escadrille pilots had bought, as mascots for their unit, two lion cubs that they named Whiskey and Soda. This was the group's favorite drinking song:

So stand by your glasses steady,
    This world is a world of lies.
Here's a toast to the dead already;
    Hurrah for the next man who dies.

Cut off from the land that bore us,
    Betrayed by the land that we find,
The good men have gone before us,
    And only the dull left behind.

So stand by your glasses steady,
    The world is a web of lies.
Then here's to the dead already,
    And hurrah for the next man who dies.

By early 1917, the Service Aéronautique had prohibited flying alone because a solitary plane was always the first to be attacked; a compact formation of several aircraft gave even superior numbers cause to hesitate. In a more crowded sky, fliers needed instantly to recognize their leaders and to tell friend from foe. German pilot Rudolph Stark described the way new Fokker aircraft delivered to his squadron were individualized: "The painter marks them with the *Staffel* Badge, the arrowhead on the wings, then paints the fuselages with the colored bands that identify individual pilots. He takes particular care with my machine, embellishing my lilac stripe with narrow black edges. Only then do the machines really belong to us." The German aces, with a certain arrogance (for the life expectancy of new Allied pilots facing them was eleven days to three weeks

in 1917), not only had their planes painted in wild color combinations (the source of the nickname "Flying Circus") but like medieval knights bearing heraldic escutcheons, even had their names painted across the top wing.

Richthofen was not the first to paint his plane completely red, but by 1917 his entire pursuit squadron flew blood-red Albatros fighters. Later that year the Red Baron took up the new Fokker triplane, in which he scored his last twenty-one victories and was shot down on April 21, 1918—not yet twenty-six years old. (There is some controversy over whether he was killed in the air by a Canadian pilot or by groundfire from Australian soldiers as he crashlanded.) In September, 1916, he had revealed something of his personal code in a memorable toast: "A glorious death! Fight on and fly on to the last

JULES ABEL FAIVRE
For France Pour Out Your Gold, ca. 1915
31½ × 45 inches
Miscellaneous Man

drop of blood and the last drop of fuel—to the last beat of the heart and the last kick of the motor; a death for a knight—a toast for his fellows, friend and foe." Baron von Richthofen was buried with full military honors by his former enemies, and his pall-bearers were Allied pilots of comparable rank. Among the funeral wreaths sent by nearby aerodromes was one from British headquarters marked "To Our Gallant and Worthy Foe."

In the spring of 1917, the Lafayette Escadrille was newly supplied with speedy Spad VIIs, and by shortly after America's entry into the war the group had raised its total of confirmed victories to twenty-four. For nearly a year longer, the Escadrille continued to fly under France's colors. The fledgling U.S. Army Air Service needed American veterans to train pilots back in the States. The French were willing to release some of them, but the Lafayette pilots were reluctant to give up flying in combat and unwilling to see the Escadrille disbanded. The well-connected Dr. Gros, now a U.S. Army major, continued acting as their go-between and brought back news that all Escadrille pilots who passed the American Army physical would be commissioned at least first lieutenants (only Thaw and Lufbery were already officers). The Escadrille voted to hold out for transfer as a group to the American air service.

In December, 1917, there were fourteen American pilots in the Escadrille, down from a record twenty, and more than one hundred (known collectively as the Lafayette Flying Corps) were serving in French squadrons. Just before Christmas the Escadrille was formally released from the Service Aéronautique; but with no active U.S. squadrons in France to join, the pilots continued flying on their own. On January 1, 1918, Norman Hall scored the Escadrille's thirty-ninth and final victory. Six days later, thirty-two-year-old Raoul Lufbery, with seventeen kills to his credit but considered overage to be a U.S. Army pilot, was given a major's commission in the American air service—and a desk job.

On February 18 what was left of the Lafayette Escadrille became the 103rd Pursuit Squadron of the U.S. Army Air Service, with Bill Thaw, now also a major, in command. After Lufbery's experience with the U.S. Army, Ted Parsons chose to remain with the French and transferred into the famous Storks group.

Of the original seven Americans in L'Escadrille Américaine, only three survived the war. A total of forty-three pilots actually served in the Escadrille during its twenty-two-month history, and nine of them were killed—six in aerial combat.

Just outside Paris, near Saint-Cloud, stands a marble memorial to the dead of the Lafayette Escadrille and to those who died in the Lafayette Flying Corps. Engraved on it is a tribute by English poet Richard Le Gallienne:

Their golden youth they gave, and here are laid
Deep in the arms of France for whom they died.

V. "THE HUN IS AT THE GATE"

The sinking of the *Lusitania* in May, 1915, marked, for many Americans, a turning point in their perception of the European war. This "uncivilized" act, which Theodore Roosevelt called "piracy on a vaster scale of murder than old-time pirates ever practiced," revivified earlier, then hardly believable stories of German atrocities in Belgium: the brutal sacking of the city of Louvain, the savage murder of its women and children, the senseless burning of its priceless medieval library. Americans who earlier thought Europe's squabbles none of their country's business began to believe with Rudyard Kipling that "the Hun is at the gate" and that America inevitably would have to step in to save Western civilization.

However, as Roosevelt had pointed out in a series of articles just after the European war began, the United States was far from prepared to wage a modern war and that simple common sense—given the explosive world situation—dictated the imminent necessity for making such preparations. Many others expressed fear that premature mobilization might shackle America with the very type of autocratic Prussian militarism the Allies were fighting. Roosevelt urgently advocated launching a program for universal military training, citing such desirable social benefits as quick assimilation of the large numbers of foreign-born that would be conscripted. As he said, "the military tent where they all sleep side by side will rank next to the public school among the great agents of democratization." President Wilson, still a determined pacifist and neutral, was against any kind of conscription or increase in militarism and told Congress so in his annual message of December 8, 1914: "We shall not alter our attitude . . . because some amongst us are nervous and excited."

Indeed, some *were* nervous. Shortly after Wilson's December speech, a number of prominent New York businessmen (among them Cornelius Vanderbilt, Henry C. Frick, and Simon Guggenheim) formed

ANONYMOUS
Are You Trained to Defend Your Country?, 1915
20½ × 27 inches
Museum of the City of New York

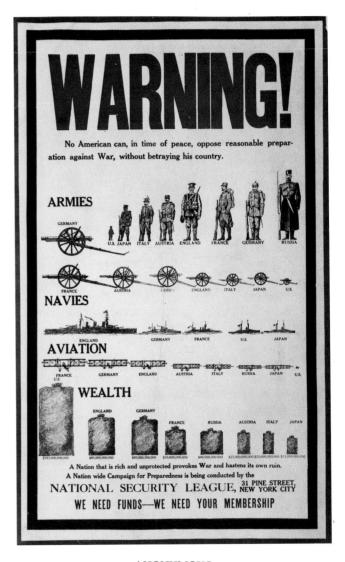

ANONYMOUS
Warning!, ca. 1915
14 × 21 inches
University of Texas at Austin

the National Security League, to press on Congress and the president the immediate need for "preparedness." In addition to universal military training, they argued for reorganization and expansion of the Army and Navy; fresh impetus was given their program when the *Lusitania* was sunk a few months later. Peace advocates, led by Secretary of State William Jennings Bryan, quickly sought to temper official reactions to this tragedy, for fear that ill-considered protests might trigger war with Germany; their fears were seconded by pro-German and anti-British elements equally anxious to prevent a hasty American entry into the conflict on Britain's side.

Wilson fully understood the possible consequences of threats, but he could not simply ignore his earlier warning to Germany that "strict accountability" for injury to neutrals would be demanded of her. He had to react strongly to the loss of American lives in this German attack or sacrifice national honor and prestige. On the other hand, too strong a protest might jeopardize his longed-for role as peacemaker by casting him as another belligerent. Nevertheless, Wilson sensed that his most effective weapon for keeping America neutral would be the very threat of her possible entry into the war; therefore, diplomatic notes to Germany concerning the *Lusitania* sinking were deliberately forceful.

Before he resigned in protest over the abrasiveness of the second note, Secretary Bryan suggested that such problems could be avoided in the future by keeping American citizens off belligerents' ships and out of the war zone. Wilson refused even to consider accepting restrictions on such hallowed tenets of American foreign policy as freedom of the seas and neutral rights. Within a few weeks of the third and last *Lusitania* note, a German U-boat sank the White Star liner *Arabic* with a loss of two American lives. The possible consequences of this sinking were also a problem for German Chancellor Theobald von Bethmann Hollweg since he was fighting his own battle to restrict provocative activities by Germany's undersea navy. Grand Admiral Alfred von Tirpitz—his powerful surface fleet impotently bottled up in port—was determined that his U-boats be given free rein to attack Allied shipping whether this forced America's entry into the war or not; this, however, was too risky a prospect for Bethmann Hollweg and the kaiser. In quashing the admiral's dangerous plan, the kaiser ordered that "America must be prevented from taking part against us as an active enemy. . . . First the war must be won, and that end necessitates absolute protection against a new enemy." With the imperial mandate and the German Navy reined in, Bethmann Hollweg issued the so-called *Arabic* pledge, which promised that passenger liners would not be subject to attack without warning or protection for human lives. Germany secretly went even further by temporarily withdrawing submarines from the west coast of Ireland and instructing U-boat commanders in the North Sea to operate under Cruiser Rules.

It appeared to the world that Wilson had boldly forced Germany to back down, that he had brilliantly championed America's neutral rights with measures still short of declaring war. Now Wilson began to face the necessity of reassuring the American people

that the nation *could* defend itself should Germany not be as rational in a future crisis. In November, 1915, the president announced his intention to put forth a program of military and naval expansion. He wanted to prepare the nation to "care for its own security and to make sure of entire freedom to play the impartial role in this hemisphere and in the world which we all believe to have been providentially assigned to it." On December 7, Wilson offered Congress a comprehensive defense plan, just four days after expelling German military attachés Karl Boy-Ed and Franz von Papen for espionage. Apparently German agents had launched a dastardly scheme to explode a bomb during a high-level naval ball in New York's Ansonia Hotel, within sight of the U.S. Atlantic Fleet at anchor in the Hudson River. Fortunately, the Secret Service had monitored the agents' phone calls and was able to intercept delivery of the bomb.

In the summer of 1915, under pressure from the National Security League and other patriotic groups, the War Department had opened a training camp in Plattsburg, New York, where Regular Army officers prepared the sons of well-to-do businessmen—completely at the trainees' own expense—to become future officers in the event of war. Twelve hundred young men attended that first summer (in response to colorful posters showing a handsome youth in neat uniform asking, "Are you trained to defend your country?"). The following summer, with additional "Plattsburgs" opened, some sixteen thousand men voluntarily showed up for military training.

President Wilson already had begun to align himself with the idea of "reasonable preparedness," and in late January, 1916, he toured the nation on behalf of his beleaguered defense program. Even this modest beginning was condemned by the pacifists, including publisher Oswald Garrison Villard in his *New York Evening Post*: "You are sowing the seeds of militarism, raising up a military and naval caste, and the future alone can tell what the further growth will be and what the eventual blossoms." Wilson defended his efforts at adjusting his nation's defenses to the world's new perils by citing the words of Ezekiel: "But if the watchman see the sword come, and blow not the trumpet, and the people be not warned . . . his blood will I require at the watchman's hand." On June 3, 1916, Congress passed the National Defense Act, which called for expanding the Regular Army rapidly from about 75,000 men to 175,000, and then to 223,000 over a five-year period. The National Guard was to be raised to 450,000 reserves, subject to Federal call, and a Reserve Officers Training Corps would be established in America's colleges.

On November 7, 1916, Wilson was reelected president (under the dual banner "Peace with Honor" and "He Kept Us Out of War"). This victory, although narrow, confirmed for him that he had pursued the right course all along—that most Americans really

ANONYMOUS
Send Off Day, ca. 1917
40 × 23 inches
Maurice Rickards

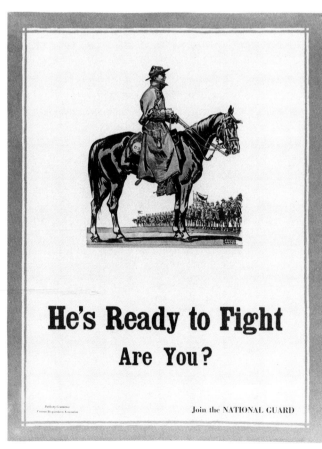

EDWARD PENFIELD
He's Ready to Fight, ca. 1917
19 × 25 inches
George M. Dembo

ANONYMOUS
Are You Trained to Do Your Share?, 1915
20½ × 27 inches
Meehan Military Posters

LES RÉALITÉS DE LA GUERRE SUR MER

L. HAFFNER
The Realities of the War at Sea, 1918
20 × 30 inches
George M. Dembo

did want peace. Colonel House recorded in his diary on November 2 what Wilson had confided: "I do not believe the American people would wish to go to war no matter how many Americans were lost at sea."

The belligerents in Europe had virtually been at stalemate since the Battle of the Marne in 1914. The year 1915 was characterized by small battles and tremendous loss of life, and 1916 saw gigantic offensives with even greater losses. The autumn of 1916 found little territorial change, with much of Belgium and stretches of France still in German hands. On December 12, 1916, the German government, recognizing its advantageous position on the battlefield, announced its willingness to negotiate with the Allies. On December 18, Wilson sent a note to each of the belligerents asking for a clear statement of acceptable peace terms. Although Wilson had tried unsuccessfully before to mediate differences between the warring parties, he decided to make one more attempt at peacemaking since ending the war seemed the only certain way to keep America out of it. But nothing had changed to make mediation more acceptable to Britain and France, and the more costly the war became the less likely it was that the Allies would simply settle for its cessation. The British responded first with terms known to be unacceptable to the Germans, "restitution and reparation," and the Germans, reluctant to give up all

territorial gains, informed Wilson that terms acceptable to them would be withheld until a peace conference was convened.

In reporting to Congress on January 22, 1917, the unsatisfactory results of his peace feelers, Wilson acknowledged that irreconcilable war aims had caused an impasse; therefore, he strongly urged the belligerents to accept a compromise, "a peace without victory"—to end the "death and ruin." He also outlined the need to establish an international organization after the war to guarantee that world peace would endure. The belligerents took no interest in his compromise, and the British were especially offended that in advocating "a peace among equals" Wilson could see no difference between Germany's evil war aims and their own crusade to rid the world of Prussian militarism.

The Germans, rebuffed in their peace overtures, had begun to sense the inevitability of America's entry into the war. Germany's admirals, so long reined in, argued that a free hand with their new U-boats could crush Britain and bring the war to an end long before the United States could effectively use her great resources against Germany. German U-boats were already sinking over half a million tons of Allied shipping each month, and British grain reserves were said to be dwindling toward a six-week supply. Bethmann Hollweg reluctantly gave in to Germany's military leaders, but as he informed the Reichstag, "I always proceeded from the standpoint as to whether an unrestricted U-boat war would bring us nearer to a victorious peace or not. Every means . . . that is calculated to shorten the war is the humanest policy to follow."

On January 31, 1917, Germany announced the resumption of unrestricted submarine warfare and her intention to sink without warning any ship that ventured into the war zone. To Wilson this was a direct challenge, a repudiation of the *Arabic* pledge and all other concessions on submarine warfare. On February 3, a U-boat sank the U.S.S. *Housatonic* (a namesake of the Union warship that was the first vessel ever to be sunk by a submarine), and Wilson had no real alternative but to sever diplomatic relations with Germany. Nearly a year earlier, when the *Sussex* was torpedoed, he had told Congress he would be forced to do so unless Germany abandoned "its present methods of submarine warfare." Wilson refrained from taking the next step, that of declaring war, because he still retained a hope of becoming the peacemaker if America could remain officially neutral.

The next major development unfolded on February 24, 1917, when the British government passed on to Wilson the intercepted text of a telegram between German Foreign Minister Alfred Zimmermann and his country's ambassador in Mexico: "We intend to begin unrestricted submarine warfare on the first of February. We shall endeavor in spite of this to keep the United States neutral. In the event of this

WILLIAM ALLEN ROGERS
Only the Navy Can Stop This, ca. 1917
20 × 25½ inches
Miscellaneous Man

not succeeding, we make Mexico a proposal of alliance on the following basis: Make war together, make peace together, generous financial support, and an understanding on our part that Mexico is to reconquer the lost territory in Texas, New Mexico, and Arizona. The settlement in detail is left to you.''

Deprived of any reason to give Germany the benefit of the doubt, Wilson released the text of Zimmermann's telegram to the press, and there was a tremendous uproar. For the first time, Americans in the West and Southwest felt themselves directly threatened by the European conflict. Still reluctant to declare war, Wilson decided that armed neutrality was to be his next step. On February 26, the president asked Congress for authority to arm merchant vessels, since shippers were increasingly hesitant to send their valuable cargoes and vessels into the war zone without better protection. Indeed, two more American ships had just been sunk, and deliveries to the hard-pressed Allies were beginning to flag. The House of Representatives approved a resolution to arm the ships, but a similar bill was blocked in the Senate

when peace advocates argued that merchant-ship captains with guns to shoot would surely plunge the country into war. Senator Robert M. La Follette of Wisconsin, long an opponent of American entry into the war, had led a filibuster to prevent passage of the measure. Furious about this, Wilson sputtered, ''A little group of willful men . . . has rendered the great government of the United States helpless and contemptible.'' Nevertheless, the administration found sufficient authority in an 1819 statute to order the arming and to instruct merchant ships to fire on any submarine sighted. During March, Germany torpedoed five American merchantmen; over the spring U-boats sank more than 850,000 tons of shipping per month, twice as much as Britain could replace.

In the middle of March, the Russian people rebelled once again in Moscow and St. Petersburg and this time forced the czar to abdicate. The new Russian government was to be formed on a democratic, constitutional basis, which assuaged Wilson's distaste for waging war as an ally of a totalitarian regime. In his War Message to Congress he would welcome

Something doing boys!
Uncle Sam's on the bridge
ENLIST

Issued by The City of Boston Public Safety Committee

the change in Russia: "The autocracy that crowned the summit of her political structure . . . has been shaken off and the great, generous Russian people have been added in all their naive majesty and might to the forces that are fighting for freedom in the world, for justice, and for peace." Now it would be an alliance of democracies battling autocracy. On March 16, German U-boats sank three more American ships, and at last Wilson's conscience was reconciled to entering the war, for that now seemed the only course left to preserve American honor and security.

On April 2, 1917, President Wilson called Congress into extraordinary session, "because there are serious, very serious, choices of policy to be made." He was confident that Congress would not "suffer the most sacred rights of our nation and our people to be ignored or violated." He went on to say: "With a profound sense of the solemn and even tragical character of the step I am taking and of the grave responsibilities which it involves, but in unhesitating obedience to what I deem my constitutional duty, I advise that the Congress declare the recent course of the Imperial German government to be in fact nothing less than war against the government and people of the United States." In conclusion the president said: "It is a fearful thing to lead this great peaceful people into war, into the most terrible and disastrous of all wars, civilization itself seeming to be in the balance. But the right is more precious than peace, and we shall fight for . . . the right of those who submit to authority to have a voice in their own governments." As Wilson returned to the White House that night, he was cheered by the crowds. "Think what it was they were applauding," he told his secretary Joe Tumulty. "My message today was a message of death for our young men."

It was not until 3:12 A.M., April 6, 1917, that the declaration of war was finally approved by 82 to 6 in the Senate and by 373 to 50 in the House, following eighteen hours of continuous debate.

VOLUNTEERISM AND THE DRAFT

"A country can choose to be a great military power, and to remain in peace times constantly upon a military footing," Senator John Sharp Williams wrote George Creel, the future head of the government's Committee on Public Information, "or it can choose to be a great democracy of hope and peace and progress, and knowing well beforehand that if it chooses to be this latter, it must muddle and suffer infinitely in men and money when war is forced upon it." Even when war *was* forced upon America, a few days after this letter was written, there was still widespread doubt that an American army would ever see action in Europe. Learned argument was put forth to prove that the Constitution did not authorize the deployment overseas of the state militias, even as federalized National Guardsmen, and the American Bar Association was forced to stage a full-fledged debate. Before a large American combat army could be fielded in France, the General Staff stated, two full years of hard training would be required. As California Senator Hiram Johnson analyzed the international situation for a newspaper editor back home, President Wilson intended to "fight with our dollars to the last Frenchman and Englishman. He expects the war to be ended by the time he can prepare to have an army ready." And yet, within two months of the declaration of war, a full American division had embarked for France. Shortly thereafter, General John J. Pershing was calling for an American Army of one million soldiers to join him in France by the following summer.

The Preparedness Movement had anticipated the need for a substantial American Army and Navy well before it became clear that the United States could not avoid entering the war. A program of universal military training had been advocated by Theodore Roosevelt and the National Security League since 1915, but its many opponents labeled the idea "Prussian to the core"—it mocked the American ideal of volunteerism. President Wilson had long opposed subjecting the country's youth to compulsory military service, but, in February, 1917, he went along with the drafting of a conscription bill. On May 18, Wilson signed the new Selective Service System into law, a month to the day after the House Military Affairs Committee came out overwhelmingly against conscription. David M. Kennedy, in his book *Over Here,* suggests that the president did not really abandon volunteerism but merely welcomed having powers of conscription if volunteers did not bring the Army to its necessary strength. For Wilson, Kennedy writes, "conscription was to serve primarily as a way to keep the right men in the right jobs at home." The president explained to a correspondent that "when men choose themselves, they sometimes choose without due regard to their other responsibilities. Men may come from the farms or from the mines or from the factories or centers of business who ought not to come but ought to stand back of the armies in the field."

The first step in raising a large army by conscription was to prepare a roster of all eligible young men between the ages of twenty-one and thirty, as the new Selective Service Act prescribed. Not too confident that a voluntary registration program would readily bring forth America's youth, Secretary of

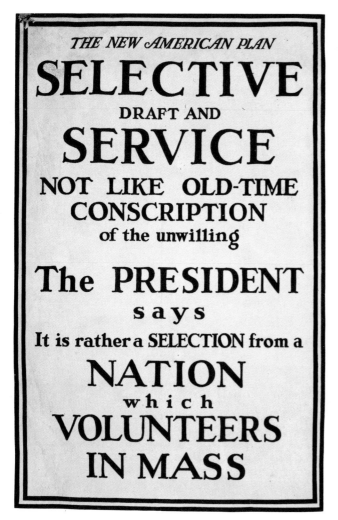

THE NEW AMERICAN PLAN

SELECTIVE
DRAFT AND
SERVICE
NOT LIKE OLD-TIME
CONSCRIPTION
of the unwilling

The PRESIDENT
s a y s
It is rather a SELECTION from a
NATION
w h i c h
VOLUNTEERS
IN MASS

ANONYMOUS
Selective Draft and Service, ca. 1917
14⅛ × 21⅝ inches
University of Texas at Austin

War Newton Baker informed the president that he was ''exceedingly anxious to have the registration and selection by draft conducted under such circumstances as to create a strong patriotic feeling and relieve as far as possible the prejudice which remains to some extent in the popular mind against the draft by reason of Civil War memories. With this end in view, I am using a vast number of agencies throughout the country to make the day of registration a festival and patriotic occasion.''

President Wilson did his part by issuing a ringing proclamation that identified Registration Day as ''nothing less than the day upon which the manhood of the country shall step forward in one solid rank in defense of the ideals to which this nation is consecrated. It is important to those ideals no less than to the pride of this generation in manifesting its devotion to them that there be no gaps in the ranks.'' On June 5, 1917, nearly ten million young men stepped forward and registered without incident. Much relieved, a blindfolded Secretary Baker began drawing registration numbers out of a fishbowl on July 20 to determine the order of the draft calls. In September the first draftees reported for duty at newly built cantonments all over the country.

The original legislation established a state quota system whereby draft calls were levied by local boards on a proportional basis. Several exemptions were available, most notably those of being a husband or conscientious objector, and inevitably, with exemption powers in the hands of a local board established politically, there was a significant degree of favoritism in the selection process. The burden of the draft, therefore, fell initially upon those with the least claim to status or connections. Recent immigrants would constitute some twenty percent of those inducted, swelling the high numbers of the poor and barely literate quickly selected. However, of all young men called for induction, one quarter were judged illiterate and another third were physically unfit.

In June, 1918, a new registration day was set to enroll those who had turned twenty-one in the interim. From April to the end of June, more men had been called to the colors than in all of 1917, and the hastily trained doughboy was sent to France at the rate of ten thousand a day over the summer of 1918. Even at that, with Germany launching one offensive after another, the desperate manpower shortage of the Allies was not easily alleviated. In August the age limits of the draft were extended in both directions, to encompass all eligible men between eighteen and forty-five. Once again Prime Minister David Lloyd George pleaded for more and more Americans on the Western Front, warning that ''the difference of even a week in the date of arrival may be absolutely vital.''

"FOOD WILL WIN THE WAR"

For months Belgian relief director Herbert Hoover had supplied President Wilson with complete details of his work, even undertaking for him a survey among Allied leaders of problems ahead if America entered the war. When Germany resumed unrestricted U-boat warfare in January, 1917, Hoover began turning over the leadership of the Commission for Relief in Belgium to nationals likely to remain neutral. Although, as a Quaker, Hoover had been

among those opposed to American military participation in the war, his opinion seems to have been altered by the sinking of several Belgian Relief ships. Shortly after the United States declared war on Germany, Wilson called him back to Washington. When asked what part food would play in the war, Hoover told the president that ''second only to military action it was the dominant factor.''

Because of desperate food shortages in Europe,

FOOD WILL WIN THE WAR
You came here seeking Freedom
You must now help to preserve it
WHEAT is needed for the allies
Waste nothing

UNITED STATES FOOD ADMINISTRATION

CHARLES E. CHAMBERS
Food Will Win the War, 1917
20 × 30 inches
George M. Dembo
The same message also appeared on this poster in Yiddish, Italian, Spanish, and Hungarian.

שפּייז וועט געווינען דיא קריעג!
איהר קומט אהער צו געפֿינען פֿרייהייט.
יעצט מוזט איהר העלפֿען זיא צו בעשיצען
מיר מוזען דיא עלליים פֿערזארגען מיט ווייץ.
לאזט קיין זאך ניט גיין אין ניוועץ
יוניטעד סטייטס שפּייז פֿערוואלטונג.

it was understood that America must find a way to feed all of the Allies—she already supplied wheat for ninety percent of Britain's daily bread. The generosity and compassion of the American people and the great agricultural resources of the North American continent (which provided fifty percent of the world's corn and twenty-five percent of its wheat) would be called upon for even greater sacrifice and industry. When offered the challenge of now helping his country feed her allies, Hoover readily accepted, on the same conditions specified in his earlier crusade. From that day forward, no one on America's side would face a day without adequate rations.

Food distribution among the belligerents in Europe was managed with authoritarian controls and rationing, enforced by police powers. Hoover felt that coercion of this sort was unsuitable and unnecessary in America and that everything could be handled on a voluntary basis. The press announcement on May 5, 1917, of his appointment as head of the U.S. Food Administration quoted his philosophy on the subject: "The whole foundation of democracy lies in the individual initiative of its people and their willingness to serve the interests of the nation with complete self-effacement in the time of emergency. I hold that democracy can yield to discipline and that we can solve this food problem for our own people and for our allies by voluntary action."

Indeed, the completely successful work of the Food Administration was carried out by 750,000 volunteers and only eight thousand full-time employees, most of whom were clerks and secretaries. Every state had its own food controller who worked through local volunteers to get the Food Administration's message across. However, little in the way of orders and regulations was sent down from the central administration, only guidance and recommendations. As Hoover told the Senate committee overseeing his work, "we must centralize ideas but decentralize execution." Though the Food Administration handled transactions totaling $7 billion, Hoover pointed out in his *Memoirs* that it was the only major agency at

CRAWFORD YOUNG
Sir, Don't Waste While Your Wife Saves, ca. 1918
21 × 29 inches
George M. Dembo

CUSHMAN PARKER
Little Americans Do Your Bit, ca. 1918
14 × 21 inches
George M. Dembo

HERBERT ANDREW PAUS
Save Food and Defeat Frightfulness, ca. 1918
56 × 36 inches
Guernsey's

JOHN E. SHERIDAN
Food Is Ammunition, ca. 1918
21 × 29 inches
Walton Rawls

Food *is*
Ammunition –
Don't waste it.

UNITED STATES
FOOD ADMINISTRATION

Save a loaf
- Help

ANONYMOUS
Save a Loaf a Week, ca. 1918
21 × 11 inches
Walton Rawls

a week -

vin the war

HOWARD CHANDLER
CHRISTY
*In Her Wheatless
Kitchen*, ca. 1918
15 × 30 inches
George M. Dembo

J. PAUL VERREES
*Can Vegetables, Fruit,
and the Kaiser too*,
ca. 1918
22 × 33 inches
University of Texas at
Austin

the end of the war that was not subjected to congressional investigation. It even returned a profit of $50 million to the government.

Twenty million Americans signed pledges of membership in the Food Administration, which obligated them to conserve scarce food so that our Allies in Europe would not have to go hungry. In addition to meat and eggs, Americans were urged to cut back on wheat, the single most vital food item, and to eat corn and barley instead, which were in good supply. Meatless and wheatless days each week were patriotically subscribed to by America's families, and children were forced to clean their plates before they could leave the table. Hoover often wondered about his standing with America's boys and girls, for he knew that his name was linked to every dreaded vegetable children were made to swallow.

"GREATEST MOTHER IN THE WORLD"

Little more than a month after Germany had invaded Belgium, the relief ship *Red Cross* had steamed out of New York harbor with a team of surgeons, 120 nurses, and tons of medical supplies to aid the war's victims. The organization that sponsored this ship had been founded in 1881 by Clara Barton, who,

CAN

Vegetables
Fruit AND
the Kaiser too

Tomatoes

Peas

Kaiser Brand
Unsweetened

Write for Free Book to
NATIONAL WAR GARDEN COMMISSION
WASHINGTON, D.C.

Charles Lathrop Pack, President   P.S. Ridsdale, Secretary

J.Paul VERREES

A. HENDEE
This Is What God Gives Us, ca. 1918
21 × 28½ inches
Museum of the City of New York

L. N. BRITTON
Eat More Corn, Oats and Rye, ca. 1918
21 × 28½ inches
Museum of the City of New York

WILLIAM McKEE
Spirit of '18, 1918
20 × 30 inches
George M. Dembo

ANONYMOUS
Helping Hoover in Our U.S. School Garden, ca. 1918
20 × 30 inches
George M. Dembo

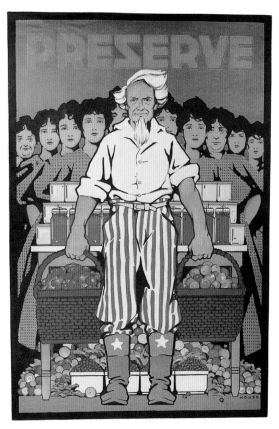

HOUSCH
Preserve, ca. 1918
28 × 41 inches
Miscellaneous Man

ANONYMOUS
Get Behind the Girl He Left Behind Him, ca. 1918
20 × 30 inches
Miscellaneous Man

122

War Gardens Victorious

Every War Garden a Peace Plant—
NATIONAL WAR GARDEN COMMISSION
— Charles Lathrop Pack, President   WASHINGTON, D.C.

MACINEL WRIGHT ENRIGHT
War Gardens Victorious, ca. 1919
23 × 29½ inches
State Historical Society of Iowa

Red Cross
Christmas
Roll Call
Dec. 16-23rd

The
GREATEST MOTHER
in the WORLD

S. A. ICIEK and
A.G. McCOY
If I Fail He Dies,
ca. 1918
28 × 21 inches
George M. Dembo

appalled by the callous neglect of the wounded at the beginning of the Civil War, formed an agency to gather and deliver medical supplies directly to the battlefield. Barton then undertook the task of supervising nurses for the Union armies in northern Virginia. Following the war, she led an agency that searched out the fate of missing soldiers. Several years later, Barton traveled to Europe and, in the wake of the Franco-Prussian War, did relief work in association with the International Red Cross, which had been founded in 1864 through the efforts of Swiss philanthropist Jean Henri Dunant. In 1859, during the Austro-Sardinian War, he had happened upon the site (a day after) of the Battle of Solferino, where forty thousand men lay dead or dying. From that moment on he labored toward the founding of a compassionate organization that would come quickly to the aid of the wounded soldier. In 1863 he assembled a conference with representatives from sixteen countries to address this humanitarian problem. The next year twelve nations met in Geneva to sign an international convenant mandating the civilized treatment of the sick, wounded, and dead in battle, as well as the prisoner of war. To further this humane mission the convention founded the International Red Cross. When Barton returned to the United States she directed her energies toward getting her

HÉLÈNE JONES
The Motor Corps of America, ca. 1918
30 × 40 inches
George M. Dembo
*Motor Corps volunteers agreed to devote sixteen hours
a week to Red Cross duties.*

ALONZO EARL FORINGER
The Greatest Mother in the World, ca. 1918
20½ × 27½ inches
Walton Rawls

"I Summon you to Comradeship in the Red Cross"

Woodrow Wilson

HARRISON FISHER
I Summon You to Comradeship in the Red Cross, 1918
30 × 39 inches
Museum of the City of New York

own country to sign the Geneva Convention and to affiliate with this benevolent association. Finally, a National Society of the Red Cross was organized in America, and from 1882 to 1904 Barton was its president. In 1905 the American Red Cross became the official disaster relief arm of the U.S. government, with America's president as its president.

As soon as war deluged Europe, the American Red Cross had started collecting supplies and enrolling medical personnel for duty on the Continent. Ample funds, however, were harder to come by, for Americans had developed the habit of donating to relief organizations only *after* catastrophe had struck—spurred to a kindhearted generosity by shocking newspaper headlines, pictures, and strident text describing the disaster. In the current situation, the Red Cross appeal was hampered both by Allied military censorship of provocative details of war's horrors and by America's widespread inclination to have nothing to do with foreign wars. But even after the United States finally entered the conflict, the situation remained so desperate that President Wilson appealed directly to the American people: "It is for you to decide whether the most prosperous nation in the world will allow its national relief organization to keep up with its work or withdraw from a field where there exists the greatest need ever recorded in history."

In early May, 1917, Wilson replaced the mostly female directorate of the American National Red Cross with a group of businessmen he named the War Council. Henry Pomeroy Davison, a banker and partner in J. P. Morgan & Company, was appointed its chairman, and he quickly outlined the challenge for America: "Thousands of old men, women, and children were homeless and starving, fleeing before a relentless enemy; whole towns and cities were crumbling into dust under the increasing pounding of the guns; food, clothing, and medicine were lacking; and disease was raising its ugly head in the wake of death and desolation. If ever the brotherhood of man was to be demonstrated and proved, the hour had surely come."

Money still remained a pressing concern, but the War Council had little idea of the sums required for the relief of suffering on a scale never before seen. For a time the figure of $25 million was thought to be an adequate beginning, but ultimately the Council decided to launch a campaign for $100 million. At that point the First Liberty Loan drive was already under way, prompting the Council to put off its fund drive until the week of June 18–25, 1917. A great financial success, the Red Cross appeal brought in pledges of more than $115 million. A second war fund drive almost a year later for another $100 million resulted in pledges of $182 million. The Council also promoted a continuing membership drive that by the end of 1917 had enrolled twenty-two million people in the Red Cross—sixteen million during the one-week drive at Christmas. By Armistice

W. B. KING
Hold Up Your End!, 1918
20½ × 27½ inches
Museum of the City of New York

HARRISON FISHER
Have You Answered the Red Cross Christmas Roll Call?, ca. 1918
28 × 30 inches
George M. Dembo

127

You can help
AMERICAN RED CROSS

WLADYSLAW THEODORE BENDA
You Can Help, ca. 1918
20 × 30 inches
George M. Dembo

Day, American Red Cross membership had grown to thirty million, almost one-third of the entire population.

Even before the first $100 million war fund drive was launched, the War Council had sent an eighteen-man commission to France to ask General Pershing what the Red Cross could do for him. "If you want to do something for me," the general replied, "for God's sake 'buck up the French.' They have been fighting for three years and are getting ready for their fourth winter. They have borne a tremendous burden, and whatever assistance we can lend them promptly will be of the greatest possible value."

By the time America entered the war, the Red Cross already had enrolled a reserve for relief work of more than eight thousand nurses and had formed base hospital units in big cities that were pledged to overseas service when called. That fateful April the organization was able to mobilize three thousand Red Cross nurses, and by October 1, 1918, a total of 14,368 nurses had been assigned to the Army and 903 to the Navy, with 2,454 more awaiting orders. Before the year was out the Red Cross had sent seventeen base hospitals to France; by the

Armistice, fifty-one complete hospitals had been turned over to the Army and five to the Navy. The Red Cross also operated forty-seven ambulance units as part of the Medical Corps of the American Expeditionary Force. Eventually, about six hundred Red Cross nurses were also sent to take care of American doughboys in French hospitals—under the slogan "American nurses for American men"—to spare them the trauma of recovering consciousness where no one spoke their language. With the help of the Society of Colonial Dames, the organization also completely outfitted two government-appropriated passenger vessels as hospital ships for the Navy; they were renamed *Comfort* and *Mercy*.

President Wilson hoped to channel all of America's relief efforts through one organization: "With its catholicity and its democracy the Red Cross is broad enough to embrace all efforts for the relief of our soldiers and sailors, the care of their families, and for the assistance of any other non-combatants who may require aid." The Red Cross, while directing massive efforts toward European relief, also sought to become the major link between America's dough-boy and his home folks. Through its chapters all over the country (which grew to a total of 3,874 by the war's end) and its Camp Service offices at every military post, the Red Cross took on the private troubles of America's servicemen, as well as those of their families, so that while fighting at the front the doughboys might be spared any worries about their folks back home. As the slogan went, "Don't pack up your troubles in your old kit bag; tell 'em to the Red Cross man." In France, the Red Cross also kept track of all American casualties and, when necessary, took photographs of identified graves for the families of dead heroes.

In addition to maintaining 781 canteens for servicemen in the United States (most of them at railroad junctions where troop trains stopped for a while to take on coal and water), Red Cross chapters produced and shipped a steady stream of supplies for the war effort—including, in one three-month period, 63 tons of chewing gum. When cotton became scarce, the Red Cross developed a substitute surgical dressing by gathering and laboriously processing tons of sphagnum moss, which absorbed more than twice its weight in liquid. By October 1, 1918, the women of America had made, packed, and shipped 253 million surgical dressings. They had also turned 2.5 million pounds of wool into socks and sweaters and had made 275 million articles of clothing for European relief.

American Red Cross hospitals provided care for France's wounded as well, and particularly made

ANONYMOUS
Our Boys Need Sox, ca. 1918
20 × 30 inches
Miscellaneous Man

128

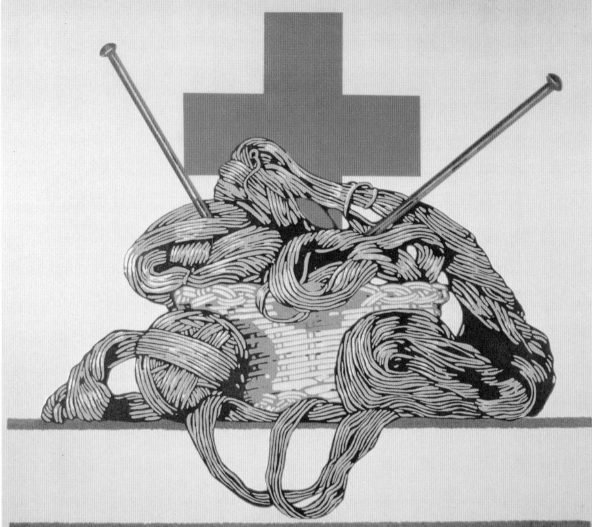

ANONYMOUS
The French Wounded Emergency Fund, ca. 1918
20 × 30 inches
George M. Dembo

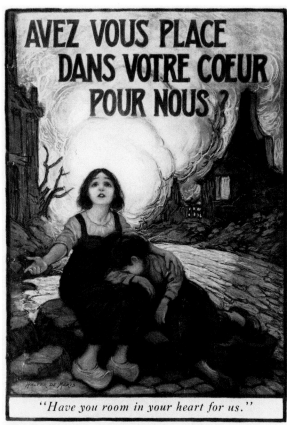

WALTER DeMARIS
Have You Room in Your Heart for Us?, ca. 1918
20 × 30 inches
George M. Dembo

efforts to save the countless children orphaned by the war. In the summer of 1917, Germany began repatriating thousands of French and Belgian families carried off in the early months of the war to work in German industry. When these enslaved workers were no longer effective, Germany returned them through Évian-les-Bains, on the south shore of the Lake of Geneva, at the rate of a thousand or more a day—forty to sixty percent of them children, and most diseased and broken in spirit. A Marseilles newspaper grimly assessed the future for France:

"There can be no real victory unless we can successfully combat child mortality. If we consider the enormous adult death rate for the war period, we can only conclude that after the war nothing will be left of France but a glorious skeleton. . . . The American Red Cross has come to aid us in the fight for our children. Because of this, if for no other reason, we owe the Society a debt of unbounded gratitude and affection."

Almost two hundred Red Cross nurses died in the line of duty.

JAMES MONTGOMERY FLAGG
Viva La France!, 1918
28 × 41 inches
Susan E. Meyer

ALL FOR ONE AND ONE FOR ALL!
VIVE LA FRANCE!

JAMES MONTGOMERY FLAGG

Allied Tribute to France: July 14, at 5 p.m.

MASS MEETING on the French National Holiday
to show we all stand together till we win Peace by Victory

OFFICIAL UNITED STATES WAR FILMS

H. Devitt Welsh

PRODUCED BY · SIGNAL · CORPS · U·S·A · AND
COMMITTEE · ON · PUBLIC · INFORMATION

VI. "A VAST ENTERPRISE IN SALESMANSHIP"

Within a week after the United States declared war on Germany, President Wilson had created a body he called the Committee on Public Information. Its purpose was to convince the American people that direct involvement in this "foreign entanglement" was now unavoidable—and right! Hundreds of writers, artists, and speakers would be enlisted to expound the idea that America ultimately entered the war, as Wilson had told Congress, to fight "for the rights of nations great and small and the privilege of men everywhere to choose their way of life and of obedience." He went on to say that "the world must be made safe for democracy. Its peace must be planted upon the tested foundations of political liberty. We have no selfish ends to serve. We desire no conquest, no dominion. We seek no indemnities for ourselves, no material compensation for the sacrifices we shall freely make. We are but one of the champions of the rights of mankind."

Wilson named progressive journalist George Creel director of this crusade. As editor of the *Rocky Mountain News* in Denver, Creel had supported Wilson's nomination and election, and he corresponded frequently with the president during his first administration. He also played an important role in Wilson's 1916 reelection campaign, writing syndicated articles about Wilson's program and publishing a book called *Wilson and the Issues.* After the president's reelection, Creel declined an invitation to join the administration in Washington, but he kept in close touch as the probability of war increased. Statements that strict censorship would be needed to safeguard military secrets particularly disturbed Creel, but, as Wilson had said, "millions of men and women of German birth and native sympathy . . . live amongst us." Indeed, about fifteen percent of the total population

was foreign born (2.5 million of German birth alone, and another 6 million of the second generation); and in the Middle West, particularly in Ohio, Wisconsin, the Dakotas, and in Texas, there were extensive communities of German-Americans steeped in the history, literature, and music of their fatherland. And numerous German-language newspapers circulated in these areas, serving as vehicles for well-

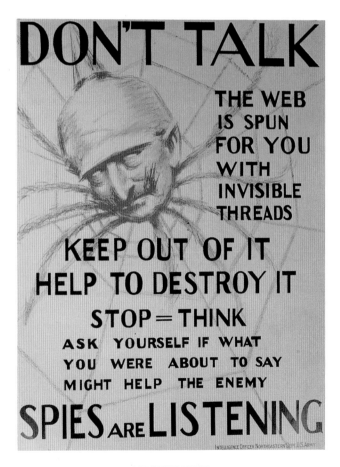

ANONYMOUS
Don't Talk, Spies Are Listening, ca. 1917
21 × 28 inches
Miscellaneous Man

H. DEVITT WELSH
Official United States War Films, ca. 1918
28¼ × 42 inches
Meehan Military Posters

ANONYMOUS
Stand Fast America!, ca. 1918
42 × 28 inches
George M. Dembo

orchestrated propaganda from the Imperial German Embassy. German-Americans represented strong voting blocs in many sections, and not only did they tend to be pro-German but antiwar and anti-big business.

On the evening of April 2, 1917, just following the president's War Message to Congress, legislation was introduced in the Webb-Culberson Bill for the groundwork of government censorship. In supporting the bill, Wilson wrote Congressman Edwin Webb "that it seems to me imperative that powers of this sort should be granted." Creel immediately reacted to news of this bill, writing Wilson to condemn censorship and arguing that "the need was for expression not repression." He urged an all-out publicity campaign to communicate our war (and peace) aims not only to all Americans but to every neutral country and to our new allies: England, France, Russia, and Italy. As for the un-American idea of censorship—never yet resorted to in our history— he insisted that all proper security needs could be met by "voluntary methods." Furthermore, the First Amendment of the Constitution forbade Congress from ever "abridging the freedom of speech or of the press." Wilson sent for Creel immediately, discussed his recommendations in detail, and quickly drafted him as chairman of his new Committee on Public Information, with the secretaries of State, War, and Navy as the other members.

Only a few months earlier Wilson had won re-election by a margin so close—just twenty-three electoral votes—that the outcome was uncertain for two days. He owed his victory to popular credit for having "kept us out of war," since for more than a year prior to this election his administration had championed strict neutrality in the European conflict. Not only that, Wilson had opposed even the movement toward preparedness for possible war—at least initially. His principal opponent, Theodore Roosevelt,

dared to characterize Wilson as cowardly for not taking the country to war over the *Lusitania* disaster, since, as Roosevelt pointed out in his speeches, "the loss of life among non-combatant men, women, and children on the ships which were torpedoed . . . has exceeded the total number of lives lost in both the Union and Confederate navies during the entire Civil War. Think of that, friends." The ex-president had written in the introduction to an English book urging American entry into the war that "a surfeit of materialism has produced a lack of spiritual purpose in the nation at large. . . . The result was a soil in which various noxious weeds flourished rankly; and of these the most noxious was professional pacifism."

Former secretary of state William Jennings Bryan was one of the leading political spokesmen for pacifism, and, even though he had left the Wilson cabinet in protest, he campaigned for the president's reelection in 1916 on the basis of his "Peace with Honor" pledge. Bryan, himself, had been the Democratic candidate for president in 1896, 1900, and 1908, and he argued that "some nation must lift the world out of the black night of war into the light of that day when peace can be made enduring by being

ANONYMOUS
The Triple Alliance, ca. 1918
14 × 21 inches
University of Texas at Austin

"Eternal Vigilance is the Price of Liberty"

American Defense Society
Vigilance Corps

AMERICANS!
Serve at the Front
or Serve at Home

This is a call to the *Vigilant Men and Women* in every community. *You are the constructive patriots of America.* You should be organized and at work. You should first discover and report every disloyal person and action in your community, and help the authorities suppress the activities of these destructive forces.

Once these are suppressed, you can proceed to really constructive work. Until then a great part of what our Government and People are doing is rendered ineffective. Will you not join with other patriotic Americans in organizing a Vigilance Corps in your community? We are actively engaged in this work and can help you. You can rely at all times upon the enthusiastic cooperation of

THE AMERICAN DEFENSE SOCIETY
National Headquarters   44 East 23d Street, New York

ANONYMOUS
Vigilance Corps, ca. 1917
14 × 22 inches
George M. Dembo

built on love and brotherhood, and ours is the nation to perform the task."

Another key figure in the pro-peace movement also had run for president—four times as candidate of the Socialist Party. Eugene Victor Debs had led the American Railway Union into the widespread Pullman Strike of 1894, and his frequent clashes with big business inevitably edged him into the Socialist Party. His opposition to war stemmed not so much from pacifism as from a conviction that war came about through capitalist greed, that ultimately it was workers who did the fighting and dying while capitalists were enriched by the profits of death. He urged "workers of all countries to refuse to support their governments in their wars."

A fourth key political figure who had opposed American involvement in the European War was Robert Marion La Follette, Republican senator from Wisconsin. As governor of his state he had broken with the old Republican leadership and begun a program of progressive reform that brought him nationwide recognition. He shared Debs's distaste

for big business, but, in contrast, he feared that without much-needed reforms the rampant greed and political machinations of capitalist tycoons would trigger a movement toward Socialist solutions.

Lawyer Amos Pinchot, another progressive reformer, a supporter of Wilson's pacifist program, and a founder of the American Civil Liberties Union, questioned George Creel in a letter written shortly after the declaration of war: "Has Wilson changed? Is he going back on himself and on us? . . . Have we got to die tomorrow for principles that yesterday the President told us were wrong? . . . the Administration, and the liberal press . . . and even much of the reactionary press, for two solid years carried on an anti-war propaganda. They were pro-Ally, but they said we had no business in it. At the end of this period the President went to the country on the issue that he kept us out of war—and won."

Pinchot's dilemma indicated the seriousness of the problem Creel faced in his brand-new endeavor: to convince America (and particularly liberal Americans earlier sold on Wilson's stand for neutrality and pacifism) that it was now right and just to go to war, not simply to save the world for democracy but to rid it of militarism, even barbarism—that America's noble mission was something really worth dying for.

As Newton D. Baker, Wilson's secretary of war, reflected on it later:

The whole business of mobilizing the mind of the world so far as American participation in the war was concerned was in a sense the work of the Committee on Public Information. . . . I think it was Mr. Creel's idea, and it was certainly a great contribution to the mobilization of the mental forces of America, to have, in lieu of a Committee on Censorship, a Committee on Public Information for the production and dissemination as widely as possible of the truth of America's participation in the war. . . . It required faith in democracy, it required faith in fact; for it is a fact that our democratic institutions . . . would enable us to deal with information safely; that, as Mr. Creel believed, if we received the facts we could be trusted.

After the war Creel published a candid though self-serving book about his adventures with the Committee on Public Information; he called it *How We Advertised America*. Describing the work of the Committee, he wrote: "In all things, from first to last, without halt or change, it was a plain publicity proposition, a vast enterprise in salesmanship, the world's greatest adventure in advertising." In dealing with the situation that Pinchot called attention to— the turnabout in Wilson's position on America's entry into the war—he commented: "During the two and a half years of our neutrality the land had been torn by a thousand divisive prejudices, stunned by the

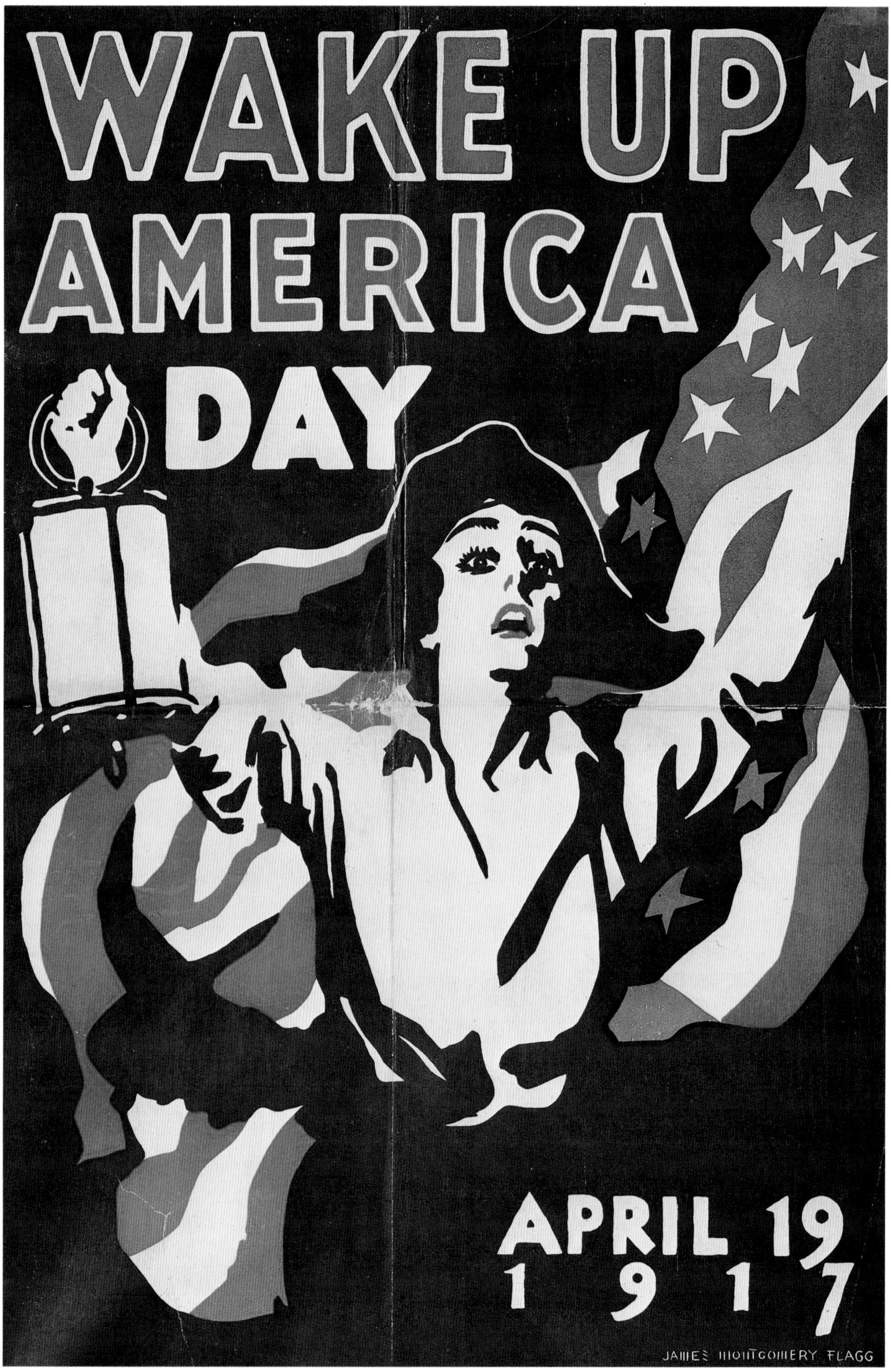
WAKE UP
AMERICA
DAY
APRIL 19
1917
JAMES MONTGOMERY FLAGG

voices of anger and confusion, and muddled by the pull and haul of opposed interests. These were conditions that could not be permitted to endure. . . . The *war-will*, the will to win, of a democracy depends upon the degree to which each one of all the people of that democracy can concentrate and consecrate body and soul and spirit in the supreme effort of service and sacrifice."

Creel went on to describe the astounding scope of his committee: "There was no part of the great war machinery that we did not touch, no medium of appeal that we did not employ. The printed word, the spoken word, the motion picture, the telegraph, the cable, the wireless, the poster, the sign-board— all these were used in our campaign to make our own people and all other people understand the causes that compelled America to take arms." More than 150,000 men and women were involved in the myriad activities of the Committee, manning separate divisions for the publication of patriotic pamphlets, the operation of a speakers bureau, the production of posters and pictorial material, the making and distribution of films and slides, and the creation and placement of advertising and cartoons supporting government aims.

The Committee's first undertaking was the preparation and dissemination of thirty-odd booklets devoted to condemning the evils of Prussian autocracy and to citing the virtues of American institutions, ideals, and purposes in entering the war. "Taken together," Creel wrote, "these pamphlets make the most sober and terrific indictment ever drawn by one government of the political and military system of another government." Among the publications in the "Red, White, and Blue" series were *How the War Came to America* (5,428,048 copies), *The President's Flag Day Address, with Evidence of Germany's Plans* (6,813,340 copies, distributed door-to-door by the Boy Scouts), and *Conquest and Kultur* (1,203,607 copies). In the "War Information" series one could select *The War Message and the Facts Behind It*

(2,499,903 copies), *The Great War: From Spectator to Participant* (1,581,903 copies), and *Home Reading Course for Citizen Soldiers* (361,000 copies). Among the "Loyalty Leaflets" were *Friendly Words to the Foreign Born* (570,543 copies), *Ways to Serve the Nation* (568,907 copies), and *A War Message to the Farmer* (546,911 copies). The Committee issued several other series, including some in German, and Creel gives the total number of booklets distributed as 75,099,023.

FOUR-MINUTE MEN

Among the most interesting activities of the Committee on Public Information was the work of a group known as the Four-Minute Men. The idea originated in Chicago just before the beginning of the war, when Donald M. Ryerson, a strong supporter of preparedness and universal military training, determined that a good time to get the attention of eligible young men was during the four-minute lull

as film reels were changed at the "nickelodeon" movie theaters. He gave the first four-minute talk on preparedness at the Grand Theater in Chicago at the beginning of April in 1917, and arrangements for similar talks were then made with theater managers all over town. Volunteer speakers were heralded by a glass slide projected on the screen that announced a talk of "four minutes on a subject of

H. DEVITT WELSH
Four-Minute Men, ca. 1917
28 × 42 inches
George M. Dembo

and at its peak some seventy-five thousand speakers were available. By August, 1917, the Four-Minute effort had broadened to include speeches delivered at churches and synagogues, lodges and labor unions, as well as at granges and lumber camps. There was even a women's division to insure that the government's messages would reach those who only attended the matinee performances. Almost every night throughout the war, Four-Minute Men were speaking on some phase of the war effort, and it is likely that few Americans above the age of six failed to hear at least one such address.

Creel decided that the topics and coverage should not be left to individual choice, so regular bulletins were prepared, each containing resource material on every aspect of the assigned topic—as well as four-minute talks already written. Among the forty-six bulletins issued (and their delivery periods) were: "Universal Service by Selective Draft" (May 12–21, 1917), "First Liberty Loan" (May 22–June 15, 1917), "Food Conservation" (July 1–14, 1917), "Maintaining Morals and Morale" (November 12–25, 1917), "War Savings Stamps" (January 2–19, 1918), "The Danger to Democracy" (February 18–March 10, 1918), "Where Did You Get Your Facts?" (August 26–September 7, 1918), "Four-Minute Singing" (to be used any time), and, following the Armistice, "What Have We Won?" (December 8–14, 1918).

The Four-Minute Men bulletins were so popular that the War Department commissioned similar ones from the Committee for troop commanders to use in delivering short, inspirational talks to their men. Among those supplied were: "Why We Are Fighting" (January 2, 1918), "Insurance for Soldiers and Sailors" (February 1, 1918), and "Back of the Trenches" (April 6, 1918). In addition, bulletins were prepared for the War Savings and Liberty Loan drives and were sent by the Bureau of Education directly to the two hundred thousand schools in all parts of the country. This was in addition to the Committee's semimonthly periodical *National School Service* that reached all of America's six hundred thousand public school teachers.

Each state director and local chairman had to maintain his own office, and every speaker not only volunteered his time but footed his own expenses. At the war's end, President Wilson paid tribute to the Four-Minute Men: "It is a remarkable record of patriotic accomplishment that an organization of seventy-five thousand speakers should have carried on so extensive a work at a cost to the government of little more than one hundred thousand dollars for the eighteen months' period—less than $1 yearly on an individual basis."

national importance." The group's name, of course, was a play on the Minutemen of April, 1775, at Lexington and Concord.

The concept was taken to Creel in Washington, who saw in it (before the advent of commercial radio) a swift and effective way of transmitting important government messages directly to the people. There were about twelve thousand movie theaters in America, in most cities and towns, and the relatively new motion-picture shows were well attended, especially when Charlie Chaplin played. Within minutes Creel had formed an official organization and named Ryerson director. Early in June, however, Ryerson was commissioned in the Navy and his job went to William McCormick Blair, another of the original Four-Minute Men. By the end of June there were 5,405 local branches of the national organization,

DIVISION OF FILMS

By the last decade of the nineteenth century, Thomas A. Edison's laboratory had developed the first practical motion-picture camera, as well as a "peep-show"

apparatus for viewing its films. Called a kinetoscope, this viewer was introduced to the New York public in April, 1894, and shortly thereafter to the citizens

LOUIS FANCHER
U.S. Official War Pictures, 1917
28 × 41 inches
Miscellaneous Man

IF YOU CAN'T ENLIST—INVEST
Buy a
Liberty Bond

DEFEND YOUR COUNTRY
WITH YOUR DOLLARS

BOSTON AMERICAN

of Paris and London. In France, the Lumière brothers copied and improved the camera, or kinetograph, and invented a way to project films so that several people could watch simultaneously. The American premiere of this new way to view "movies" took place in April, 1896, at Koster & Bial's Music Hall in New York City. For a decade, motion pictures continued to be seen in America as either "peep-shows" or projected on screen in vaudeville acts—a theatrical routine that reached its apex in 1914 when cartoonist Winsor McCay began interacting with the animated star of *Gertie the Dinosaur* in his "lightning sketch" presentation.

About 1905, theaters opened to show just films, and their five-cent admission fee gained them the nickname "nickelodeon." The theaters projected single-reel action films of about ten minutes' duration (a reel could hold one thousand feet of film), and early special effects were especially enjoyed by the large semiliterate and immigrant audiences. The first film of any length to be shown in America was the four-reel *Queen Elizabeth*, imported from France in 1912 and starring Sarah Bernhardt. Hollywood's initial multireel feature was *The Squaw Man* of 1913, a joint venture of Jesse Lasky, Cecil B. De Mille, and Samuel Goldwyn. With the release in 1915 of *The Birth of a Nation* by D. W. Griffith, Americans first realized the great dramatic and aesthetic potential of this new form of entertainment.

It was clear to George Creel that he could not ignore the motion picture as a way of stirring hearts and minds about the sacrifices America's boys were making "over there." But since the War Department prohibited civilian photographers in France, or, for that matter, in any military establishment or munitions factory, authentic battlefield scenes were not available to commercial film studios. However, a photographic section had been formed in the Army Signal Corps to compile the historical record of America's part in the conflict, and Creel asked the secretary of war to let him view the photography on a regular basis, with the idea of selecting suitable pictures and films to show for patriotic purposes. As a result, the Committee on Public Information became the official distributor for both stills and movies taken by military cameramen—but Creel was to discover that the historical section of the Signal Corps hardly even existed. Quickly surveying the body of experienced photographers available in America, both motion and still, Creel urged the Corps to "draft" an adequate force from among them to serve at home and abroad.

Some experienced photographers had little need to be coaxed. As Edward Steichen wrote in *A Life in Photography*: "I wanted to be a photographic reporter, as Mathew Brady had been in the Civil War, and I went to Washington to offer my services." Steichen was given the rank of lieutenant in the Signal Corps and sent to Europe in the first convoy of American troops. In France he was transferred into the Air Service and subsequently became the head of its photographic section, with the rank of lieutenant colonel and an office in General Pershing's headquarters at Chaumont. Nevertheless, his kind of photography was not exactly suitable for Creel's purposes. Citing the "wartime problems of making sharp, clear pictures from a vibrating, speeding airplane ten to twenty thousand feet in the air," Steichen defined his work as follows: "Photograph enemy territory and enemy actions, record enemy movements and gun emplacements, pinpoint the targets." It was information, he went on to say, "that, conveyed to our artillery, enabled them to destroy their targets and kill."

When films and photographs of Americans at war began to arrive from France (censored of hardship, mutilation, and atrocity), the Committee would make duplicate prints of those thought most useful to the

HOWARD CHANDLER CHRISTY
The Spirit of the Red Cross, ca. 1918
28 × 41 inches
George M. Dembo
A Flagg poster for a Flagg film.

MARTINY
Under Four Flags, ca. 1918
28½ × 41½ inches
George M. Dembo

war effort and distribute them to the news media, to libraries, and to historical societies. The bulk of the motion-picture footage shot at the front was made available, for a fee, to the weekly film-news syndicates: Hearst-Pathé, Universal, Mutual, and Gaumont. Experienced film editors did what they could to put the remaining footage into stirring movies to distribute free among state councils of defense and various patriotic societies. But Creel felt that the growing pictorial assets of the Signal Corps were not being fully cultivated, so the Committee went into the motion-picture business as a producer and exhibitor.

The Committee's first feature film was *Pershing's Crusaders*, followed at intervals of six weeks by *America's Answer* and *Under Four Flags*. The plan was to open each film officially before an invited audience to demonstrate its worth and to create public interest, then prints were to be sold, leased,

STONER
Official United States War Films, ca. 1918
28 × 40 inches
Museum of the City of New York

or rented to local exhibitors. George Bowles, who had handled the distribution of *The Birth of a Nation*, was put in charge of this endeavor. *Pershing's Crusaders* was officially presented by the Committee in twenty-four cities, *America's Answer* in thirty-four, and *Under Four Flags* in nine. Each of these showings was preceded by a press campaign of about two weeks, with several hundred posters and window-cards of various sizes prominently displayed. *America's Answer* broke all records for any previous feature for range of distribution, with nearly six thousand theaters exhibiting the film. Revenues from the Committee's pictures totaled $852,744.30, and that included other features such as *Our Bridge of Ships* and *Our Colored Fighters*.

The Film Division also had a Scenario Department that developed scripts for one-reel pictures needed by various government departments. These were offered free to independent producers, who were simply required to give the film the widest possible commercial circulation. Among those independently made were *Keep 'Em Singing and Nothing Can Lick 'Em* and *A Girl's a Man for a' That*, the story of women in war work. Both were done by Paramount-

ELBERT McGRAN JACKSON
If Your Soldier's Hit, ca. 1918
28 × 42 inches
George M. Dembo

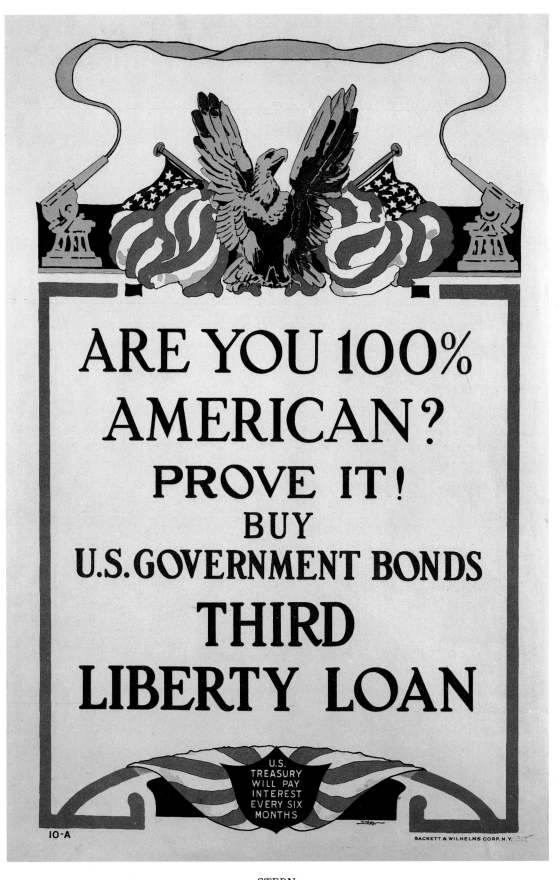

STERN
Are You 100% American?, ca. 1918
20 × 30 inches
Museum of the City of New York
*Many were concerned with the possible disloyalty of
the foreign born.*

Bray Pictograph. Pathé did *Solving the Farm Problem of the Nation*, which dealt with the U.S. Boy's Working Reserve, and Universal produced *The American Indian Gets into the War Game*. C. L. Chester made a similar presentation in *Colored Americans*, as well as *There Shall Be No Cripples*, about rehabilitating the wounded.

Several two-reel pictures were produced by the Division on its own, notably *If Your Soldier's Hit*, on the treatment of casualties; *Our Horses of War*, on training mules and horses for the artillery and the cavalry; *The Storm of Steel*, on the production of guns and munitions; and *The Bath of Bullets*, showing the development and use of machine guns.

In addition, there was a Department of Slides that supplied official photographs in steropticon form at fifteen cents each for the use of lecturers, school-teachers, ministers, and others. The first of the illustrated war lectures was "Ruined Churches of France," which came with fifty slides and a prepared text. Others followed in quick succession and included "Our Boys in France," one hundred slides; "Trenches and Trench Warfare," seventy-three slides; and "Flying for America," fifty-four slides. Barely in existence a year, the Department distributed a total of two hundred thousand slides.

THE SPEAKING DIVISION

A dynamic force in the Committee on Public Information was the Speaking Division, which was founded in September, 1917. President Wilson felt that a speaking campaign would "give to the people that fullness of information which will enable and inspire each citizen to play intelligently his part in the greatest and most vital struggle ever undertaken by self-governing nations."

The man put in charge was Arthur E. Bestor, president of the Chautauqua Institution, a movement that began in 1874 as a Methodist assembly to organize Sunday-school courses; it spread nationwide from Lake Chautauqua, New York, and grew into a popular traveling circuit of lectures on every subject imaginable. The Division acted as a source for speakers on all aspects of American life and provided a network through which war-effort spokesmen could be guaranteed a large audience wherever they were routed. Eventually a roster of ten thousand important opinion-makers was assembled, and this was winnowed to a select list of three hundred effective speakers.

The Division took charge of practically every national tour, especially those of foreign visitors, who ranged from British Attorney General Sir Frederick E. Smith, "who proved only irritating and offensive," to the French warrior-priest Captain Paul Perigord, who made 152 talks over a seven-month period. The priest had won a battlefield commission when he led a charge at Verdun after every officer in his sector had been killed. Another outstanding speaker was Wesley Frost, the consul at Queenstown, Ireland, where many *Lusitania* victims had washed ashore. He was the official reporter of eighty-one U-boat sinkings, and made sixty-three addresses in twenty-nine states.

THE ADVERTISING DIVISION

The advertising community got off to a bad start when representatives approached officials in Washington with a well-worked-out campaign for the First Liberty Loan. In his book, Creel pointed out that "advertising was regarded as a business, not a profession, and the majority looked upon the advertising agent with suspicion, even when he was not viewed frankly as a plausible pirate." *Voluntary* was the proper catchword in Washington at the time, and when it became clear to the Liberty Loan Army that the agents' campaign was based upon government *purchase* of advertising space, the agents were very brusquely shown the door. One creative representative of the advertising community subsequently came up with what was named the "Chicago Plan," whereby the agents themselves first obligated patriotic individuals or organizations to purchase advertising space, which was then generously donated to the government. For the First Liberty Loan, a million dollars' worth of space was contributed.

In preparation for the Second Liberty Loan, Creel persuaded President Wilson to establish a Division of Advertising. In his executive order, Wilson defined its role as "receiving through the proper channels the generous offers of the advertising forces of the nation to support the effort of the government to inform public opinion properly and adequately." Creel estimated that donated advertising space saved the government at least five million dollars. Besides contributions under the "Chicago Plan," some eight hundred publishers of monthly and weekly periodicals gave regular space to the Division of Advertising, and advertisers themselves volunteered their long-term contracted space for government purposes.

Of course, the Committee on Public Information sponsored many additional activities of significance,

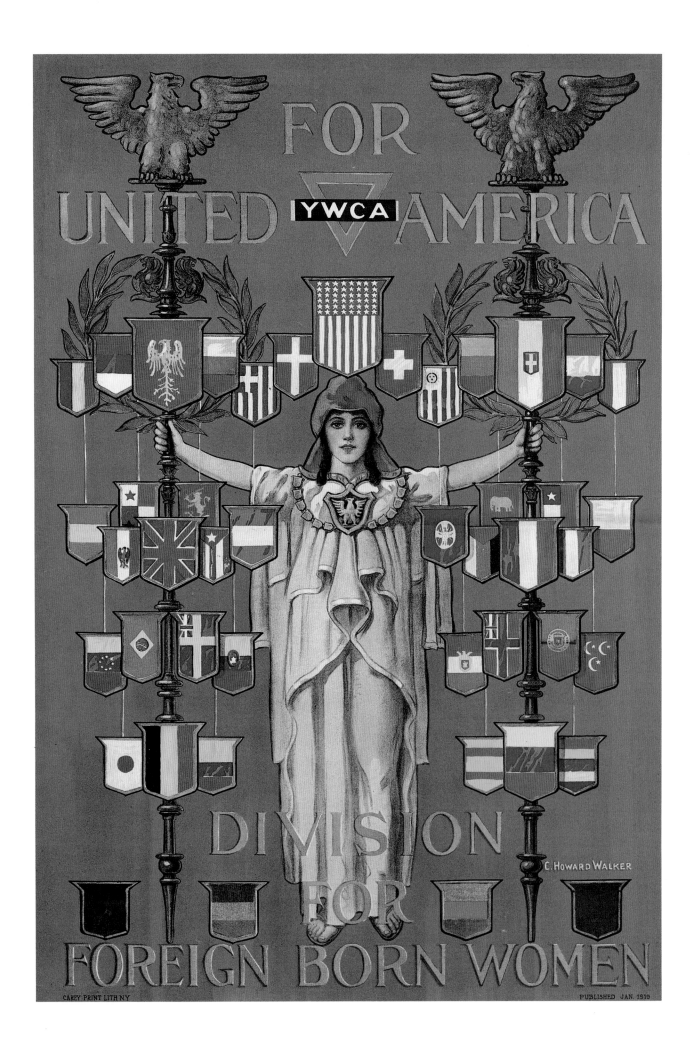

including the publication of the country's first daily *Official Bulletin*. Posted in every military camp and fifty-four thousand post offices, it recorded, as they happened, all new government orders, regulations, laws, and proceedings of official bodies (a service deemed so important that it eventually evolved into the *Federal Register*). The Committee also initiated divisions of Women's War-Work and War Expositions, which are considered elsewhere in this volume; and an entire section of the Committee was devoted to dealing with the foreign born and to sending, through its World News Service, America's democratic message to countries everywhere. For this book, the most important activity of the Committee on Public Information was the Division of Pictorial Publicity, which mustered nearly three hundred of America's most famous artists into government service. Its operation is the subject of the next chapter.

C. HOWARD WALKER
For United YWCA America, 1919
28 × 40 inches
Museum of the City of New York
Both the YWCA and the Committee on Public Information concentrated on the foreign born.

CAN YOU DRIVE A CAR?
WILL YOU DRIVE ONE IN FRANCE?
IMMEDIATE SERVICE AT THE FRONT!

American Field Service

40 State Street

Boston, Mass.

VII. "HOW ART PUT ON KHAKI"

Less than two weeks after America entered the war, the Society of Illustrators held a meeting in New York City to examine the ways in which artists might rally to their country's cause. Many of the members were already backers of preparedness through anti-pacifist, patriotic groups such as the Vigilantes—in particular Howard Chandler Christy, who, when he lived in Ohio, was known to fly Old Glory daily and to fire his cannon on the Fourth of July. Christy went eagerly to Cuba in the Spanish-American War, on assignment for *Harper's*, *Scribner's*, and *Leslie's Weekly*, and his combat drawings earned him renown as a war artist and also the friendship of Theodore Roosevelt—who appeared in his book *Men of the Army and Navy*. During this meeting, society president Charles Dana Gibson, America's highest-paid artist, received a telegram from George Creel asking him to appoint a committee to help in producing whatever artwork the government would need. As Gibson later wrote to Creel:

> It always struck me as more than fortunate that your telegram on the night of April 17, 1917, should have reached me when and where it did. It was at a dinner at the Hotel Majestic, the first gathering of artists after the declaration of war. We were there to offer our services to the country, but were in some doubt as to the method of procedure. We were sparring for an opening. . . . the speeches were about half over and some of them threatened to get us off track, when just at the psychological moment your telegram was handed to me and we had a focusing point. If it had all been prearranged it could not have happened better.

On April 22 Gibson met with Creel at the latter's

HOWARD CHANDLER CHRISTY
Patriotic League, 1918
20½ × 28 inches
Museum of the City of New York

home in New York City, and the Division of Pictorial Publicity of the Committee on Public Information was formally launched, just nine days after Creel received his mandate from President Wilson. Creel later described his feelings:

> Even in the rush of the first days . . . I had the conviction that the poster must play a great

CHARLES DANA GIBSON
Can You Drive a Car?, ca. 1917
14 × 22½ inches
Museum of the City of New York

CHARLES DANA GIBSON
House Manager, 1917
15¼ × 20½ inches
University of Texas at Austin

---

part in the fight for public opinion. The printed word might not be read, people might not choose to attend meetings or to watch motion pictures, but the billboard was something that caught even the most indifferent eye. . . . What we wanted—what we had to have—was posters that represented the best work of the best artists—posters into which the masters of the pen and brush poured heart and soul as well as genius. Looking the field over, we decided upon Charles Dana Gibson as the man best fitted to lead the army of artists.

In 1886, at the age of nineteen, Gibson had sold his first drawing to the original *Life* magazine. By 1888 he was drawing regularly for that periodical, as well as for *Puck* and *Tid-bits*. Earlier he had been an apprentice to sculptor Augustus Saint-Gaudens and had studied with Kenyon Cox, William Merritt Chase, and Thomas Eakins. In 1890 he created in the pages of *Life* the spirited and stylish young socialite who would be widely admired and imitated as the Gibson Girl. Her image not only appeared weekly in *Life* but on teacups, silver spoons, and wallpaper; there were songs about her and even a

play. Her creator's talents were likewise much admired by numerous publishers, and *Collier's* tempted Gibson with a lucrative contract to publish his work exclusively. But Gibson would not abandon the magazine that gave him his start; to publish Gibson's drawings at all, *Collier's* would have to share him with *Life*. In 1903, Gibson signed a *Collier's* contract that paid him one thousand dollars each for one hundred drawings over a four-year period.

As America's most famous illustrator Gibson was an ideal leader for the Division of Pictorial Publicity; he had favored entering the war from the moment Germany first invaded Belgium, and since 1916 he had produced prowar political cartoons. Gibson felt even more compelled to serve his country now that she was at war, as his biographer Fairfax Downey describes: "The war had moved him as politics never had been able to do. The scorn, the elation, the passionate conviction which make a great cartoonist now were his. Color for a time was forgotten in the power which surged genii-like from his ink bottle. Never had he drawn with such vigor and verve. His soldiers fixed bayonets and leapt into action. Columbia's robe swept back outlining her beautifully molded body as she rushed forward toward victory."

Headquarters for the Division of Pictorial Publicity was opened in New York City (with branches in Chicago, Boston, and San Francisco), and within a month the organization had enlisted most of the best-known illustrators in America. Frank De Sales Casey, art manager of *Collier's*, was chosen to be vice chairman and secretary, because, as Gibson said, "Casey knows every artist in town." Besides Gibson and Casey, the original members of the committee that formed the Division were Charles Buckles Falls, Henry Reuterdahl, Louis Fancher, Charles D. Williams, Robert J. Wildhack, and Fred G. Cooper. The associate chairmen of the Division were Herbert Adams, Edwin H. Blashfield, Ralph Clarkson, Cass Gilbert, Oliver D. Grover, Francis Jones, Arthur Matthews, Joseph Pennell, Edmond Tarbell, and Douglas Volk. Architect Cass Gilbert, whose Woolworth Building was then the tallest in the world, defined their mission: "To visualize to the people the facts of the great contest; to make the story of the war and what it meant a story that 'one who runs may read,' and to place upon every wall in America the call to patriotism and to service—to tell to over one hundred million of our fellow countrymen the story of courage and suffering, heroism and confidence in victory, so necessary to the conduct of the war—and so effective in securing the victory."

H. Devitt Welsh of Philadelphia went to the Washington office of the Committee to serve as "contact

---

CHARLES DANA GIBSON
Here He Is, Sir, ca. 1917
27 × 41 inches
Guernsey's

U. S. NAVY

Courtesy of Life

Drawn by Charles Dana Gibson

"Here he is, Sir."
We need him and you too!
Navy Recruiting Station

man." His job was to make certain that the heads of important government branches knew that America's artists were duly mobilized and eager for wartime service. Welsh compiled lists of the pictorial requirements of each department and forwarded them on to Gibson in New York City, who oversaw the work like the art director of a topflight illustrated magazine. Unlike other volunteer organizations, the Division never held open competitions for assignments, because Gibson felt the best artists were already available to him and that a mountain of well-meaning submissions would result in extra work. Usually it was Frank Casey who recommended the artist for each job.

The muster roll of the Division of Pictorial Publicity contained the names of 279 artists and 33 cartoonists. Among them were such well-known painters as George Bellows, Edwin H. Blashfield, Kenyon Cox, Arthur G. Dove, William Glackens, F. Luis Mora, Joseph Pennell, Henry Reuterdahl, Frank E. Schoonover, Albert Sterner, and N. C. Wyeth. Of course the roster included the famous illustrators Howard Chandler Christy, Harrison Fisher, James Montgomery Flagg, Charles Dana Gibson, John Held, Jr., Rea Irvin, Francis and Joseph Leyendecker, Edward Penfield, Coles Phillips, and Jessie Willcox Smith. In addition there were those whose work for the Division would help in making them famous: L. N. Britton, Charles Livingston Bull, Dean Cornwell, Harvey T. Dunn, Charles Buckles Falls, Gordon Grant, Wallace Morgan, Herbert Paus, Henry Raleigh, William A. Rogers, John E. Sheridan, Adolph Treidler, and Ellsworth Young. The names of numerous other well-known artists are linked to familiar World War I posters, but their work was done under the auspices of other organizations, including various art schools. The School of Printing and Graphic Arts of the Wentworth Institute in Boston produced an especially accomplished series of posters.

The pictorial publicity campaign for the Navy was conducted independently by the Navy Recruiting Bureau, first under Captain K. M. Bennett and later under Lieutenant Commander O. F. Cooper. Lieutenant Henry Reuterdahl, a member of Gibson's executive committee, served also as the executive officer and artistic adviser to the Navy. The Marine Corps' pictorial publicity needs were met separately, under the direction of Major T. G. Sterrett. The artists involved in these programs were essentially the same as those of the Division of Pictorial Publicity, with the notable exceptions of Frank Brangwyn, a well-regarded muralist and member of the British Royal Academy, and Louis Raemaekers, a Dutch artist who had worked primarily in England with the National Committee for Relief in Belgium. After the war,

EDWIN HOWLAND BLASHFIELD
Where Columbia Sets Her Name, ca. 1918
20 × 30 inches
Miscellaneous Man

WENTWORTH INSTITUTE
Find the Range of Your Patriotism, ca. 1918
23 × 33 inches
Meehan Military Posters

Secretary of the Navy Josephus Daniels applauded the efforts of artists in his sector of responsibility: "Striking posters which aroused patriotism and pictured the opportunity for service in the War for Democracy and the Freedom of the Seas proved one of the most effective features of our notably successful recruiting campaign. These were designed by distinguished artists who volunteered their services, considering it a privilege to make these contributions to the cause."

Gibson described his division's operations in a *New York Times* article: "We have a meeting every Friday night. This takes place at our headquarters, 200 Fifth Avenue, where we meet men who are sent to us with their requests by the different departments in Washington. The meeting is adjourned to Keen's Chop House, where we have dinner." (Later the membership of the Division grew so large that the meeting place was changed from the West 36th Street restaurant to the Salmagundi Club on lower Fifth Avenue.) Gibson continued: "Suppose we have with us someone from the Food Administrator's office, sent to us so that we can get more clearly in mind the needs of his division through personal contact. Casey, once having got the suggestion, picks out two

HENRY REUTERDAHL
All Together!, 1917
43 × 31½ inches
Walton Rawls

ENLIST IN THE NAVY

LOUIS RAEMAEKERS
Enlist in the Navy, ca. 1917
40 × 30 inches
Miscellaneous Man

of the best men he thinks can be found for the work, and at dinner he places them on each side of the official emissary. In the course of the dinner views are exchanged on all sides, and we come to understand one another pretty thoroughly."

Gibson had said that the artist "should think right" to be able to communicate clearly through his art, so the weekly dinners of the Division were opened to speakers of national prominence who volunteered the wisdom of their varied backgrounds and experience. Among them were Charles M. Schwab, head of the United States Shipping Board (a prodigious user of posters); banker Otto H. Kahn; war correspondent Floyd Gibbons of the *Chicago Tribune* (who had been wounded covering the action); Britain's famous cartoonist Captain Bruce Bairnsfather; evangelist Gypsy Smith; sculptors Frederick McMonnies and Daniel Chester French; and poet Bliss

Carman. Every meeting was also attended by American or Allied war heroes who electrified the gathering with tales of their adventures, including the best-selling author Sergeant Guy Empey. Once there was even a hero dog from France that had been cited for saving a regiment at Verdun. As Gibson explained it: "This is a schoolroom. All are welcome. We come here to learn from each other, to get inspiration, and get religion for the great task the Government has set for us. No artist is too great to come and give his best. We are fortunate to be alive at this time and to be able to take advantage of the greatest opportunity ever presented to artists."

Every week Casey journeyed to Washington with at least seventy-five pounds of sketches and drawings for approval by government agencies, though many officials of the time knew nothing at all about art. At first Gibson, himself, spent hours in government offices soliciting the chance to show officials sketches by some of the most famous names in contemporary illustration. As he explained it, "the suspicion with which some of those in Washington looked upon the artists was not to be wondered at and bothered me less as I became better acquainted with the men I met down there. After all, we were offering something for nothing, and that in itself was suspicious." Through it all Gibson was patient and persistent, and at last the importance of what he had to offer penetrated official consciousness.

However, even among members of Gibson's executive committee differences arose about the merit of certain artists in the Division. Albert E. Gallatin, a painter, collector, and art critic, who mounted the Allied War Salon for showing artists attached to the armies in France, was to publicly express his low regard for the creations of James Montgomery Flagg and Howard Chandler Christy in his book *Art and the Great War*. Flagg, on the other hand, took little

AFTER A ZEPPELIN RAID IN LONDON
"BUT MOTHER HAD DONE NOTHING WRONG, HAD SHE, DADDY?"
Prevent This in New York
Invest in
LIBERTY BONDS

LOUIS RAEMAEKERS
After a Zeppelin Raid in London, ca. 1917
14 × 20 inches
George M. Dembo

DANIEL SMITH
Knowledge Wins, ca. 1918
20 × 30 inches
George M. Dembo

notice of the kind of art that Gallatin favored and was capable of observing of Renoir that "his banalities were apparently painted with pillow feathers and lipstick."

Not only were artists of the Division subject to call, like militiamen, but in regular weekly meetings their patriotic mission was analyzed for them in detail, with everyone present contributing criticism, ideas, and inspiration. Gibson constantly admonished his co-workers to make their posters represent ideas, not events (a problem for artists accustomed to illustrating the narrative highpoints in articles and books): "We must see more of the spiritual side of the conflict. We must picture the great aims of this country in fighting this war. They already have been pictured in words by the President, and I want to say now that he is the greatest artist in the country today, because he is an idealist. He is the great Moses of America. He points out the promised land, the milk and honey. The work of the artist will be made easy by putting into pictorial form the last message of the President."

Gibson said that "there wasn't an artist in the

BOOKS
WANTED
FOR OUR MEN
„IN CAMP AND
OVER THERE"
TAKE YOUR GIFTS TO
THE PUBLIC LIBRARY

CHARLES BUCKLES FALLS
Books Wanted for Our Men, ca. 1918
27½ × 33 inches
Museum of the City of New York

JOHN E. SHERIDAN
Hey Fellows!, 1918
20 × 30 inches
Meehan Military Posters

"Hey Fellows!"

YOUR MONEY BRINGS THE BOOK WE NEED WHEN WE WANT IT

American Library Association

United War Work Campaign - Week of November 11·1918

JESSIE WILLCOX SMITH
*Have You a Red Cross
Service Flag?*, 1918
21 × 28 inches
Museum of the City
of New York

JESSIE WILLCOX SMITH
Welfare Federation, ca. 1920
14 × 20 inches
Miscellaneous Man
*A relief poster done after
the war.*

WELFARE FEDERATION

20 Hospitals   26 Children's Organizations   21 Family Agencies
15 Nursing and Health Groups   22 Neighborhood Houses
13 Character Building Agencies

Unaided by Federal or State Funds

THIS IS YOUR RESPONSIBILITY

November 12 to November 28

country, man or woman, who didn't offer the best that was in him. . . . the single one who hesitated was a Quaker, and he was only able to hold out for a short time." Gibson may have been referring to Maxfield Parrish, who was then living in New York, but his biographer Coy Ludwig writes:

It is not known whether the poster that Parrish designed for the Red Cross during the First World War was ever actually used as a poster. The unusual design consisted of four panels in a single wooden frame. Two upper panels each contained a red cross inside a garland or wreath. In the lower left panel an old man and children, some of whom wear wooden shoes, receive Red Cross food packages. In the right panel a Red Cross nurse attends to a wounded serviceman, who rests in a deck chair. There is an attempt to unify the four panels by making the sky continuous throughout. As interesting as the individual panels might be, when taken together . . . they are not representative.

Jessie Willcox Smith, who would illustrate more than thirty-five children's books (among them, in 1916, Charles Kingsley's hugely successful *Water Babies*) and two hundred covers for *Good Housekeeping*, produced only one war poster, the well-known "Have You a Red Cross Service Flag?" However, she participated in a division program in which artists volunteered to do portraits of patriotic citizens whose purchases of Liberty Bonds went into the thousands of dollars.

For the Third Liberty Loan, Lieutenant Reuterdahl and N. C. Wyeth, the distinguished illustrator of *Treasure Island*, *Robinson Crusoe*, and other classics, worked jointly on a painting ninety-feet long and twenty-five-feet high, which was displayed outside the Sub-Treasury Building in New York City. Wyeth painted the left half, showing American troops going over the top, and Reuterdahl did his specialty, the war at sea, on the other half. Wyeth designed only one poster during the war—for the Red Cross. It shows a medic helping a wounded soldier from the battlefield while his comrades continue their charge

FREDERICK DUNCAN
A Man May Be Down But He's Never Out!, 1919
30 × 40 inches
Miscellaneous Man

SIDNEY H. REISENBERG
Civilians—When We Go Through This, 1918
22 × 33 inches
Miscellaneous Man

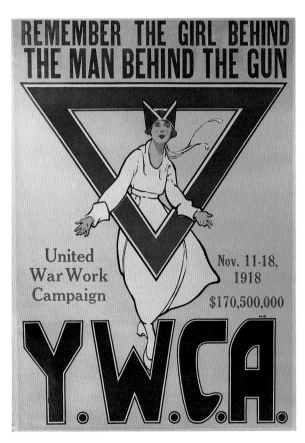

M. B.
Remember the Girl Behind the Man Behind the Gun, 1918
21 × 19 inches
Miscellaneous Man

BURTON RICE
See Him Through, 1918
20 × 30 inches
George M. Dembo

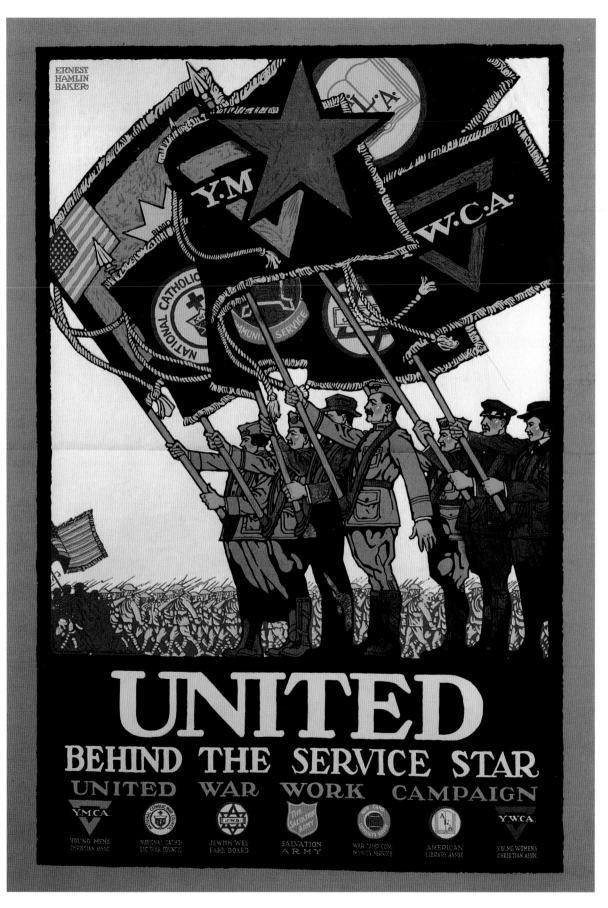

ERNEST HAMLIN BAKER
United Behind the Service Star, ca. 1918
28 × 40 inches
Museum of the City of New York

in the background. For the Fourth Liberty Loan, Reuterdahl made three paintings in Washington, D.C., each over twenty-feet wide.

Also during the Fourth Liberty Loan drive, twenty-two artists from the Division set up painting easels on Fifth Avenue in front of The New York Public Library, which along with The Metropolitan Museum

of Art was a popular site for spectacles of patriotism. During the United War Work Campaign, seven division artists had painted in front of the Library and two in front of the Metropolitan. Their aim was to call attention to the needs of the Y.M.C.A., the Knights of Columbus, the Salvation Army, the Jewish Welfare Board, the American Library Association, the Y.W.C.A., and the War Camp Community Service in providing comfort and support to doughboys here and "over there." For the Liberty Loan campaign, the artists made stirring sketches to be offered as inducements to bond-buyers for raising their subscriptions to higher denominations. The artists were assigned Allied countries to commemorate in paint, and the pictures would then be used to decorate Fifth Avenue shop windows during the Liberty Loan drive. William Glackens was given Russia, F. Luis Mora was assigned beleagured France, Charles Buckles Falls got Japan as his subject, Howard Chandler Christy was asked to memorialize Italy, and so on. James Montgomery Flagg was awarded Belgium, and evidently what came to his mind was a particular headline of August, 1914, when Germany was tearing through Belgium: "Huns Kill Women and Children!" It was the inspiration for his famous poster "Tell That to the Marines!" Flagg shows a man, fighting mad after reading the headline on a newspaper, who is tearing off his civilian jacket on the way to joining the Marines. Shortly after the appearance of this poster, the following poem appeared in the *New York Herald*:

ERNEST HAMLIN BAKER
For Every Fighter a Woman Worker, ca. 1918
28 × 42 inches
Ada Rodriguez

ALBERT HERTER
His Home Over There, 1918
23 × 41½ inches
Walton Rawls

LUCIEN HECTOR JONAS
Four Years in the Fight, ca. 1918
28 × 42½ inches
Walton Rawls

ADOLPH TREIDLER
For Every Fighter a Woman Worker, ca. 1918
30 × 41 inches
Museum of the City of New York

NEYSA MORAN McMEIN
One of the Thousand Y.M.C.A. Girls in France, 1918
42 × 28 inches
Museum of the City of New York

THE APPEAL OF A POSTER
By N. A. Jennings

"Huns Kill Women and Children!"
  It was staring him in the face.
Telling the tale in headlines
  of the deeds of a hellborn race;
Telling of dastards' doings,
  Black murder hurled down from the skies
On nursing babes and mothers—
  Such a slaughter as Germans prize.

"Huns Kill Women and Children!"
  And the words seared into his soul;
His heart grew sick with horror
  At the thought of the pitiful toll.
Then rage filled all his being
  And he took an oath then and there.
"Those black fiends must be punished,
  And, by God! I will do my share!"

"Huns Kill Women and Children!"
  With each moment his anger grew;
Grim, determined, jaw hard set.
  He was fighting mad through and through.
Gentle with child or woman,
  Full of courage and fine and clean,
Showing in all his make-up
  True type of the fighting Marine!

"Huns Kill Women and Children!"
  They are doing it now today—
Murdering Red Cross nurses,
  Dropping bombs on children at play.
Get in the fight to stop them;
  In France men are showing you how;
Join the Marines! Go to it!
  And the time to enlist is NOW!

In its twenty months of existence between April, 1917, and November, 1918, the Division of Pictorial Publicity submitted seven hundred poster designs to fifty-eight separate government departments and patriotic committees requesting artwork. In addition it produced 122 car, bus, and store-window cards, 310 advertisements, 287 cartoons, and 19 seals, buttons, and banners. The major recipients of the Division's work were the American Red Cross, War Savings Stamps, the Liberty Loans, the Shipping Board—Emergency Fleet Corporation, the War Camp Community Service, the food, fuel, and railroad administrations, and the Division of Films. For the military proper, the Division prepared eighteen posters for the Ordnance Department, four for the Signal Corps, one for the aviation branch, one for

JAMES MONTGOMERY FLAGG
Tell That to the Marines!, ca. 1918
30 × 40 inches
Museum of the City of New York

M. LEONE BRACKER
Keep 'em Smiling!, 1918
28 × 42 inches
Walton Rawls

the Tank Corps, and five for the Marine Corps.

In addition, the War Department asked the Division to recommend eight artists to accompany the Army to Europe to document the fighting and the sacrifices of America's doughboys. Among those chosen were Wallace Morgan and Harvey Dunn, whose work from the front was often used in the posters. The others were J. Andre Smith, Ernest Peixotto, Harry Townsend, George Harding, William J. Aylward, and W. J. Duncan, all commissioned captains in the Army. About three hundred drawings were done by these men, of which two hundred were selected for a traveling exhibition, and fifty-one were reproduced in various national periodicals.

Enlisted for the duration of the war as unpaid members of the Division—not even as dollar-a-year men—American painters, designers, illustrators, and cartoonists donated highly paid artistic services to their country. One of the illustrators commented, "They were big men who would ordinarily receive $1,000 to $10,000 for a sketch, so you can see what the nation is saving." (Once Flagg even stomped out of a meeting when an artist dared to broach the subject of remuneration for government work.) This was the first time in any American war that colorful, patriotic posters were used to help win it, or that

WALLACE MORGAN
Feed a Fighter, ca. 1918
21 × 29½ inches
Museum of the City of New York

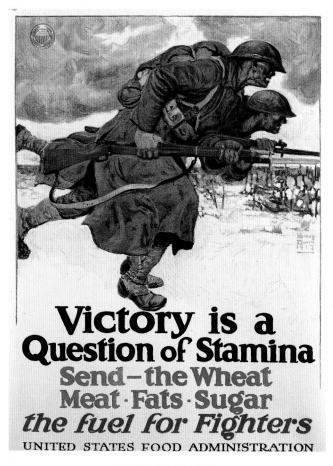

HARVEY T. DUNN
Victory is a Question of Stamina, 1917
21 × 29 inches
Museum of the City of New York

the fine arts were officially recognized for a role in achieving victory. A high government official summed it up: ''Charles Dana Gibson and the Division of Pictorial Publicity did work of immense value in helping to win the war. Their services were of more value to the Government in forming public opinion than all other agencies put together. No other group, no other profession did as much.''

At the Victory Dinner of the Division of Pictorial Publicity on February 14, 1919 (appropriately launched with rounds of Gibson cocktails), Cass Gilbert paid tribute to Gibson: ''No one else could have done what he did. The great character of the man, rising above all personal considerations, shone forth in his intense earnestness and patriotic fervor; he moulded the divergent views of the active minds around him into one composite impulse of *service*—service for the nation, service for the greatest cause that the Nation could undertake. . . . His enthusiastic advocacy brought into play the finest and most co-operative effort of that group of the most brilliant men among the illustrative artists of America.''

The following poem was featured in the commemorative booklet for the Victory Dinner:

THOUGHTS
INSPIRED BY A WAR-TIME BILLBOARD
BY WALLACE IRWIN

I stand by a fence on a peaceable street
   And gaze on the posters in colors of flame,
Historical documents, sheet upon sheet,
   Of our share in the war ere the armistice
     came.

And I think about Art as a Lady-at-Arms;
   She's a studio character most people say,
With a feminine trick of displaying her
     charms
   In a manner to puzzle the ignorant lay.

But now as I study that row upon row
   Of wind-blown engravings I feel
     satisfaction
Deep down in my star-spangled heart, for I
     know
   How Art put on khaki and went into action.

There are posters for drives—now trium-

phantly o'er—
  I look with a smile reminiscently fond
As mobilized Fishers and Christys implore
  In a feminine voice, "Win the War—Buy a
    Bond!"

There's a Jonas Lie shipbuilder, fit for a
    frame;
  Wallie Morg's "Feed a Fighter" lurks deep
    in his trench;
There's Blashfield's Columbia setting her
    name
  In classical draperies trimmed by the
    French.

Charles Livingston Bull in marine
    composition
  Exhorts us to Hooverize (portrait of bass),
Jack Sheridan tells us that Food's Ammuni-
    tion—
  We've all tackled war biscuits under that
    class.

See the winged Polish warrior that Benda has
    wrought!
  Is he private or captain? I cannot tell
    which,

For printed below is the patriot thought
  Which Poles pronounce "Sladami Ojcow
    Naszych."

There's the Christy Girl wishing that she was
    a boy,
  There's Leyendecker coaling for Garfield in
    jeans,
There's the Montie Flagg Guy with the air of
    fierce joy
  Inviting the public to Tell the Marines.

And the noble Six Thousand—they count up
    to that—
  Are marshalled before me in battered
    review.
They have uttered a thought that is All in
    One Hat
  In infinite shadings of red, white, and blue.

And if brave Uncle Sam—Dana Gibson,
    please bow—
  Has called for our labors as never before,
Let him stand in salute in acknowledgment
    now
  Of the fighters that trooped from the stu-
    dio door.

"I SHALL EXPECT EVERY MAN WHO IS NOT A SLACKER TO BE AT MY SIDE THROUGHOUT THIS GREAT ENTERPRISE."

Woodrow Wilson

To All Employees: A CALL TO *Action!*

This plant is executing a contract for the United States Navy

As patriotic Americans you can render a great service by doing your work promptly and doing it well

Remember: Your work is an important factor in this fight for freedom. On land and sea our soldiers and sailors are depending on you to
DO YOUR PART
IN THE WINNING OF THE WAR

VIII. "A CALL TO ACTION"

Shortly after America declared war on Germany, the premier of France sent President Wilson the following cable:

> It is desired that in order to cooperate with the French Air Service, the American government should adopt the following program: the formation of a flying corps of 4,500 airplanes—personnel and matériel included—to be sent to the French Front during the campaign of 1918. The total number of pilots, including reserves, should be 5,000 and 50,000 mechanics. Two thousand planes should be constructed each month, as well as 4,000 engines by the American factories. That is, during the first six months of 1918, 16,300 planes (of the latest type) and 30,000 engines will have to be built. The French government is anxious to know if the American government accepts this proposition, which would enable the Allies to win the supremacy of the air.

Forty-five hundred airplanes! Five thousand pilots! That was a tall order for a country whose aviation industry had built fewer than eight hundred aircraft in its entire history and whose generals had bought exactly 152 military airplanes. The Army's Aviation Section then consisted of 65 officers (just half of them experienced pilots) and about 1,000 enlisted men. Only another 113 were in flight training.

Although the invention of the flying machine is credited to two American brothers from Ohio, it was two French brothers who really invented flying—more than a century earlier. Indeed, France can boast of the first three ever to fly in an aircraft: a sheep, a duck, and a rooster. In the last quarter of the eighteenth century, Joseph de Montgolfier sat in front of a smoldering fire on his hearth and pondered Spain's tactical problem with England's fortress on Gibraltar: the Spanish had not been able to oust the British by land or sea—leaving air, he playfully

HERBERT ANDREW PAUS
A Call to Action!, ca. 1918
29 × 43 inches
George M. Dembo

deduced, as the only untried element. While coming to terms with the hopelessness of Spain's situation, he found himself another problem to ponder as he watched bits of ash break loose from his burning logs and sail up the chimney: could hot air provide sufficient power to lift other light things into the air? The next day he built a cloth-covered frame that actually rose to the ceiling when he burned wads of paper directly beneath it.

With the help of his brother Etienne, Joseph built and tested several increasingly larger containers (or balloons, from *balloné*, "distended" in French) until, in May, 1783, he was ready to demonstrate his invention publicly. That balloon, constructed of wallpaper-backed strips of cloth held together by eighteen hundred buttons, was filled with hot air from a fire of straw and wool, and it soared to a height of six thousand feet. It was on the next flight, for the benefit of Louis XVI, that the three animals flew for two miles and landed safely. Oddly, the first humans to leave Earth in an aircraft were not the Montgolfier brothers but two volunteers who soared above Paris in an ornate seventy-foot-tall *Montgolfière*—the premiere performance of manned flight. Hot-air balloons did not quickly become vehicles of the sky, for one could not reliably predict a destination; indeed, the inventor was quite surprised to discover that balloons could not be rowed through the skies by oarsmen. A century and more would pass before the world saw an airship that was steerable (*dirigeable* in French)—and self-propelled.

Wilbur and Orville Wright, of Dayton, Ohio, were bicycle mechanics who became totally absorbed in the idea of flying just before the turn of the century. Like other pioneer experimenters with flight, they first concerned themselves with controlling the movements and improving the stability of gliders. Earlier they inquired of the Smithsonian Institution whether any books had ever been written on the subject. "Contrary to our previous impression," Wilbur noted, "we found that men of the very highest standing in the professions of science and invention had attempted the problem." Basing their designs on model tests in their own wind tunnel, they built a series of biplane gliders and flew them successfully on a beach recommended for steady wind velocity near Kitty Hawk, North Carolina. Their No. 3 glider

MECHANICAL TRAINING

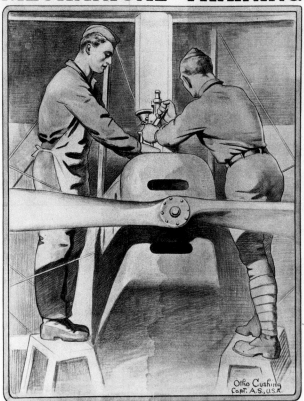

ENLIST IN THE AIR SERVICE

OTHO CUSHING
Mechanical Training, ca. 1919
19 × 25½ inches
George M. Dembo

---

had a movable tail and a single control that, through wires, "warped" its carefully shaped wings (the result of two hundred wind-tunnel tests) to alter the flight's lateral direction. By the fall of 1903, on the next aircraft, the Wrights had added a light-weight gasoline engine to drive a propeller intended to push their craft through the air. On December 17, at Kitty Hawk, they tested what they hoped would be the first manned, heavier-than-air, self-propelled flying machine. With Wilbur piloting and Orville alongside to steady the wings, the machine rolled down a track and lifted itself ten feet up into the air, where it flew one hundred feet before settling back to earth. Orville proudly evaluated their ac-complishment: "This flight lasted only twelve sec-onds, but it was nevertheless the first in the history of the world in which a machine carrying a man had raised itself by its own power into the air in full flight, and sailed forward without reduction of speed, and had finally landed at a point as high as that from which it had started."

Back in Dayton, the Wright brothers built an im-proved machine they flew more than one hundred

times in 1904. The next year they constructed an even better aircraft, and by the fall of 1905 one brother had taken a flight of thirty-eight minutes' duration that covered twenty-five miles. After ac-complishing that, the Wrights decided to stop all flying, for fear that some genius carefully watching their flights might copy their invention before they could patent it and sell the manufacturing rights. Their caution was not misplaced, for in 1906 an experienced Brazilian aeronaut named Alberto San-tos-Dumont flew a distance of 715 feet in France. Since the turn of the century, he had designed and flown gasoline-powered balloons and airships, mak-ing round trips between the Eiffel Tower and Saint-Cloud.

Although the Wrights had promptly announced their achievement to the press, *Scientific American* protested that "no public demonstration has ever been made by them." The magazine then offered a prize to anyone who could fly a plane over a desig-nated one-kilometer course. Held on July 4, 1908, without the Wrights, the contest was won by Glenn Curtiss, a motorcycle manufacturer and racer whose aircraft *June Bug* had first flown in March, 1908. Along with Alexander Graham Bell and a few others, Curtiss in 1907 had founded the Aerial Experiment Association.

Surprisingly, the Wright brothers were not im-mediately successful in selling rights to their invention in America. As a result, in 1907 Wilbur had gone to Europe, where several inventors were already getting machines up into the air. Unlike Americans, the French showed great interest in flying, but the Wrights refused to demonstrate their invention again until it was safely protected by a business based on their patents. Finally, after the American government ordered a Wright Flyer in February, 1908—launching the world's first military air service—a French syn-dicate licensed rights to manufacture the brothers' plane. The Wrights then began to fly again, and their demonstrations soon led to manufacturing con-tracts in England, Germany, and Italy as well.

In July, 1909, Louis Blériot flew the English Channel in an airplane for the first time. Shortly thereafter the War Ministry of France bought a Wright Flyer, while urging French manufacturers to build planes particularly for military use—a challenge eagerly taken up. Before the end of 1910, the French gov-ernment had thirty aircraft and fifty-two military pilots. The world's first commercial airline had been started in 1909 when Germany put Count Ferdinand von Zeppelin's engine-powered dirigibles into regular service. By 1914, the dirigibles had completed more than 1,588 trips at forty miles per hour without a mishap.

CHARLES LIVINGSTON BULL
Be an American Eagle!, ca. 1917
21 × 27 inches
University of Texas at Austin

JOIN THE
ARMY AIR SERVICE
BE AN AMERICAN EAGLE!
CONSULT YOUR LOCAL DRAFT BOARD. READ THE ILLUSTRATED
BOOKLET AT ANY RECRUITING OFFICE, OR WRITE TO THE CHIEF
SIGNAL OFFICER OF THE ARMY, WASHINGTON, D.C.

ANONYMOUS
Join the Air Service, ca. 1918
20 × 30 inches
University of Texas at Austin

LOUIS FANCHER
Over There, ca. 1918
29 × 39 inches
Richard E. Davis

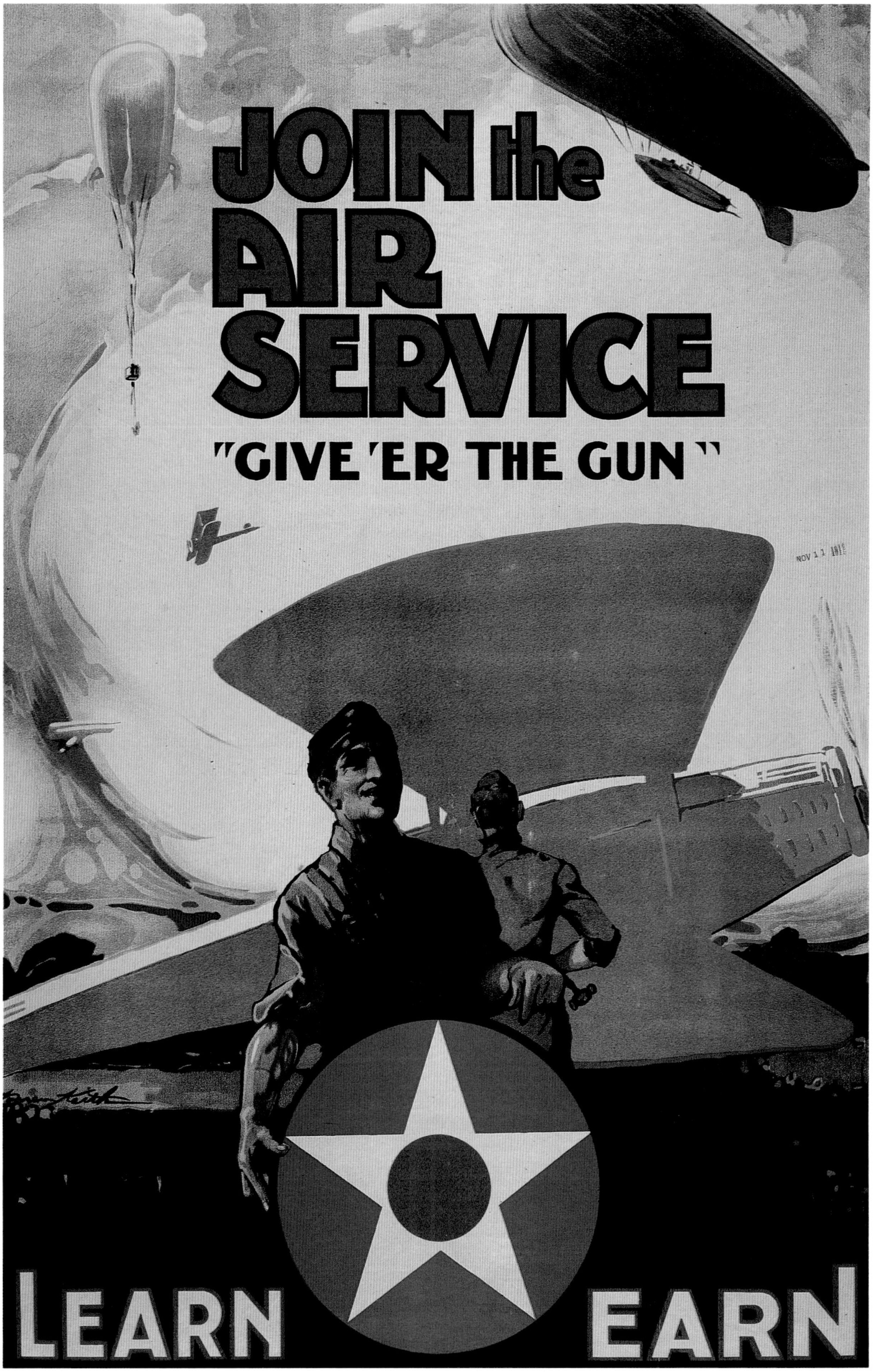
JOIN the
AIR
SERVICE
"GIVE 'ER THE GUN"
LEARN
EARN

In 1910 alone, thirty-seven daring aviators died piloting their machines, and Orville Wright was responsible for a regrettable first in that area as well. In September, 1908, while flying acceptance tests for the U.S. Army at Fort Myer, Virginia, Orville crashed a new plane, killing his passenger Lieutenant Thomas E. Selfridge—the world's first aviation fatality. Fortunately for the Wrights, the American Army already had taken the step of buying its first airplane, and other armies were following suit. By the beginning of World War I, France (with 160 aircraft and 15 airships) and Germany (with 246 aircraft and 7 Zeppelins) had the two largest military air forces in the world. Britain had built 113 aircraft and 6 airships, of which 63 were sent to France with the British forces in August, 1914.

In July, 1914, Congress had created the Aviation Section of the Army Signal Corps, authorizing a body of 60 officers and 260 enlisted men. America could then boast just 65 licensed aircraft pilots—only 35 of them in government service—but military flight training had just begun the previous year at the Signal Corps Aviation School in College Park, Maryland. Assigned twenty-eight aircraft, the school quickly lost nine of them as more than one quarter of the men receiving flight training were killed in the process. Eleven of the remaining planes were subsequently condemned for safety's sake, and by the time the war began in Europe the school had only five flyable aircraft left. Another aviation school had·been established at North Island in San Diego, but its director had halted training until safer planes could be found. Private schools, such as that of plane-builder Glenn Curtiss in San Diego, were still producing pilots, and Curtiss's reliable dual-control JN-4, or "Jenny," was available to become the Army's basic trainer.

In 1916, President Wilson had sent eight of the Army's thirteen tactical airplanes to Mexico with General John J. Pershing's mission to punish Pancho Villa. Unfortunately for America, those outmoded aircraft almost completely discredited flying in the military mind by continually breaking down or crashing. Pershing's soldiers were then diverted from their punitive mission to rescue stranded pilots. By the time America declared war on Germany, the Army had fifty-five serviceable aircraft, but none stood a chance in the kind of combat that had evolved in two years of aerial warfare in Europe. The National Advisory Committee on Aeronautics (established by Congress on March 3, 1915) rated fifty-one of the planes obsolete and the other four obsolescent. Meanwhile, the Europeans had taken aviation from a maximum ground speed of 80 to 90 miles per hour—with a twenty- to forty-minute climb to an altitude of ten thousand feet—to 132 miles per hour—with an eight-minute ascent to ten thousand feet. Part of the reason Europe's industry was able to progress so rapidly was that a plane was basically a skeleton of hardwood strips braced with steel wire and covered with fabric stretched taut by paint. "We literally thought of and designed and flew the airplanes in a space of about six or eight weeks," said builder T. O. M. Sopwith, whose Camel was the most successful fighter of the war. Planes were mostly made by hand, so there was no great investment to be lost when existing parts, machinery, and dies were abandoned in favor of radical developments. However, this flexibility in design and speed of production also led to insufficient testing of significant alterations (with planes falling apart in mid-air) and to problems of maintenance and scarcity of spare parts—which explains the following ditty sung by Britain's Royal Flying Corps:

Take the cylinder out of my kidneys,
The connecting rod out of my brain, my brain,
From the small of my back take the camshaft,
And assemble the engine again.

In September, 1914, a German General Staff report identified the role that aircraft were to play: "Experience has shown that a real combat in the air such as journalists and romancers have described should be considered a myth. The duty of the aviator is to see; not to fight." As a matter of fact, the early planes were known as "scouts" and went out unarmed, with an officer observer in the rear seat and the enlisted pilot considered his chauffeur. To the military strategist, aircraft were flying horses, and their role would be similar to that of the cavalry—the eyes and ears of the infantry and artillery. Indeed, the British Army had been saved from encirclement at Mons in the first days of the war by observation planes that spotted the German advance. With the emergence in late 1914 of single-seat fighter planes and the growing romanticization of the pilots themselves, this attitude changed rapidly. Said British Prime Minister David Lloyd George of the pilots, "They recall the legendary days of chivalry not merely by the daring of their exploits but by the nobility of their spirit."

The first casualty to aerial combat was a German observation plane forced to land in a field by three British aircraft and then set on fire with a match. Weapons were brought into play when it became necessary to prevent enemy observers from going behind one's lines and to protect one's own aircraft on similar missions. Pilots first took rifles and pistols aloft, even though American Colonel Isaac Newton Lewis already had adapted his air-cooled machine gun for use in Wright biplanes. The American military refused to have anything to do with the idea, so in 1913 Lewis had gone to Belgium and begun manufacturing the aerial machine gun himself.

WARREN KEITH
Join the Air Service, ca. 1918
20 × 30 inches
University of Texas at Austin

Although the French experimented early with the mounting of machine guns to fire forward without endangering the aircraft's propeller, it was not until February, 1915, that they actually began arming planes with Hotchkiss machine guns. These guns were placed above the top wing. Early in the spring of 1915, the British began mounting Lewis guns on the rear cockpit of their two-seaters for defensive use by the observer. Even though the French first figured out a rudimentary way to fire a machine gun through a propeller's arc, the Germans developed a better system, which synchronized a gun's rate of fire with the propeller revolutions so that a pilot could accurately place his shots by aiming his entire plane. The mechanism did not always work correctly (partly because the guns did not consistently fire at an even rate), but it did give the Germans a decided advantage over the Allies into the second winter of the war—until the French developed an even better device.

PREPARING FOR PREPAREDNESS

Although not totally unaware of the rapid developments Europeans had made in aviation during the war, most Americans had never even seen an aircraft in the sky (including many who were to become pilots). Few Americans were convinced that their country would ever need to have such specialized contraptions or that the United States would ever get dragged into the European conflict. After America had actually declared war on Germany, few (even in high places) gave much thought to what the next step would be. As he was justifying the enormous increase in a War Department budget appropriation at a Senate Finance Committee hearing, a government official was interrupted by the chairman with a loud cry of disbelief: "Good Lord! You're not going to send soldiers over there, are you?" Even the secretary of the Treasury was heard to reassure citizens that dollars would be "substitutes for American soldiers."

Colonel George Owen Squier, Orville Wright's first official passenger at the Army airplane tests in 1907, had been sent to the Western Front early in the war as an American military observer. Squier came back with the novel idea that because of the military stalemate on the ground the war would be won in the air, but no one in the Army would listen to him. The Air Service, then a section of the Signal Corps and restricted to unmarried men under the age of thirty, had little prestige in America and offered ambitious young officers no possibility for career advancement. Ironically, the official guidelines used in selecting men for aviation cautioned recruiters that "immature, high-strung, over-confident, impatient candidates are not desired"—a rejection of the very characteristics of most aces on both sides of the conflict in Europe!

As the possibility of involvement in the war became more threatening, the attitudes of some Americans toward the military began to change. President Wilson had presented a comprehensive plan for national defense in December, 1915, and had toured the country on behalf of "limited preparedness" early the following year. "We are participants, whether we would or not, in the life of the world," Wilson told a meeting of the League to Enforce Peace. "What affects mankind is inevitably our affair as well."

Finally facing the fact that something had to be done about our lack of readiness in case of war, on August 29, 1916, Congress established a new government body called the Council of National Defense. Although the pacifist spirit of the country made members of Congress uneasy about taking concrete steps toward mobilizing the country's military power, they were equally uncomfortable with public accusations voiced by preparedness spokesmen that they were being derelict in their duty. If war came it was clear that the country's major industries would have to operate on a radically different footing, but there was no official understanding of just what America's capabilities were—or her deficiencies. The tycoons of our laissez-faire industrial infrastructure played close to the chest, sharing little information about their stockpiles of raw materials or the capacity of their plants. Therefore, Congress found it necessary to set up the council as a way to begin effecting the "coordination of industries and resources for the national security and welfare"—should war ever come.

In June, 1917, in response to the rather overwhelming appeal of the French premier for planes and pilots, the Council of National Defense determined that with an appropriation of $300 million the United States could build 19,000 planes by 1920. But, for 1918, the War Department's program was calling for 22,625 airplanes and 44,000 engines (operational reliability, the Allies learned, required that most planes have a spare engine). On July 21, Congress debated the program for less than an hour and exuberantly appropriated $640 million for aviation, the greatest sum then ever voted by that body for one program. Undeterred that the aviation branch hardly existed, Congress authorized its expansion to 345 combat formations and founded the Aircraft Production Board, with Howard E. Coffin of the Hudson Motor Company as its head. General James E. Fechet commented that "the greatest madhouse in air history was opened for business."

J. PAUL VERREES
Join the Air Service and Serve in France, 1917
25 × 37 inches
Museum of the City of New York

THE LIBERTY ENGINE AND THE LIBERTY PLANE

The Aircraft Production Board's first piece of business was to design and set up a production line for an engine to power the tens of thousands of planes that were to be built for the Allies. Americans had earned an international reputation for getting things done quickly and efficiently, and indeed a prototype airplane engine was ready for testing in twenty-eight days. The story is told that automotive engineers Jesse G. Vincent and Charles Hall checked themselves into a Washington hotel with their drafting boards and designed a three-hundred-horsepower, eight-cylinder engine from scratch in just four days. But it is more likely that this prototype was based upon an automobile engine Vincent was then developing for Packard, and it was subsequently amplified into a four-hundred-horsepower, twelve-cylinder behemoth. Before July 4, 1917, the first so-called Liberty Engine had come off the assembly line, and by the Armistice 150 were being produced daily.

Secretary of Agriculture David Franklin Houston, in summarizing for the Academy of Political Science what programs the government had launched in the early days of the war, particularly praised the work of the Aircraft Production Board: "The building program . . . will be expedited by reason of a great and interesting achievement, that of a standardized engine, something which no European nation has developed even after three and a half years of war. This accomplishment is in line with the best American traditions, and was made with unique speed. What standardization of the engine and of its parts means in respect to speed and quantitive production, in repairs and economy of materials, need not be dwelt upon." Indeed, Howard Coffin had earlier achieved national prominence by strongly advocating standardized auto parts; there were as many as 450 American car-makers in 1915. But little prior thought seems to have been given to what kind of airplane the new engine was to power. It was not until June, 1917, that the Army first sent engineers to Europe to study the basic designs of airplanes the Allies had been developing in three years of aerial combat. The American aviation industry was then seen to be so ill-equipped to produce advanced aircraft that the engineers ultimately recommended buying U.S. Air Service fighter planes from the French. The Aircraft Production Board would also have to get their airplanes abroad, too.

The Liberty Engine was designed without a specific airframe in mind; as it turned out, it was too large and heavy for any existing European airplane—with the exception of the British De Havilland-4, a rather stocky two-seater known for poor pilot visibility. Since the French were counting on receiving thousands of speedy single-seat fighters, the Board decided it would find a way of modifying and improving France's outstanding Spad fighter as America's contribution toward "darkening the skies over Europe." But the Board was to suffer the humiliation of having to cancel a contract for three thousand Spads when it discovered that it was impossible to adapt that well-tested airframe to the Liberty Engine. There was then no choice but to license manufacturing rights to the DH-4 from De Havilland and to get on with installing the growing number of Liberty Engines into some kind of airframe. Too heavy and unresponsive to perform as a fighter, the Liberty Plane, as it was named, finally was fitted out for bombing and reconnaissance.

By the end of 1917, only 529 of the thousands of combat planes the French were expecting in 1918 had been built, and only 2,390 Liberty Engines had come down the production line. This poor showing,

HOWARD CHANDLER CHRISTY
Fly with the U.S. Marines, 1920
30 × 40 inches
Meehan Military Posters
The DH-4, or Liberty Plane, in flight.

L. N. BRITTON
Warning!, ca. 1917
27 × 41 inches
University of Texas at Austin

coupled with the expenditure of millions of dollars, led to a Senate investigation of the aviation program in the spring of 1918, and, later, to a presidential inquiry headed by Charles Evans Hughes, the man Wilson had defeated in 1916. By the Armistice, 3,227 DH-4s had been built, of which 1,885 had been delivered to France over the summer of 1918. However, since most of the planes required rebuilding in France, only 200 or so actually were used in the war. American ace Captain Eddie Rickenbacker described their performance in combat: "From every side Fokkers were diving on the clumsy Liberty machines which, with their criminally constructed fuel systems, offered so easy a target to the incendiary bullets of the enemy that their unfortunate pilots called this boasted achievement of our Aviation Department 'Flaming Coffins'." The only American-built aircraft to fly in combat during World War I, it found its rightful place in government service after the war as a U.S. Mail plane.

The Aircraft Production Board was not without accomplishments; it did satisfactorily build some three thousand of the Curtiss "Jenny" as a basic flight trainer and six hundred of the Thomas-Morse S-4-C "Tommy" as an advanced trainer. American pilots were to discover, however, that both were poor preparation for the Spad VIIs and Sopwith Camels they actually flew in combat; but, fortunately, the real advanced flight training took place at airfields in England, France, and Italy. In America, the Air Service had quickly expanded its original two training fields to twenty-seven, for there was no shortage of young men longing to fly—38,000 volunteered. Ground schools were established at ten colleges, and 23,000 men were accepted for the three-month course, with about three-quarters of them going on to flight training at military airfields. Before the war ended America had graduated 4,028 from advanced training schools and had placed 1,238 pilots and observers on flying duty at the front.

AN EXPLOSIVES SITUATION

A. N. PALMER
Not Just Hats Off, ca. 1918
40 × 60 inches
Meehan Military Posters

It is not surprising that America failed to produce the enormous number of fighter planes called for by France, since that required the mastery of brand-new technologies developed principally in Europe during the war. Nor would it have been reasonable to expect the United States to go into full-scale mobilization of war production before even entering the war; but it is hard to justify so little contingency planning by government and industry in the months just prior to April, 1917. From the war's beginning, American military observers at the front anxiously reported that the scale and destructiveness of modern warfare made the country's previous experience in combat almost worthless. Yet, America's military leaders seem to have discounted the warnings and failed even to compile and analyze important front-line reports before filing them for future study at the War College. When Frank A. Scott was made head of the General Munitions Board in March, 1917, he naturally sought to quickly acquaint himself with the potential problems of procuring weapons and allocating them to tactical units. Scott called upon the Army's General Staff for copies of their latest studies, but, to his surprise, there *were* none.

Nevertheless, a few good businessmen, no doubt influenced by the preparedness movement, had understood the necessity for making industrial preparations in case Wilson ultimately was unable to keep the country out of war. As early as 1915 the Chamber of Commerce of the United States had formed the Committee on National Defense to make plans for producing war goods. Since reports from the front indicated that America's military equipment was woefully and totally obsolete, some manufacturers envisioned huge orders for a vast new range of matériel. Noting that production of goods for the

Allies had lifted the American economy out of a recession in 1914, the Chamber of Commerce exercised more perspicacity than the government in launching a survey of the country's factories and natural resources so that its members might prepare for an onslaught of expected orders.

The explosives industry in particular had responded to the needs of the Allies by expanding production of war's basic requisite some three thousand percent in the thirty or so months between August, 1914, and April, 1917. However, since almost every speck of gunpowder that could be produced was being shipped to the Allies, it should have been clear that if (or when) America entered the war an entirely new reservoir of high explosives would have to be opened; the fortunes of the Allies could not be jeopardized by the United States' commandeering of their major source of supply. And yet it was months before the War Department recognized the dilemma. What brought the situation to a head was the signing of the Interallied Ordnance Agreement late in the fall of 1917, which obligated the United States to produce even more powder for the Allies. Just weeks earlier the secretary of war had begun negotiating with the DuPont Company to build a giant new powder plant, but even that proposed facility could not have sufficiently raised production capacity. In mid-December, 1917, the War Department named engineer Dugald Caleb Jackson to be the director of U.S. government explosives plants. He quickly concluded arrangements with DuPont to build the new powder plant in Nashville and personally directed the construction of another explosives plant at Nitro, West Virginia. Although at the Armistice the combined average daily production of the two new powder plants was five hundred thousand pounds, or less than one-third of planned capacity, this scale of production was indeed a great accomplishment; when construction of these plants had begun there was less than a year remaining in the war.

EQUIPPING THE DOUGHBOY FOR BATTLE

Failure to face the gunpowder problem expeditiously was not an isolated fact in America's preparations for war. Although the machine gun, the submarine, and the torpedo, like the airplane, had all been American inventions (indeed, of the major weapons introduced in World War I, only poison gas and the tank were not American innovations), each had been developed to deadliest perfection by European belligerents—and all were initially denigrated by the American military establishment. For instance, senior American naval officers at the turn of the century uniformly considered the submarine a death trap—indeed, thirty or more men (including the inventor) had drowned in testing its first true prototype. However, according to John P. Holland, the inventor of subsequent underwater craft, the real reason that the admirals lacked interest in submarines was that "there's no deck to strut on."

German generals had quickly recognized the defensive importance of the machine gun in trench warfare, for one automatic gun was more than a match for dozens of charging riflemen; as a result, German tactical units were issued machine guns on a scale unheard of. The Allies quickly followed suit, and American military observers dutifully reported this significant development to the General Staff, who gradually began to be aware that America's army not only was underequipped with machine guns but that those it did have were obsolescent. In the fall of 1916, the secretary of war appointed a board of military and civilian experts to look into the matter. However, the experts could not agree among themselves on which machine gun to adopt. Although Colonel Lewis's air-cooled machine gun was widely used and respected in Europe, it once

SIMAY
Subscribe to the Liberation Loan, ca. 1918
31¼ × 44 inches
George M. Dembo

again failed to meet the requirements of the U.S. Army. Nevertheless, the board did announce that the Army would sponsor competitive tests for machine guns in May of the following year.

Among the inventors who showed up with new machine guns at the Springfield (Massachusetts) Armory on May 1, 1917, was John Moses Browning, who had already designed an automatic pistol for the Army. After witnessing just ten days of competitive firing, two members of the board hurriedly left for Washington to inform the War Department that Browning's gun was far in advance of anything available—both as a weapon and in the simplicity of its design for manufacture. The board was unanimous in recommending Browning's heavy machine gun and anxious that the Ordnance Department make quick arrangements for its manufacture. The board representatives met with the secretary of war on May 11, but it was not until July that the War Department placed an order for twenty-two thousand Brownings with the holder of the inventor's patents, Colt's Patent Firearms Manufacturing Company. Colt's, however, was already operating at capacity and could not then accept the order. It was not until October, 1917, that production got under way, with an order for sixty-five thousand guns, and not until

May, 1918, that the guns were produced in significant quantity. Eventually, nearly one hundred thousand Brownings were manufactured, but for many months American soldiers trained with obsolete Maxim and Colt machine guns; in France they fought with the Hotchkiss. Even when the Browning guns began to be available in France, there was little opportunity for the troops to exchange weapons during the fighting. Nevertheless, after July 1, 1918, units of Pershing's doughboys did embark for France fully equipped with Brownings. Had production begun in the summer of 1917 instead of the late fall, fully three-quarters of the American Expeditionary Force could have sailed with Browning heavy machine guns.

In the spring of 1917—with America no longer a neutral—Allied military missions began to arrive from Europe with hopes of replenishing the tons of munitions and equipment used up or destroyed in the fighting. Initially, both sides of the Atlantic believed that America's legendary industrial output was to be her greatest contribution to winning the war and that machinery and matériel, rather than soldiers, would be her benefaction to the Allies. Having exhausted their own production resources, the Allies turned eagerly to America for their salvation, believing that with the push of a button all

L. N. BRITTON
To Everyone in This Plant, ca. 1918
18 × 23¾ inches
George M. Dembo

GEORGE HAND WRIGHT
Hip—Hip! Another Ship, ca. 1918
40 × 60 inches
George M. Dembo

the supplies they could possibly use would start rolling off American assembly lines. Imagine, then, their consternation when they discovered that the United States had barely begun organizing for war production and that much of the armamentaria the Allies desperately counted on would not be forthcoming. Indeed, America had let three years go by without seriously embracing preparedness or considering the plight of the Allies. Most people seemed to hope that Wilson would continue to keep the country out of war. Ironically, an industrial and technological giant like America had to do most of its fighting in the Great War with borrowed European equipment—airplanes, machine guns, and artillery manufactured in Great Britain and France. America's doughboys, who first sailed to Europe in felt campaign hats, had to be equipped with the British Tommy's distinctive steel helmet to stand a chance of surviving in the trenches.

It is hard to fault American industry for the lag in full mobilization when official orders for war supplies were so slow in coming. Nineteen years earlier, in gearing up to fight against Spain, the War Department had seen its venerable procurement and supply systems break down under the strain, but little seems to have been done in the interim to modernize the department's operations. When war was declared on Germany, each of the department's bureaus—regarding all others as deadly competitors—went quickly into action to corner all the military supplies it could possibly use. This sudden, enormous increase in demand for practically all raw materials and all manufacturing facilities produced chaos among existing war industries. The situation—coupled with colossal transportation snarls—got so far out of control that in January, 1918, the chairman of the Senate Committee on Military Affairs, Senator George E. Chamberlain, informed a National Security League gathering that "the Military Establishment of America . . . has almost stopped functioning." Indeed there was much truth to this assertion, but by that late date order was finally being brought to military procurement through overall direction. There were to be only ten months left in the war, but once under way the mobilization of America's industrial might was an accomplishment unrivaled by any other country in any period. The world had never seen such rapid progress on such a scale; that it resulted in so little material effect at the front must be blamed on a late beginning.

THE WAR INDUSTRIES BOARD

On
The
Job
For
Victory

**United States Shipping Board
Emergency Fleet Corporation**

It was not until the summer of 1917 that the government began to recognize the difficulties besetting industrial production, and not until then were the first steps taken toward complete control of industry. The War Department was but one customer for American industry's products; it competed for a share of the same scarce materials and facilities with, among others, the Purchasing Commission for the Allies, the Navy Department, and the Shipping Board. No existing agency was in a position of authority to rationally allocate raw materials to essential industries, but it was clear that centralized control would be necessary if America's industrial might were to produce the necessities of war efficiently. The procurement situation did not really improve until the spring of 1918, a full year into this country's belligerency. Part of the problem lay with the very nature of American free enterprise, which saw government interference with business as patently un-American. In the United States, a businessman prided

ANONYMOUS
On the Job for Victory, ca. 1918
21 × 28 inches
George M. Dembo

OVERLEAF
JONAS LIE
On the Job for Victory, ca. 1918
56 × 38 inches
Museum of the City of New York

ON THE JOB

·UNITED STATES SHIPPING BOARD

FOR VICTORY

EMERGENCY FLEET CORPORATION

CHARLES DANA GIBSON
Together You Will Win!, ca. 1918
18 × 25 inches
George M. Dembo

himself on deciding what he wanted to produce and what he would sell it for—subject only to the universal laws of supply and demand. Although no one would have believed it possible in America, the government ultimately was to annul even these formerly immutable laws.

With some four million young men pulled out of industry and farming for service in the Army and Navy, a scarcity of labor was added to that of materials. Not only was the absence of these men a burden on those remaining in the factories and fields, but those same soldiers and sailors increased the demand for all products in considerably greater degree than their numbers. Soldiers seem to wear out, lose, or destroy their equipment and clothes at a rate four times that of civilians. Stated another way, for a field coat on a soldier's back (estimated to last three months), there had to be one in reserve in France, one in transit, one in reserve in the United States, and one in the process of manufacture. And the military supply line—which stretched three thousand miles through railroad cars to warehouses to ships to other warehouses in Europe to more railroad cars to, ultimately, supply depots—had to be kept filled to capacity so that a reliable stockpile was available to sustain the troops in France. In addition, there was the problem for industry of producing the entirely

PFIFER
Let Us All Pull Together, ca. 1918
19 × 25 inches
University of Texas at Austin

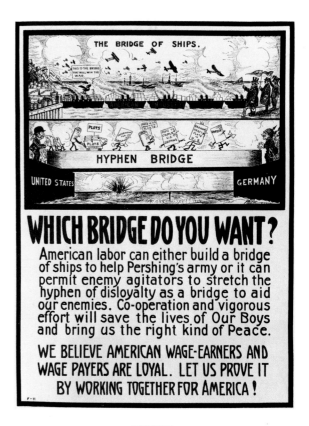

PFIFER
Which Bridge Do You Want?, ca. 1918
19 × 25 inches
University of Texas at Austin

*Two of a series of ten posters combating disloyalty, especially among foreign-born,
or "hyphenated," Americans.*

HIBBERD V. B. KLINE
Teamwork Wins, ca. 1918
26½ × 41 inches
Miscellaneous Man

Will YOU supply
EYES for the NAVY?

NAVY SHIPS NEED BINOCULARS AND SPY-GLASSES.

Glasses will be returned at Termination of War, if possible.
One Dollar will be _paid_ for Each One Accepted.

Tag each Article with your Name and Address and express or Mail to
Hon. Franklin D. Roosevelt, Ass't. Sec'y. of Navy.
℅ Naval Observatory - Washington D.C.

WILL YOU HELP US "STAND WATCH" ON A DESTROYER?

new range of paraphernalia required for war. Manufacturers not only had to learn to make unfamiliar products but often had to create special machinery and facilities overnight. With patriotic dedication, industry might have managed without the four million men gone to war; but it could not cope with a quadrupling of demand without some independent control of scarce resources. It was well known that nitrates, rubber, and tin (all absolutely essential to war industry) were not among the country's abundant natural resources; but at the outset, there was little idea of what raw materials *were* available or where they could be found. Nor—beyond what the Chamber of Commerce had undertaken—was there any useful survey of the range of manufacturing facilities available in this vast land, their locations, what they were capable of, or which could be converted to war production in the least amount of time. There was also the problem of important goods America had never felt the need to manufacture. For instance, the country had imported all of its optical glass from world-renowned makers in Germany and Austria—countries with which America was now at war. Providing the greatly expanded Army and Navy with sufficient telescopes, range finders, photographic lenses, and sextants proved to be a real problem. Initially, the situation was so desperate that the Navy issued a poster by Gordon Grant that showed a naval officer blindfolded and helpless on the deck of a ship at sea with the legend "Will you supply eyes for the Navy?"

The United States desperately required an organization to locate and mobilize the country's raw supplies, to control access to them, and to oversee their equitable distribution among manufacturers of priority products for the military. That organization had to discover first what was available, then what was needed, and make sure that the number of an item produced was neither too few nor too many. It had to control what was scarce and develop new sources where supplies were inadequate to the country's needs—all to the end that America's great resources might be directed toward the war effort in the fastest and most efficient fashion. In August, 1916, Congress had taken tentative steps in this direction by setting up the Council of National Defense—with a scarcely adequate appropriation of two hundred thousand dollars. Consisting of the secretaries of War, Navy, Interior, Agriculture, Commerce, and Labor, the Council was assisted by an advisory commission of business and industrial experts representing the major sectors of economic life. The members of the commission were Daniel Willard, president of the Baltimore & Ohio Railroad; Howard E. Coffin, vice president of the Hudson Motor

Company; Bernard M. Baruch of Wall Street; Dr. Hollis Godfrey, president of Drexel Institute; Samuel Gompers, president of the American Federation of Labor; Dr. Franklin Martin, secretary-general of the American College of Surgeons; and Julius Rosenwald, president of Sears, Roebuck & Company. To deal with so many quartermaster generals and admirals with acute supply problems, Rosenwald jokingly argued that his vast experience with Sears entitled him to a military title also: General Merchandise. Although the Council's work was slow in the beginning, its pace quickened when war seemed inevitable after Germany resumed unrestricted submarine warfare in January, 1917. By the time war was declared, the Council and its committees had filled one of the largest office buildings in Washington.

Within the Council, committees were formed to investigate the adequacy of certain supplies and facilities, such as food, fuel, and railroad transportation. Gradually, some of these committees became branches of the Council and then independent agencies, such as the United States Food Administration, the United States Fuel Administration, and the United States Railroad Administration. The General Munitions Board was another branch that would become independent. Organized initially to coordinate the production of war matériel for the War and Navy departments, its first job was to oversee construction of the many new army camps by mobilizing con-

MINE MORE COAL

PRESIDENT WILSON
DEMANDS COAL TO WIN THE WAR

"The existing scarcity of coal is creating a grave danger—in fact the most serious which confronts us—and calls for prompt and vigorous action on the part of both operators and miners. * * *

"The only worker who deserves the condemnation of his community is the one who fails to give his best in this crisis; not the one who accepts deferred classification and works regularly and diligently to increase the coal output.

"A great task is to be performed.

"The operators and their staffs alone can not do it; but both parties, working hand in hand with a grim determination to rid the country of its greatest obstacle to winning the war, can do it.

"It is with full confidence that I call upon you to assume the burden of producing an ample supply of coal."

WOODROW WILSON.

UNITED STATES FUEL ADMINISTRATION

GORDON GRANT
Will You Supply Eyes for the Navy?, ca. 1917
20½ × 29 inches
Museum of the City of New York

ANONYMOUS
Mine More Coal, 1918
24 × 29 inches
George M. Dembo

WALTER WHITEHEAD
Mine More Coal, 1918
20 × 30 inches
George M. Dembo

tractors and procuring and delivering the huge quantities of building materials required. The Board bravely attempted to organize procurement for the military but began to founder in the chaos that resulted from all government bureaus competing simultaneously in the marketplace. Throughout the spring and summer of 1917, the Board struggled to impose—without adequate authority—some order on the war-supply program, but it failed completely. This failure, however, made it clear that absolute government control of industry was the only way to end the chaos.

On July 28, 1917, the General Munitions Board was reorganized, with vastly greater authority, as the War Industries Board; but it was still under the chairmanship of Frank A. Scott. Gradually the various procurement agencies began to accept the direction of the Board, and by late autumn of 1917 industrial production was more or less under the control of a central organization. Part of this was due to the efficiency of the Board itself, which reduced the entire spectrum of industrial production to four administrative branches, each directed by a single executive. Bernard M. Baruch was in charge of raw materials, Judge Robert S. Lovett set priorities, Robert S. Brookings oversaw finished products, and Hugh Frayne was concerned with the labor supply. Each branch was further subdivided. Raw materials, for example, had fifty-seven separate commodity sections, and their heads decided what to purchase of their particular material and what to pay for it. Although each commodity section duly consulted with committees of their suppliers on costs, the Board ultimately determined the prices of materials and soon put an end to financial competition for raw materials by assigning priorities. Without proper direction, industry might, for instance, have used scarce supplies of iron and hardwood on wheels for delivery wagons when artillery wheels were in short supply—or vice versa. And a foundry might have built up an enormous quantity of giant howitzers, only to discover that munitions factories by concentrating on other caliber shells had provided them with nothing to fire. Some overall authority had to ensure that the right quantity of everything was being produced.

Establishing which companies would get what raw materials from limited supplies and produce which finished goods led to unaccustomed interferences with a businessman's individual freedom. It was not unusual for irate manufacturers who had been shut down for lack of crucial materials to challenge the allocation decisions of Judge Edwin Brewington Parker, who became commissioner of priorities. "We never used any compulsion," explained Judge Parker. "Of course, if a man didn't like the priority schedule and didn't want to play with us, he found he couldn't get any fuel or any railroad cars or any materials or any labor or anything; but we never used any compulsion. The man was a free agent." The control of all these facilities was solidly in the hands of the government.

In the first few weeks of the winter of 1917, America's vast but fragmented railway system virtually braked to a halt through lack of coordination in moving the products of the heavily industrialized Northeast to ports of embarkation clustered along the Atlantic Seaboard. In December the government found it necessary to take control of the railroads to undo the tangle and to get the supply trains moving again. And Daniel Willard, who had succeeded Scott as chairman of the War Industries Board, resigned in January to lend a hand at his former post with the Baltimore & Ohio, one of the key railroads in the East.

On March 4, 1918, President Wilson, having been awarded full power under the Overman Act to reshape the government for greater wartime efficiency, appointed Bernard M. Baruch the chairman of the War Industries Board and vested him with plenary authority. Fifty years old, Baruch was a Wall Street veteran of the commodities business who always identified his occupation as "speculator." Wilson defined the scope of the newly empowered Board:

1. the creation of new facilities and the disclosing and, if necessary, the opening up of new or additional sources of supply;

2. the conversion of existing facilities, where necessary, to new uses;

3. the studious conversion of resources and facilities by scientific, commercial, and industrial economies;

4. advice to the several purchasing agencies of the government with regard to the prices to be paid;

5. the determination, wherever necessary, of production and of delivery and of the proportions of any given article to be made immediately accessible to the several purchasing agencies when the supply of that article is insufficient, either temporarily or permanently;

6. the making of purchases for the Allies.

In summarizing Baruch's role, Wilson wrote that "he should act as the general eye of all supply departments in the field of industry." From that point on, one man controlled the destiny of American businesses with absolute authority. Free enterprise was a thing of the past, and the laws of supply and demand were preempted by government fiat. No manufacturer was exempt from government control. Prices rose or fell, businesses prospered or failed, workers went where they were told—all on government orders. Not even Germany so completely controlled her citizens. Nevertheless, the War Industries Board was to operate at peak authority for just over six months, until Armistice ended the war at least a year earlier than expected. But the Board's power was exercised long enough for Baruch to characterize the mobilized industry of America as a "weapon of offense or defense more potent than anything the world has ever seen, more terrible, I think, than the mind of any man has ever imagined."

ANONYMOUS
Keep 'em Going!, 1918
20 × 30 inches
George M. Dembo

IX. THE LIBERTY LOANS

Congressman Cordell Hull of the House Ways and Means Committee estimated in 1919 that the Great War had cost the United States something over $30 billion (the Civil War had cost the Union $13 billion). Fully two-thirds of this enormous sum was raised through the four Liberty Loan and final Victory Loan campaigns.

Once war was declared, Congress next addressed the great problem of financing the new role America would play in the European conflict. Should the stupendous costs of rapidly preparing the country for a foreign war be met through increased taxation (a graduated income tax had just been enacted in the Revenue Act of 1916), or by issuing government bonds, or by a combination of both? In his War Message to Congress, President Wilson had advocated "well conceived taxation. . . . because it seems to me that it would be most unwise to base the credits which will now be necessary entirely on money borrowed." On the other hand, Treasury Secretary William Gibbs McAdoo (who was Wilson's campaign manager in the 1912 presidential race) questioned the political wisdom of a Democratic administration's being responsible for heavier taxation. J. P. Morgan, Jr., had advised McAdoo to raise no more than twenty percent of the necessary war revenues through taxation; for the remainder, the Treasury could always count on loans patriotically subscribed to by the wealthy. McAdoo took Morgan's advice on taxes but

FRED STROTHMANN
Beat Back the Hun, 1918
20 × 30 inches
Museum of the City of New York

ANONYMOUS
Buy a Liberty Bond, 1917
20 × 30 inches
George M. Dembo

ANONYMOUS
Liberty Loan and War Savings Service Buttons,
ca. 1918
Loans, ½ inch; W.S.S, ¾ inch
William A. Brennan

ANONYMOUS
You'll Be Uncomfortable Without Your Honor Button, 1918
8 × 22 inches
Maurice Rickards
A car card that shows other cards in their place of duty.

not on loan subscribers. In his book *Crowded Years*, he wrote, "We went direct to the people, and that means to everybody—to businessmen, workmen, farmers, bankers, millionaires, school-teachers, laborers. We capitalized the profound impulse called patriotism. It is the quality of coherence that holds a nation together; it is one of the deepest and most powerful of human motives."

After much debate, Congress voted in late April to initially authorize a bond issue of $5 billion—characteristically postponing a decision on hiking America's taxes. Ultimately, war revenue was raised in three major ways: the government borrowed for short-term needs from the newly founded Federal Reserve System, issued Liberty Bonds and War Savings Stamps, and passed special revenue bills that greatly increased rates on the new income tax, as well as instituting a tax on excess profits. Through these taxes, the Treasury brought in nearly $9.5 billion for the war effort.

In all the loan campaigns combined, the Treasury offered the public a total of $18.5 billion in interest-bearing bonds—which America patriotically oversubscribed by more than $5 billion. One authority, in illustrating the magnitude of this twenty-four-billion-dollar sum, said that laid out in rows of silver dollars it would encircle the Earth nearly twenty times. In contrast, during the full four years of the European war, neither Britain nor France could raise more than $20 billion each through loans. As Maurice Rickards, in his seminal book on the First World War, viewed this accomplishment: "The war-bond technique, perennial standby of the European belligerents, went American. Through high-powered publicity and all the techniques of a rapidly developing public-relations and promotion industry the American government persuaded the American people to lend it money. But where Europe had merely tinkered with the idea, America went all out."

Bonds were something quite new to the average American. A year before the first Liberty Loan campaign subscribed two billion dollars' worth, the grand total of all outstanding U.S. government bonds was just $1,378,124,593—nearly all of it held by financial institutions or wealthy businessmen. Many a patriotic citizen, who in the Liberty Loan campaign purchased his first bond ever, failed to understand the nature of the obligation and pestered the Treasury with naive questions—mostly about when to make interest payments. Secretary McAdoo issued a statement explaining that purchasers were in fact lenders who would *receive* interest, and that the bonds were so named because the proceeds of the public's generosity were "to be dedicated to the cause of human liberty." For the Second Liberty Loan campaign, the government prepared a poster that read—above a painting of the Treasury Building—"Lend Your Money to Your Government" and "U.S. Treasury will pay you interest every six months" across the bottom. Despite America's early innocence of high finance, estimates are that nearly one-third of the country's entire population bought at least one Liberty Bond; the pressure to "do one's bit" was considerable. Every purchaser received a Liberty Button to wear—proudly, or to be spared the social embarrassment of appearing buttonless. In one Liberty Loan ad, Charles Dana Gibson crowned his inimitable Columbia with a tiara emblazoned "Public Opinion." Striding purposefully forward, right fist clenched and left arm upraised, she delivered the following message:

I AM PUBLIC OPINION
All men fear me!
I declare that Uncle Sam shall not go to his knees
to
beg you to buy his bonds. That is no position for
a fighting
man. But if you have the money to buy and do not
buy, I
will make this No Man's Land for you!
I will judge you not by an allegiance expressed in
mere words.
I will judge you not by your mad cheers as our
boys
march away to whatever fate may have in store
for them.
I will judge you not by the warmth of the tears
you
shed over the lists of the dead and the injured
that come
to us from time to time.
I will judge you not by your uncovered head and
solemn
mien as our maimed in battle return to our shores
for loving care.
But, as wise as I am just, I will judge you by the
material aid you give to the fighting men who are
facing
death that you may live and move and have your
being in a
world made safe.
I warn you—don't talk patriotism over here
unless
your money is talking victory over there.
I AM PUBLIC OPINION!
AS I JUDGE, ALL MEN STAND OR FALL!

From the First Liberty Loan in May, 1917, to the Victory Liberty Loan in early 1919, the United States Bureau of Printing and Engraving produced more than one hundred billion separate bond certificates

LEND HIM A HAND

CHARLES NICHOLAS SARKA
Leslie's, April 6, 1918
10¼ × 14 inches
Norma Hughes

CHARLES NICHOLAS SARKA
Lend Him a Hand, 1918
12 × 19 inches
George M. Dembo
Numerous magazine covers were turned into posters.

"Lend Him a Hand"
BUY
LIBERTY BONDS

of all denominations—the greatest undertaking in printing history. For the First Liberty Loan, 6,060,500 bonds were printed; for the Second Loan the figure was 17,363,000. Not at first prepared for so formidable a task, the Bureau experienced numerous delays in production and delivery—many purchasers failed to receive the actual certificates for weeks or months. But by the time of the Third Loan, when more than twenty-five million bonds were printed, the Bureau was fully geared up for the tremendous workload; thereafter the bond certificates were available for delivery during each loan campaign.

Fine paper for the certificates was specially produced in New England mills, and a strict inventory was kept of every sheet until the printed securities, banded in stacks of consecutively numbered thousands, were safely stored in the Treasury vaults. Each surety bore the official signature of Houston B. Teehee, the register. Born a Cherokee in Indian Territory (which became the state of Oklahoma in 1907), Teehee was not a citizen until 1910, when he was granted full rights by the secretary of the interior. Prior to his appointment as register, Teehee already had served as a U.S. probate attorney, state legislator, and mayor of Tahlequah, Oklahoma (the end of the Cherokees' Trail of Tears). His real name was Di-hi-hi, but he took the surname Union Army buddies bestowed on his father during the Civil War.

In addition to his cabinet position as secretary of the Treasury, McAdoo was chairman of the Federal Reserve, a system of twelve regional banks coordinated by a central board in Washington. Since the system (instituted in 1913) was intended to function as the central bank for banks in the United States, it was chosen as the organizational base for soliciting and processing Liberty Loan sales. McAdoo became the head of what was called the Liberty Loan Army, a force whose total in its sales, publicity, and speaking branches fluctuated between one and two million people dedicated to the selling of Liberty Bonds.

FIRST LIBERTY LOAN

Offered $2,000,000,000; subscribed $3,035,226,850; accepted $2,000,000,000. Number of subscribers 4,000,000. Denominations: bonds with coupons attached $50, $100, $500, and $1,000; registered bonds, $100, $500, $1,000, $5,000, $10,000, $50,000, and $100,000. Date of maturity, June 15, 1947; redeemable on or after June 15, 1932. Interest three and one-half percent, payable June 15 and December 15; non-taxable. Loan opened officially May 14, closed June 15, 1917.

The congressional authorization to issue bonds was approved by President Wilson on April 24, 1917, and shortly thereafter McAdoo announced a public subscription offer of two billion dollars in Liberty Bonds. He set the interest rate at three and one-half percent, slightly less than what savings banks offered, so as not to tempt citizens to withdraw their savings from the private sector. The banking community doubted that bonds offered below the going rates would ever sell, so McAdoo was persuaded to sweeten this first offering with tax-exempt status. Since this was of real value only to the rich it was later eliminated, but interest rates for Liberty Bonds were never raised to a competitive level. Preliminaries for the first drive were launched on May 4, and early subscriptions from banks began pouring in at the rate of $330,166 a minute. By the second day, almost one-sixth of the goal had been subscribed.

To publicize the bond drive, three posters were initially prepared. All of them featured the Statue of Liberty, a popular embodiment of freedom from European autocracy. Perhaps the most memorable of the posters was the one by G. R. Macauley, which showed an aggressively determined Miss Liberty pointing a finger at every passerby and demanding, "You buy a Liberty Bond lest I perish." In this rendition, Liberty is shown half length and with her torch switched to the left hand while she points with her right. The second poster (rather rare) shows Liberty full length and pointing with her left index finger as she holds the torch aloft in the accustomed hand. In both cases, license has been taken with her pose, but Liberty's dramatic admonition remains the same and the inscribed tablet normally in the crook of her left arm is absent. Shortly after the war, a New York company, Rusling Wood, claimed in *Printers' Ink Monthly* to have lithographed the very first Liberty Loan poster. As the story is told, the company was contacted on a Saturday morning by Frank DeSales Casey (known to them as art manager of *Collier's*) on behalf of an unfamiliar committee, which was, of course, Gibson's Division of Pictorial Publicity. Casey informed the company representative that a poster was needed to advertise the first Liberty Loan, and that one of the biggest lithographers in the country had said it would take no less than two to three weeks to prepare. The committee needed the poster as soon as possible. The response from the Rusling Wood spokesman was "bring on your poster. For the United States I will break all records. You will be able to ship Tuesday night." The narrator continued: "The committee came to my office Saturday noon. Instead of a poster they had only the rough sketch for a poster by Adolph Treidler. I sent John Speth, one of our reproducing artists, to Mr. Treidler's studio, and he waited until the finished drawing was completed. Mr. Speth brought it back with him, and transferred it to the lithographing plates Sunday, and Monday the presses were running. Tuesday night the whole job, fifty thousand posters,

G. R. MACAULEY
You Buy a Liberty Bond Lest I Perish, 1917
30 × 40 inches
Museum of the City of New York

ANONYMOUS
You Buy a Liberty Bond Lest I Perish, 1917
20 × 30 inches
Meehan Military Posters

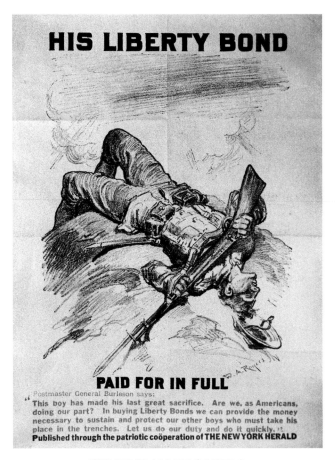

WILLIAM ALLEN ROGERS
His Liberty Bond Paid for in Full, 1917
7 × 10 inches
George M. Dembo

ADOLPH TREIDLER
Have You Bought Your Bond?, 1917
21 × 28 inches
George M. Dembo
Probably the first Liberty Loan poster.

was shipped." The poster, in black and olive green on a blue background, showed a completely realistic Statue of Liberty with the message, "Have you bought YOUR Bond? Liberty Loan Subscriptions Received Here." Perhaps as many as two million posters were printed for the first Loan, and display sheets were prepared for eleven thousand billboards. One had Uncle Sam pointing a finger as he said, "You buy a Liberty Bond; I'll do the rest." In another, the old gentleman grasped a man's coat lapel and asked pointedly, "Where is your button?" The campaign was carried on in every movie theater as well, where film trailers entreated each citizen to "Buy a Liberty Loan Bond." Even churches were called upon to participate in the drive on Liberty Loan Sunday. Hundreds of thousands of everyday folk dropped

everything to become bond salesmen.

On the closing day of the drive, McAdoo pronounced the Liberty Loan a success—"a genuine triumph for democracy. It is the unmistakable expression of America's determination to carry this war for the protection of American life and reestablishment of peace and liberty throughout the world to a swift and successful conclusion." More than four million individuals had responded to the appeal, oversubscribing the offer by more than one billion dollars. Ninety-nine percent of the purchases were in denominations from fifty to ten thousand dollars, and these pledges were accepted by the Treasury. Those who spoke for larger sums had their subscriptions scaled back proportionately, to limit the government's obligation to the original offering of two billion.

SECOND LIBERTY LOAN

Offered $3,000,000,000; subscribed $4,617,532,300; accepted $3,807,891,900. Number of subscribers 9,400,000. Date of maturity, November 15, 1942; redeemable on or after November 15, 1927. Interest four percent; payable November 15 and May 15. Loan opened officially October 1, closed October 28, 1917.

For the Second Liberty Loan campaign, announced on September 27, 1917, Secretary McAdoo offered to accept a subscription of $3 billion "or more." Urged by the financial community to make the yield represent more than mere patriotism, Congress had agreed to raise the interest rate to four percent— but the bonds were no longer to be completely tax

MAURICE INGRES
Let's End It Quick, 1917
23 × 41 inches
Museum of the City of New York

free. Solicitation got off to a faster start this time, since the Liberty Loan organization was now well-established nationwide; the public also had a much better idea of what a government bond was. Greater efforts were made to reach beyond cities and towns to rural communities, and the Treasury Department sent out a barrage of post cards—"All About Liberty Bonds"—on which answers to typical questions were offered. *What are they?* "Liberty Bonds are engraved certificates bearing the guarantee of the Government and People of the United States to repay in gold the full amount loaned with 4% interest every year. Liberty Bonds are as safe as the United States." *Why should I buy them?* "Because we are at war. Because we must have dollars as well as men in the fight for freedom. Because every bond you buy helps to win the war. Because they are the safest investment in the world to-day." The card goes on to illustrate the terms of purchase for a fifty-dollar bond: put a dollar down during the campaign, pay nine dollars the next month, then twenty dollars each for the next two months. It also indicates the possibility of "still easier terms": a dollar down and a dollar a week. The card ends with the assurance that "you can sell Liberty Bonds at any time at any bank whether or not you have completed your payments. Most banks will lend you 90% on Liberty Bonds."

Certain days were set aside for special emphasis during the campaign, including Aviation Day, October 20, when soldiers were given leave from their training camps to "bomb" (or distribute) Liberty Loan materials on city streets. October 24 was named Liberty Day by President Wilson, and the Boy Scouts were given a week of their own to try their hand at solicitation—with the slogan, "Every Scout to Save a Soldier." Millions of dollars' worth of bonds were subscribed this way. A record was set in Baltimore when a total of twenty million dollars was pledged at a single meeting. Even prison inmates were solicited with good result. In addition, distinguished personalities such as Secretary McAdoo went out on speaking tours. Arthur Guiterman characterized McAdoo's indefatigable efforts in the following:

He's always up and McAdooing.
From sun to star and star to sun,
His work is never McAdone . . .
I don't believe he ever hid,
A single thing he McAdid.

But not everyone was completely sold on Liberty Bonds, given the knowledge of who might benefit from (or be harmed by) the funds garnered. There were large groups in America of Irish Catholic extraction who were disinclined to be of any material aid to Britain. Jews with direct knowledge of Russia's pogroms were determined not to see any of their money reach America's new ally. And many Americans of German heritage who would never have supported the kaiser's militaristic program were

ANONYMOUS
Ring It Again, 1917
21 × 28½ inches
Museum of the City of New York

reluctant to see German *Kultur* crushed. Those of Danish, Swedish, and Norwegian backgrounds tended to adopt the neutrality of the Scandinavian countries, and there were ardent pacifists who refused to contribute to any kind of war. Still others—Socialists, Anarchists, Wobblies—who were outright enemies of the capitalist system, saw the war as the result of the greedy machinations of international bankers and munitions-makers and wanted nothing at all to do with it. In many instances, "Americanizers" were not sympathetic to these other points of view, and they resorted to rather harsh measures to persuade "German sympathizers" to buy Liberty Bonds, including publicizing the names of suspected shirkers, splashing their establishments with yellow paint, and subjecting them to public harassment. Secretary McAdoo even asked that he be sent the names of any slackers so unpatriotic as to hinder the activities of the Liberty Loan Army: "A man who can't lend his government $1.25 per week at the rate of 4% interest is not entitled to be an American citizen."

The first of the posters for the Second Loan carried a statement attributed to McAdoo but delivered by

DAN SAYRE GROESBECK
Shall We Be More Tender?, 1917
20 × 30 inches
Museum of the City of New York

ANONYMOUS
Remember Your First Thrill of American Liberty, 1917
20 × 30 inches
Museum of the City of New York

Uncle Sam: ''Shall we be more tender with our dollars than with the Lives of our Sons''—a quote repeated in at least one more poster. Another memorable work was designed to appeal to latecomers to these shores whose loyalty Americanizers tended to question. Similar to others issued in several middle-European languages, this one showed, in soft reds, blues, and grays, an immigrant ship passing the Statue of Liberty en route to Ellis Island, under the rubric ''Remember Your First Thrill of American Liberty.'' The poster stresses that ''YOUR DUTY'' is to buy bonds. On a thematically similar poster made for the Food

Administration by Charles E. Chambers, the message is even more explicit: "You came here seeking Freedom / You must now help to preserve it." This campaign also introduced a characterization of the enemy in Liberty Loan posters as the savage "Hun"—the first one showed just a bloody hand-print.

The results of this drive were that nearly 9.5 million Americans bought bonds, subscribing $1.5 billion more than in the last campaign. Of this amount, the Treasury accepted $3,807,891,900.

R. H. PORTEUS
Women! Help America's Sons, 1917
20 × 30 inches
Museum of the City of New York

J. ALLEN ST. JOHN
The Hun—His Mark, 1917
20 × 30 inches
Museum of the City of New York

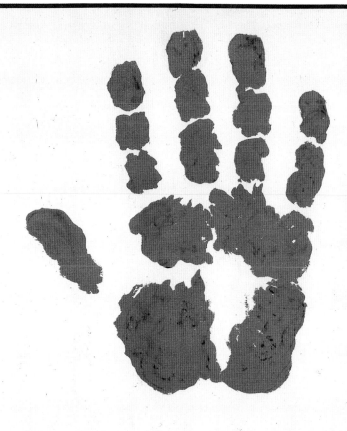

The Hun ~ his Mark

Blot it Out

with

LIBERTY
BONDS

THIRD LIBERTY LOAN

Offered $3,000,000,000; subscribed and accepted $4,176,516,850. Number of subscribers 18,308,325. Date of maturity September 15, 1928; redeemable date of maturity. Interest four and one-quarter percent, payable March 15 and September 15. Loan opened officially April 6, closed May 4, 1918.

The opening day of the Third Loan, April 6, 1918, was the first anniversary of the American declaration of war, and it was designated a holiday in virtually every state. Evening bond rallies were held on April 12 in thousands of local schoolhouses, and on Sunday, April 21, a Liberty Loan sermon was delivered in more than one hundred thousand churches. The movie stars Douglas Fairbanks and Mary Pickford attracted myriad crowds to rallies they addressed, as did Arthur Guy Empey, an American veteran of the British Expeditionary Force in France and author of

ANONYMOUS
Coming War Train, ca. 1918
20 × 30 inches
Maurice Rickards

the 1917 best-seller *Over the Top*. April 27 was named National Liberty Loan Day.

A new feature of this campaign was the honor flag, which was awarded to communities reaching their subscription quotas. The competition to be first in a particular area to win the flag was so keen that forty-nine cities earned the honor in the initial minute of this drive. Additional stars were conferred whenever a town doubled its quota, and many communities flew honor flags with several stars. The top Liberty Loan city in the country, Carthage, Ohio, boasted forty-seven stars on its banner.

Another popular feature of this campaign, and the next one, was the war exhibit train, six of which were fitted up with captured enemy trophies and war-torn artifacts of trench warfare likely to attract a flag-waving crowd. These trains were routed initially through the St. Louis, Dallas, and Atlanta districts of the Federal Reserve and were accompanied by combat veterans from all the Allies as well as Liberty Loan speakers of national reputation. Indeed, practically every cabinet member went on the road to support the bond campaign. Even the president participated. The war exhibit trains, stopping in nineteen cities, brought in $1,432,261.36.

For the Third Loan, Gibson's Division of Pictorial Publicity was in full swing, and posters by such renowned illustrators as Howard Chandler Christy, Joseph Christian Leyendecker, and Joseph Pennell appeared. Columbia (the personification of America that first appeared in the eighteenth century), Uncle Sam (her male counterpart), Abraham Lincoln, Independence Hall, the Liberty Bell, and, of course, the Stars and Stripes were time-honored symbols liberally made use of; the relatively new Statue of Liberty, now imbued with wide-ranging symbolism, was beginning her virtual eclipse of Columbia. One poster—with oblique reference to those of "hyphenated" or potentially divided loyalties because of foreign birth—asked, "Are You 100% American? Prove It!"

The most financially productive exploit of this campaign was brought about through a challenge made by the president. Wilson announced that even though he already had overextended himself in purchases of Liberty Bonds, he would still subscribe for yet another fifty-dollar bond—this time on the installment plan. He called on all patriotic Americans to "match" his effort, and the Liberty Loan Army immediately turned to the Committee on Public Information for aid. Within days, fifty thousand Four-Minute Men were delivering the president's challenge to every community in the United States. The results of this effort to "Match the President" in financial sacrifice exceeded $100 million in bond subscriptions. In all, more than eighteen million citizens invested in this campaign.

HOWARD CHANDLER CHRISTY
Fight or Buy Bonds, 1917
20 × 30 inches
Museum of the City of New York

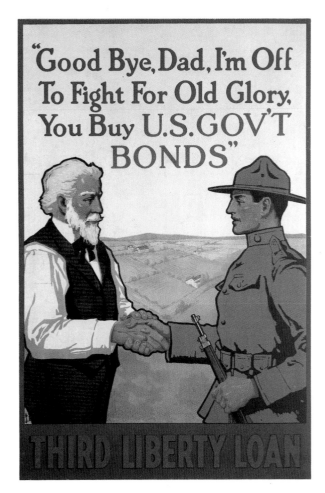

LAWRENCE HARRIS
Good Bye, Dad, 1918
20 × 30 inches
Museum of the City of New York

HENRY PATRICK RALEIGH
Halt the Hun!, 1918
20 × 29½ inches
Museum of the City of New York

ANONYMOUS
Remember the Flag of Liberty, 1918
20 × 30 inches
Maurice Rickards

JOSEPH CHRISTIAN LEYENDECKER
Weapons for Liberty, 1918
20 × 30 inches
Museum of the City of New York

OVERLEAF
HERBERT ANDREW PAUS
To Make the World a Decent Place to Live, 1918
56 × 36 inches
Guernsey's

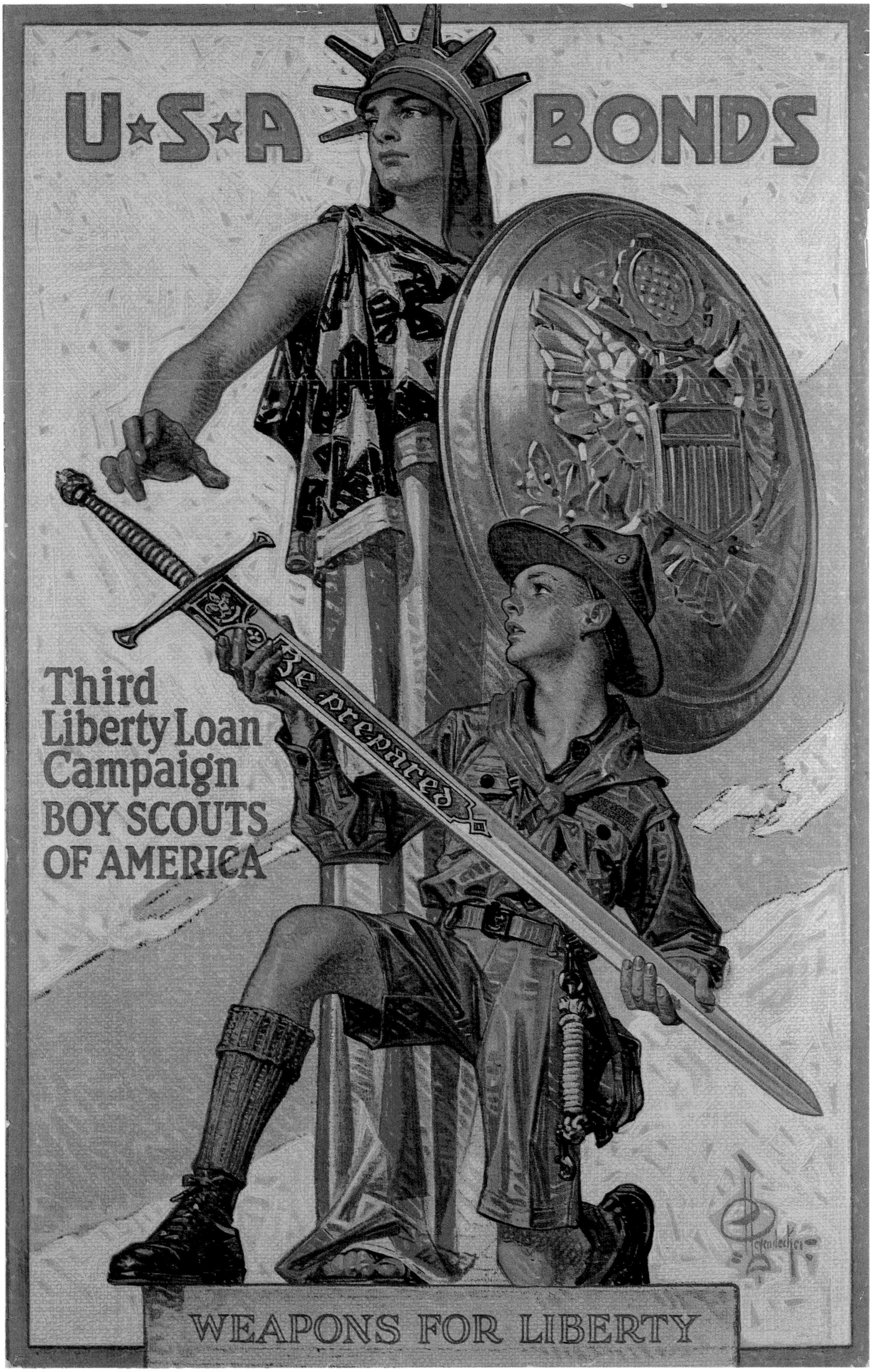
U★S★A BONDS
Be prepared
Third Liberty Loan Campaign
BOY SCOUTS OF AMERICA
WEAPONS FOR LIBERTY

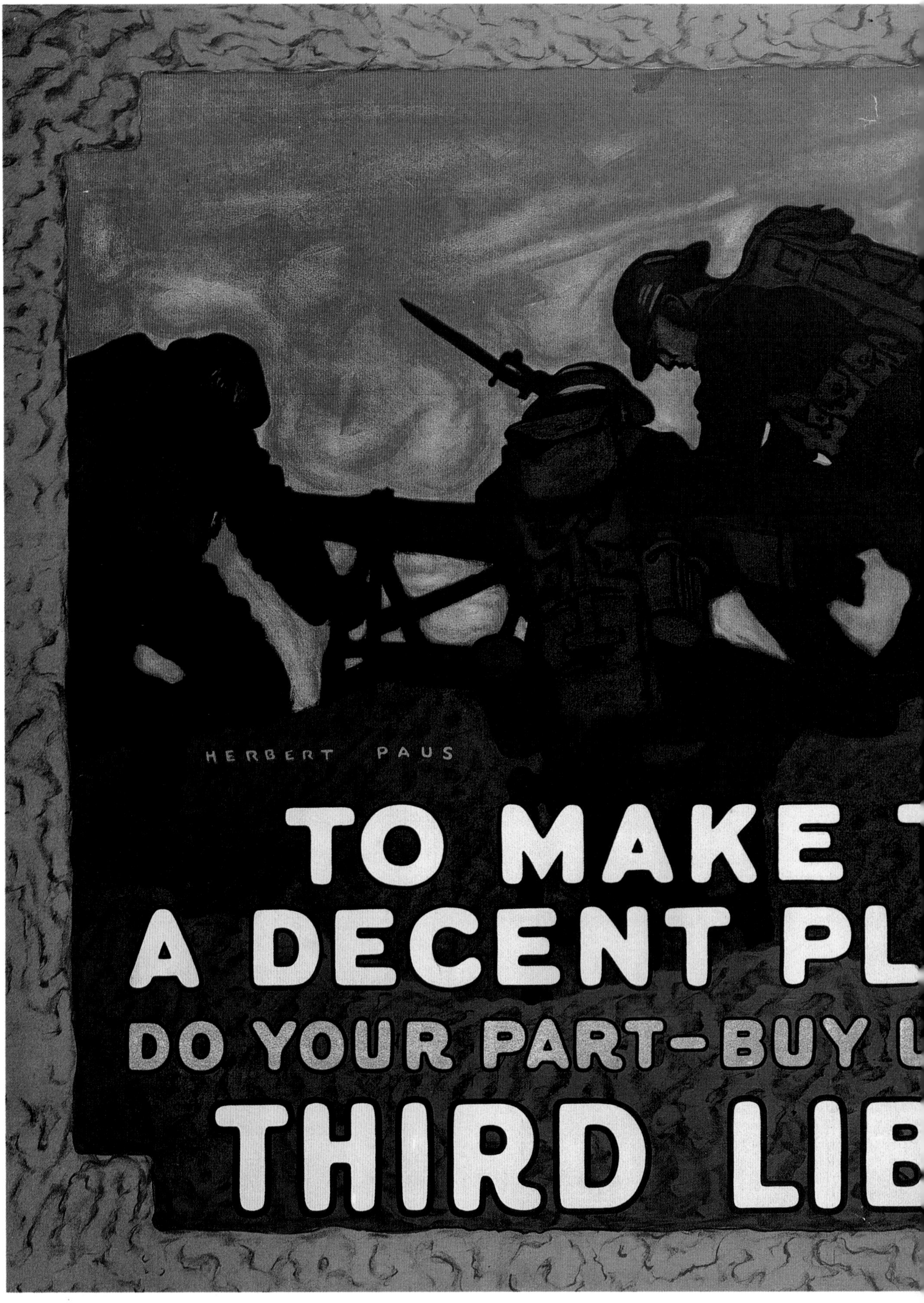

HERBERT PAUS

TO MAKE T
A DECENT PL
DO YOUR PART-BUY L
THIRD LIB

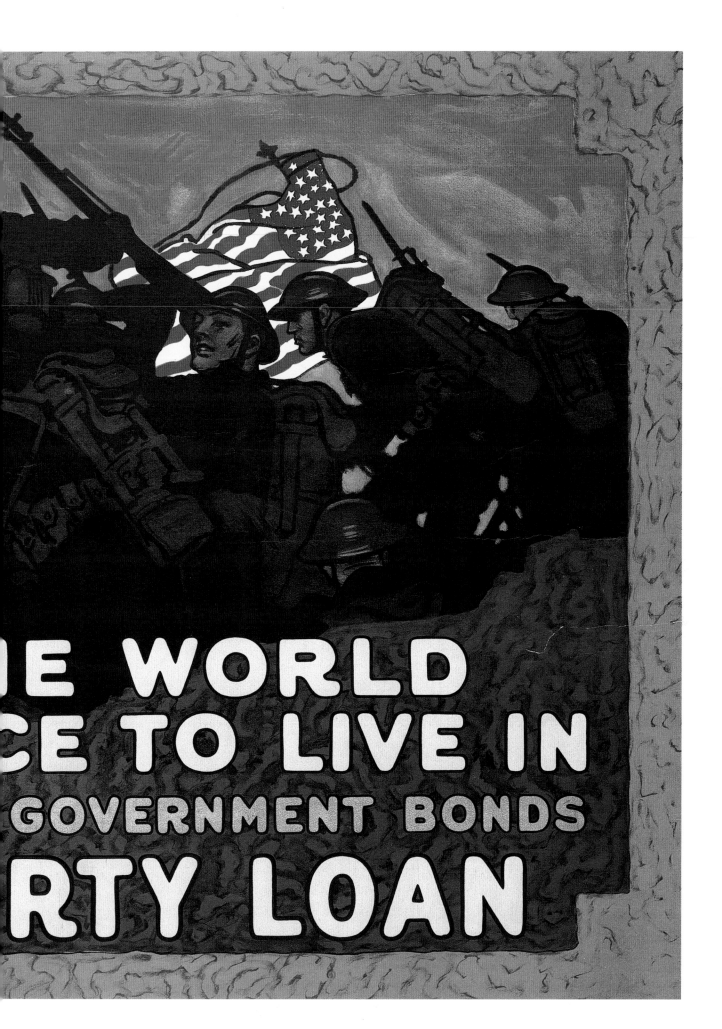

John Norton

keep these off the U.S.A

Buy more LIBERTY BONDS

5 B

THE STROBRIDGE LITHO. CO. CINCINNATI & NEW YORK

WAR SAVINGS STAMPS

Halfway through 1918, while the quickly trained American doughboy was displaying his mettle at Château-Thierry and Belleau Wood, the costs of conducting the war were mounting so rapidly that it was necessary to find substantial new sources for money. The Third Liberty Loan closed in early May and the Fourth would not open until September, but by late June the billions raised in the earlier drive were nearly gone. At this point, the National War-Savings Committee was commandeered into raising funds in the three- or four-month gaps between Liberty Loan campaigns. In late June, a concerted drive to raise money through sales of War Savings Stamps was officially launched on a poster by James Montgomery Flagg; it showed a stern-faced Uncle Sam, arms akimbo, presenting this message: "*I am telling you* / on June 28th I expect you to enlist in the army of war savers to back up my army of fighters."

When it was launched in the fall of 1917, the War Savings movement was not designed simply to raise money for waging war. Its true purpose was something rather more complex, an attempt at remedying domestic problems that arose from rapid conversion to an all-out war economy. Initially this campaign might have seemed a way to make even young boys and girls feel a part of the War Loan Organization—given the low cost of its twenty-five-cent Thrift Stamp. Indeed, several of the War Savings Stamp posters that first come to mind seem directed toward enlisting children in the war effort. For instance, Flagg produced one with Uncle Sam presenting this earnest message to a couple of attractive youngsters: "Boys and Girls! You Can Help Your Uncle Sam Win the War. Save Your Quarters. Buy War Savings Stamps." Another poster showed a boy and girl standing in the presence of General Pershing, attentively absorbing the words, "Help Him Win by Saving and Serving." But there was also the Haskell Coffin poster, "Joan of Arc Saved France," which exhorted "Women of America, Save Your Country." Another, by Herbert Paus, was obviously directed toward parents: "Save Your Child from Autocracy and Poverty." Yet another showed adults of all ages and ethnic backgrounds lined up before a sales wicket where Uncle Sam is selling War Savings Stamps.

The primary mission of the War Savings movement, which followed the lead of its British counterpart, was to entice discretionary or surplus money out of hands that might tend to squander it on luxuries. The plan was intended to deal with the fact that in a war economy, with a radical change in the nature and volume of goods to be produced and with millions of men drawn from their regular jobs for military service, there was a severe shortage of labor as well as a scarcity of raw materials for producing essential war goods. To remedy the situation, certain nonessential (or luxury) product lines had to be curtailed for the duration of the conflict, so that their materials and labor could be allocated to better effect. However, because of the open-ended need for war matériel at practically any cost and the scarcity of labor, the laws of supply and demand greatly raised the wages offered men who could be hired for essential production—as well as their discretionary income after providing basic necessities. This unaccustomed surplus cash in the pockets of American labor (following years of low wages and recession) was sure to be devoted to buying long-coveted consumer goods and luxuries—which established companies naturally wanted to continue producing in a burgeoning market. It was not then possible—before the War Industries Board was in full operation—to tell manufacturers

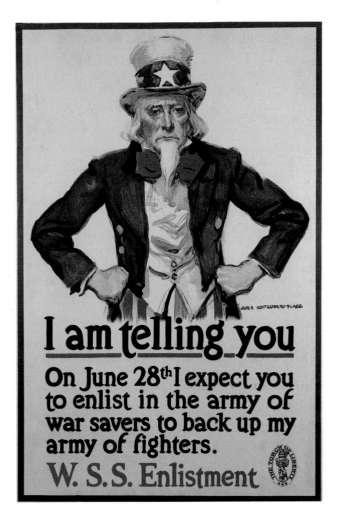

JAMES MONTGOMERY FLAGG
I Am Telling You, 1918
20 × 30 inches
Museum of the City of New York

JOHN NORTON
Keep These Off the U.S.A., 1918
30½ × 40 inches
Museum of the City of New York

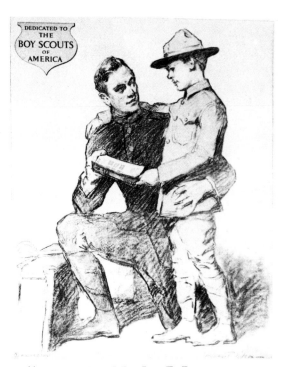

JAMES MONTGOMERY FLAGG
Boys and Girls!, 1918
20 × 30 inches
Museum of the City of New York

URQUHART WILCOX
We'll Help You Win the War, Dad, 1918
20 × 30 inches
George M. Dembo

ANONYMOUS
W.S.S. for Sale Here, 1918
40 × 29¾ inches
Meehan Military Posters

HASKELL COFFIN
Joan of Arc Saved France, 1918
20 × 30 inches
Walton Rawls

KEEP HIM FREE

W.S.S.
WAR SAVINGS STAMPS
ISSUED BY THE
UNITED STATES
GOVERNMENT

BUY

WAR SAVINGS STAMPS

ISSUED BY THE UNITED STATES TREASURY DEPT.

T. D. McGILL
Your Stamp of Approval, 1918
13¾ × 22½ inches
George M. Dembo

ADOLPH TREIDLER
Help Stop This, 1918
20½ × 28 inches
George M. Dembo

of nonessential goods such as fast sports cars or grand pianos or fur coats or fine china to cease and desist from pursuing their livelihoods. The government's initial idea was to limit the attractiveness of luxury goods by diminishing the money available to spend on such things.

One way this was accomplished was through the Liberty Loan drives, which took billions out of the hands of the man on the street and permitted the government to redirect those dollars to essential uses. The next goal was to curtail expenditures on nonessential goods whose fabrication rivaled war industries for labor and raw materials. For instance, the same fine metals, machinery, and craftsmen used in making strings for a grand piano were needed for the struts and wires that held airplanes together. In terms of competing for scarce materials, this situation was true of practically everything necessary for the war effort. To a certain extent it was possible—through huge orders and profitable terms—to induce manufacturers of fine wool topcoats to adjust their

yardage, patterns, and machinery to the production of army overcoats, or blanket-makers to limit their range of colors and patterns to olive drab for the war's duration; but there were other users of scarce commodities who could not so easily convert their product lines to war goods. And even though there was still a demand for the latter's products (stimulated by the American worker's newfound wealth), it was not beneficial to the country to have these goods available at the sacrifice of servicemen's needs.

This then was the original purpose of the War Savings movement: to curb an excessive demand even among everyday Americans for nonessentials, so that workers in a labor force severely diminished by the need for fighting men would transfer out of jobs in declining nonessential endeavors into better-paying jobs in war industries. In addition, raw materials consumed in manufacturing luxury goods would then be available for producing essential goods. Of course, with the creation of the War Industries Board, when all scarce materials eventually were allocated from a central source, this kind of subtle influence on the marketplace became obsolete. In the beginning, however, this was regarded as a more American way of dealing with the problem.

The War Savings Stamps campaign was not pre-

CHARLES LIVINGSTON BULL
Keep Him Free, 1918
20 × 30 inches
Museum of the City of New York

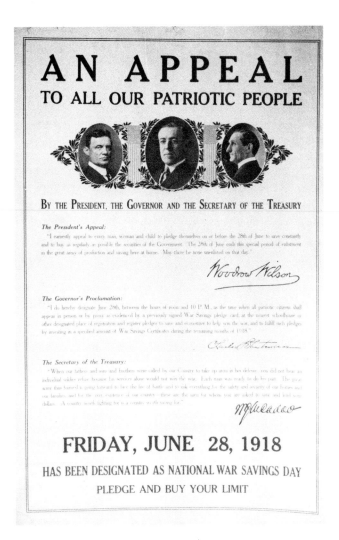

ANONYMOUS
An Appeal, 1918
28 × 42 inches
George M. Dembo

cieties, were set up all over the country to sell Savings Stamps, which were in effect small-denomination securities available in stores, hotels, theaters, and even in booths set up on the sidewalks.

Technically, the War Savings Stamp was a discounted promissory note, purchasable at a sum less than the face value it could be redeemed for later. The Thrift Stamp was sold for twenty-five cents and the War Savings Stamp had a face value of five dollars. As one purchased Thrift Stamps, they were attached to Thrift Cards that had spaces for sixteen stamps that cost a total of four dollars. This card could then be applied toward a War Savings Stamp that the government would redeem for five dollars five years later. The interest rate was four percent compounded quarterly, which did not quite earn a dollar over the five-year term, so a few extra pennies were needed in addition to the Thrift Card to purchase a War Savings Stamp. In January of a given year, the five-dollar stamp would cost $4.12; each month thereafter one cent would be added to the cost until the price would be $4.23 in December. After that, a new series of stamps with a year-later redemption date would be issued, and the price would start again at $4.12.

sented to the American public in quite these terms—at least not in the posters. The rationale most often offered was that no contribution to the war effort was too small, that even collected in nickels and quarters the money could be used by the government to hire workers and purchase raw materials that would help win the war. One brochure from the War-Savings Society Bureau urged Americans to back the country's fighters by lending their savings to the government: "Help to reduce competition with the Government for labor, materials and transportation needed for these men. That means that you will spend less for things you do not need *now*. . . . At the same time the savings that you put into War Savings Stamps will be a reserve to protect yourself and your family." Committees, or War-Savings So-

ANONYMOUS
War Savings Stamps (in Yiddish), 1918
14 × 21 inches
George M. Dembo

CASPER EMERSON, JR.
Help Them, 1918
20 × 30 inches
Museum of the City of New York

221

The promotion of War Savings Stamps sales was conducted by a wide variety of grass-roots organizations, including women's clubs, schools, labor unions, and the Agriculture Department's home demonstration agencies—all of them receptive to the task of instilling habits of thrift and systematic savings for long-term goals. Not only did schoolteachers see lessons in thrift as eminently beneficial for their young charges, but labor leaders favored setting up savings programs for the betterment of their rank-and-file members. Both the National Education Association and the American Federation of Labor conventions endorsed the Thrift and Savings movement and urged the government to continue offering small-denomination securities that their constituents could afford, even after the war ended. Furthermore, many large industrial corporations alerted their stockholders to the investment value of Savings Stamps by including with their dividend checks a public-service message from the Treasury Department.

By means of intensive campaigning, the government was able to bring in more than a billion dollars through the sales of Thrift and War Savings Stamps.

FOURTH LIBERTY LOAN

Offered $6,000,000,000; subscribed and accepted $6,992,927,100. Number of subscribers 22,777,680. Date of maturity October 15, 1938. Redeemable October 15, 1933. Interest four and one-quarter percent, payable April 15 and October 15. Loan opened officially September 28 and closed October 19, 1918.

This was the greatest of the Liberty Loan campaigns, both in terms of subscribers and of monies pledged, but it was also the drive with the most exceptional difficulties to overcome. The German government, feeling the effects of full American participation in the war, had made much clearer overtures to peace. And while the necessity for continuing to raise huge sums of money began to seem less urgent to the general public (press censorship downplayed the hardships at the front), the costs of maintaining our huge army overseas were escalating far beyond expectations; the proceeds of the previous loans already had been spent. Unfortunately, the country was also in the grips of a spreading pandemic of virulent influenza, and the recognized dangers of contagion made it necessary to prohibit nearly all public gatherings in many parts of the country— which virtually stripped the Liberty Loan Army of the use of its most efficient techniques for soliciting bond sales.

Like the last earlier pandemic of influenza, in 1889–90, this one is believed to have originated in China. It is also thought to have been brought to Europe by Indo-Chinese soldiers in March, 1918, and to have been transmitted to America across the bridge of ships supplying the Allied war effort. However, as early as 1916, influenza had been reported epidemic in twenty-three American states; and, long before March, 1918, outbreaks had been recorded in American Army training camps, naval bases, and on ships. Highly communicable, influenza spread quickly in the close quarters of army barracks, where, historically, disease was often more dangerous to a soldier than bullets on the battlefield. (In the war with Spain, typhoid leveled twenty percent of the troops in American camps.) At first called "three-day fever" among the armies on the Western Front (by the fall of 1918 American soldiers were dying from it at the rate of 250 per day), influenza had been known to Europe in epidemic form since the twelfth century. Its name, a borrowing from astrology, originated in mid-fourteenth-century Italy; for since influenza appears so suddenly, spreads rapidly, and affects so much of the population, it was thought to be brought on by the *influence* of the stars.

Although the first worldwide wave of influenza in the spring of 1918 was acute, it was not as deadly as it would become. There was a lull over the summer, and then in the fall the second wave struck America like an artillery barrage—first in Boston—with an appalling rate of mortality. In October and November, twenty percent of those afflicted died of pulmonary complications in just a few hours. The Public Health Service reported that in twelve large cities for which records existed twenty-two percent of all inhabitants had caught the flu. Normally the very old and the very young succumb first to influenza, but in this virulent form the disease was especially fatal to the healthy young. Twenty million Americans may have contracted influenza during the pandemic, and more than three hundred thousand of them died in 1918 alone. After the third wave of flu hit in January, 1919, lasting through March, the total of American dead probably surpassed five hundred thousand— not including fifty thousand doughboys. Throughout the world, more than twenty million died before the pandemic ran its course. Often referred to as Spanish influenza, in America the disease was also known as swine flu because of concurrent outbreaks among pigs—first thought to have been carriers of the disease but apparently victims of human transmission. Some scientists think this same viral agent caused an encephalitis pandemic in the 1920s and that exposure to the virus during the pandemic has

---

HOWARD CHANDLER CHRISTY
Clear the Way!!, 1918
20 × 30 inches
Museum of the City of New York

CLEAR-THE-WAY-!!
BUY BONDS
FOURTH
LIBERTY LOAN
Howard Chandler Christy.
10-B.

MUST
CHILDREN DIE
AND MOTHERS
PLEAD IN VAIN
?

Buy More
LIBERTY BONDS

led, decades later, to a high incidence of Parkinsonism and Alzheimer's disease.

At the same time, outright opposition to another huge public loan campaign was beginning to be heard, for many people felt that middle-class Americans had bought all the government bonds they could reasonably afford to carry and that future issues should be aimed exclusively at the banks and the very wealthy. Others maintained that new incentives were absolutely necessary to make the securities attractive and that they should be tax free again or pay more competitive interest rates. Furthermore, a secondary market in earlier Liberty Bond issues had led to deep discounts off their par value, and this raised doubts that another popular subscription could possibly be successful. Nevertheless, the Treasury took little notice of the putative difficulties facing the Fourth Liberty Loan and demonstrated full confidence in American patriotism by not even raising the interest rate.

As in the last campaign, the popular war exhibit trains were put into service, displaying battle trophies selected from shiploads of captured matériel fresh from the Western Front. In the Fourth Loan, these rail-borne exhibits covered almost one hundred thousand miles and attracted more than eight million people. Making four stops a day in mostly rural areas, the trains drew thousands of residents from a forty- to fifty-mile radius, swelling crowds occasionally to ten times a town's population.

A variant of this exhibit was the War Exposition, which was staged in twenty-one cities, usually in conjunction with state fairs. At the West Coast expositions, advance tickets were exchangeable at the gate for an admission ticket *and* a twenty-five-cent War Savings Stamp. The most notable of the expositions was presented on Chicago's lakefront. With a daily average attendance exceeding that of the 1893 World's Columbian Exposition, it attracted more than two million citizens; an admission price of a quarter for adults and two and a half cents for children garnered $583,731.24 for the war effort. George Creel described the attractions in Chicago: "Along the great stretches of promenade were distributed the trophies captured from the enemy by soldiers of the United States and the Allies—great thirty-five-thousand-pound guns taken in hand-to-hand struggle, battered remnants of U-boats that sent women and children to their death, reservoirs for poison gas, German planes brought down as they hovered over villages and hospitals, helmets, gas-masks—all the paraphernalia of war." The *Chicago Herald and Examiner*, in urging attendance, saw the exhibits in slightly different terms:

HENRY PATRICK RALEIGH
Must Children Die?, 1918
30 × 40 inches
Museum of the City of New York

ANONYMOUS
War Exposition, 1918
30 × 40 inches
Meehan Military Posters

Go and see the 'German 77's', the favorite field piece of the Hun army, captured in battle, battered and made useless by Allied shells. See the big torpedo, captured by the British Navy and known to be a mate to the one with which the Germans sank the *Lusitania*. Look on the 6,000 pound anti-aircraft gun captured by American troops, and notice how they perforated and riddled it with steel before they took it. See official French photographs of Hun atrocities. See the offical photographs, which cannot be denied. Walk through the trenches, and look at the dugouts in which our boys live, the helmets and gas masks they must wear, the weight of the packs they must carry, and try to imagine the hum of bullets, the roar of exploding shells, and the smash of showers of shrapnel aimed at them. . . . Go down to the War Exposition and picture to yourself that hail of shell, that smudge of poison gas, that shower of machine gun bullets, all the atmosphere of treachery and hate and unfair fighting our boys had to face. When you get that realization you will be

And NOW
The Fighting Fourth

NORMAN ROCKWELL
And Now the Fighting Fourth, 1918
14 × 16 inches
George M. Dembo

---

readier to do your full share here at home. And THAT is the sole reason for the exposition.

Another special attraction of the Chicago exposition was the sham battle staged every afternoon by the Army and Navy. As Creel reported, "this daily spectacle of men going over the top to the rattle of rifles and machine guns, and the roar of navy ordnance, aroused the assembled thousands to the highest pitch of enthusiasm." Secretary McAdoo later applauded the value of this kind of "spectacle": "Any great war must necessarily be a popular movement. It is a kind of crusade; and like all crusades, it sweeps along on a powerful stream of romanticism."

The most striking poster of this drive was designed by Joseph Pennell. It shows, in red and purple on a yellowish ground, a headless Statue of Liberty, broken torch at her feet, across the harbor from a New York City in flames and under attack by enemy bombers. Pennell had made his first sketch while returning to Philadelphia by train after a meeting of the Division

of Pictorial Publicity. When asked there for poster ideas, he had volunteered an image, which he described as "New York City bombed, shot down, burning, blown up by an enemy." Pennell's original concept was titled "Buy Liberty Bonds or You Will See This," but officialdom changed it to "That Liberty Shall not Perish from the Earth Buy Liberty Bonds." Some two million prints of this image are said to have been issued (the artist maintained that a lithographed poster was "a multiplication of the original and not a reproduction of it"), and its impact was so great that Pennell wrote a small book detailing its creation. Another memorable poster was Ellsworth Young's visual reference to the Rape of Belgium in a silhouetted image of a German soldier in his spiky *pickelhaube* helmet dragging off a very young girl. And a twenty-four-year-old Norman Rockwell—already exhibiting an unmistakable style—contributed to "The Fighting Fourth" through a poster created for the Women's Liberty Loan Committee of New England.

Much of the hoopla of earlier campaigns was absent this time, at least in areas where the deadly flu was rampant, but American patriotism was hardly diminished. On the relatively untroubled West Coast, a single packing company with large holdings in Alaska subscribed that territory's entire allotment of bonds in the early hours. Four days into the drive, Iowa and Oregon tied for recognition as first state to subscribe its quota, while in the East influenza forced one community after another to abandon well-developed and widely publicized plans for centralized bond rallies and door-to-door canvasses. In addition, certain factions in the country were doing an effective job of publicizing the German peace moves, spreading the notion that the war was virtually over. The effect was particularly significant in sections heavily settled by German, Austrian, and Hungarian immigrants. Nevertheless, the diligent and indefatigable Liberty Loan Army—aided by public appeals from both President Wilson and Secretary McAdoo—developed imaginative stratagems to outdo previous efforts in spite of the many difficulties. In addition to patriotic satisfactions, successful bond salesmen and saleswomen were rewarded with captured German helmets (some eighty-five thousand of them) and medals that had been cast from enemy cannon. Intact German fieldpieces were awarded to cities with good Liberty Loan records, and three hundred top cities were given the honor of naming a ship built by the Emergency Fleet Corporation. On the final day of the campaign, the St. Louis Federal Reserve District (also first in the last drive) reached its quota, and before the night was out all the rest of the twelve districts had reported success.

JOSEPH PENNELL
That Liberty Shall Not Perish, 1918
30 × 41 inches
Museum of the City of New York

IOSEPH PENNELL DEL.

THAT LIBERTY SHALL NOT PERISH FROM THE EARTH BUY LIBERTY BONDS

FOURTH LIBERTY LOAN

VICTORY LIBERTY LOAN

Offered $4,500,000,000; subscribed $5,249,908,300; accepted $4,500,000,000. Number of subscribers 11,803,895. Date of maturity May 20, 1923; redeemable on June 15 or December 15, 1922. Interest three and three-quarters percent and four and three-quarters percent according to issue. Loan officially opened April 21, 1919, and closed May 10, 1919.

When the Victory Loan opened, the war to end all wars had been over for more than five months, but two million American doughboys still remained in France and Germany, requiring the country's continued attention and sustenance until they could be returned home safely. And although Congress was quickly canceling contracts and writing off $15 billion

in appropriations for war matériel ordered but no longer needed, the government nonetheless was spending $2 billion a month on obligations related to the war. It was still necessary to raise money, and this idea was best characterized in Gerritt A. Beneker's poster, "Sure! We'll Finish the Job," where a workman sporting buttons from the four earlier drives once again proudly digs his hand into the pocket of his overalls. This could be seen as the counterpoint to LeRoy Baldridge's poster reproducing a note from "Private A.E.F., On the Rhine, 1919": "To the folks back home"—"We are finishing our job. Are you finishing Yours?"

For this campaign, the head of the Liberty Loan Army was Carter Glass, who had been appointed secretary of the Treasury after McAdoo's resignation in January, 1919. Glass, a sixteen-year veteran of

HENRY PATRICK RALEIGH
Hun or Home?, 1918
20 × 30 inches
Museum of the
City of New York

GERRIT A. BENEKER
*Sure! We'll Finish
the Job*, 1918
26 × 28 inches
Museum of the
City of New York

INVEST I
VICTORY LIBI

THEY KEPT THE
SEA LANES
OPEN

L.A. SHAFER

THE W.F. POWERS CO. LITHO, N.Y.

THE
RTY LOAN

L. A. SHAFER
They Kept the Sea Lanes Open, 1919
39 × 29¼ inches
Museum of the City of New York

Congress, had been a member of the House Committee on Banking and Currency and had drafted the measure that created the Federal Reserve System in the Owens-Glass Act of December 13, 1913. As in the last drive, there were those who felt it was not possible to expect an overextended middle class to buy any more bonds (unless the interest rate were raised), that American patriotism alone could not be counted on to float a subscription of $4.5 billion—especially since the war incentive was gone.

Glass addressed this subject in a talk before the Pittsburgh Chamber of Commerce:

> When I am told of the difficulties which will beset the Victory Loan, I refuse to lose faith in the enduring patriotism of the American people; I decline to believe that the fathers and mothers who gave four million sons to die, if need be, that liberty might survive, will now haggle over the material cost of saving the very soul of civilization from the perdition of Prussian tyranny. . . . I should doubt our ability to cope with the problems of peace if we so quickly should forget the obligations of war. . . . The honor of the Government is involved. Being your Government, it is your honor that is involved; and I know that the appeal of the American Government to the American people will meet a response of which the nation will be proud.

As Glass predicted, the Victory Loan was a successful test of American patriotism, with nearly twelve million people subscribing $749,908,300 more than was asked for. Both Michigan and Iowa, always among the earliest, reported exceeding their quotas by the third day of the campaign. And two days before the end of the drive, for the third consecutive time, the St. Louis Federal Reserve District became the first district in the country to reach its goal.

C. LeROY BALDRIDGE
To the Folks Back Home, ca. 1919
20 × 30 inches
Meehan Military Posters

In the war loan campaigns' two-year history, the total number of individual pledges reached 66,289,900; and the gross amount subscribed to was $24,072,111,400.

HOWARD CHANDLER CHRISTY
Americans All!, 1919
27 × 40 inches
Museum of the City of New York

OFFICIAL U. S. WAR FILM
RELEASED BY
COMMITTEE ON PUBLIC
INFORMATION
GEORGE CREEL, CHAIRMAN

PERSHING'S CRUSADERS

AUSPICES OF THE

UNITED STATES GOVERNMENT

-THE FIRST OFFICIAL AMERICAN WAR PICTURE-

TAKEN BY U.S. SIGNAL CORPS AND NAVY PHOTOGRAPHERS

X. "DRUMS ARE DRUMMING EVERYWHERE!"

General John Joseph Pershing's earliest childhood memory was of gunfire—when Confederate raiders shot up the family home near Laclede, Missouri. Born September 13, 1860, in a border state badly divided over Civil War issues, toddler John had watched his father march off with Union infantry as a sutler. Family lineage predated the American Revolution, and Pershing noted in his biography that "each generation furnished pioneers as the frontier moved westward. . . . Their log cabins have dotted every state from Pennsylvania to the Pacific." After some prior undergraduate schooling, Pershing took the competitive exam for West Point and was graduated with the class of 1886, as first captain of the Cadet Corps and thirtieth in a class of seventy-seven.

Commissioned a second lieutenant in the cavalry, Pershing was posted to a fort in New Mexico, where his unit's mission was to track down and capture Chief Geronimo and a band of hostile Apaches who had bolted the reservation. After four years in the Southwest (sixteen months spent in pursuit of Geronimo), Pershing was transferred to South Dakota to help quell the dangerous Sioux uprising known as The Ghost Dance. While guarding the perimeter of what was to be called the Wounded Knee Massacre, he saw action in a brief skirmish.

For a time, Pershing taught "military science and tactics" at the University of Nebraska, where he also earned a law degree and temporarily considered abandoning an army career. His next assignment was hunting down renegade Indians in Montana Territory as a troop commander with the 10th (Negro) Cavalry. It was this posting, when he subsequently returned to West Point as a none-too-popular in-

JAMES MONTGOMERY FLAGG
Our Regular Divisions, ca. 1917
21 × 28 inches
Susan E. Meyer

structor, that led cadets to christen him "Black Jack." In New York City, on his way to the military academy, he was a guest in the same horse-show box as Theodore Roosevelt, then police commissioner. Old Indian hands, the two "hit if off" immediately; when next they saw each other it was on Cuba's San Juan Hill.

ANONYMOUS
Pershing's Crusaders, 1918
30 × 45 inches
Museum of the City of New York

235

Help him to help U.S.!

Help the
Horse to
Save the
Soldier

JAMES MONTGOMERY FLAGG

THE AMERICAN **RED STAR** ANIMAL RELIEF

National Headquarters, Albany, N.Y.

At the outbreak of the Spanish-American War, Pershing was desperate to see action. He arranged to leave his West Point teaching post and return to the 10th (Negro) Cavalry in the only position open, that of its quartermaster. When his unit landed in Cuba, along with sixteen thousand other soldiers, most were in blue flannel uniform coats and missing essential equipment. Only the volunteer Rough Riders were properly outfitted for the tropics in khaki; but in the chaos of embarkation at Tampa half that regiment got left behind in Florida, along with *all* of their horses. When Lieutenant Colonel Theodore Roosevelt charged (on foot) up San Juan Hill with his First U.S. Cavalry Volunteers, Black Jack Pershing and the 10th Cavalry Regiment shared that adventure—but not the publicity. Cited as the "coolest man under fire" ever seen, Pershing was recommended for the Silver Star by his brigade commander.

Promoted to captain, Pershing was next sent to Washington, D.C., where he helped plan military governments for the islands just won from Spain.

He was then posted to the Philippines, where he found the Moslem Moros in the southern islands no happier with American administration than they had been with Spanish rule. During the first three years of the occupation, there were almost three thousand skirmishes with the Moros; in one surprise attack an entire U.S. infantry company was massacred. Pershing's success in the pacification of the Moros led to his selection, over more senior officers, to command a major expedition against one well-entrenched band. Correspondent Henry Savage Landor of the London *Mail*, who accompanied Pershing, wrote that "the Bacolod campaign entitled him to a high place among military commanders of the world." News of Captain Pershing's triumphs preceded his return home in 1903 and led to a presidential invitation to the White House—from his old friend Teddy Roosevelt.

During the years that Pershing was stationed in the Philippines, Secretary of War Elihu Root had attempted to modernize the Army. Outraged by the

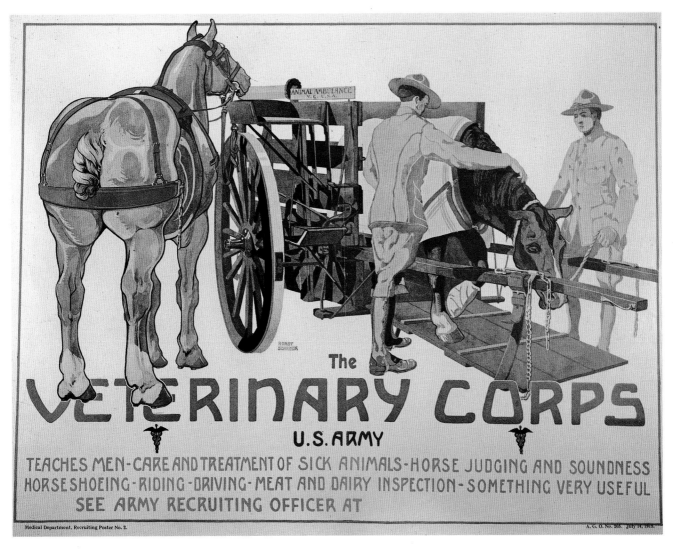

JAMES MONTGOMERY FLAGG
Help Him to Help U.S.!, ca. 1918
23½ × 33 inches
Museum of the City of New York

HORST SCHRECK
The Veterinary Corps, 1919
25 × 19 inches
State Historical Society of Iowa

FORTUNINO MATANIA
Help the Horse to Save the Soldier, ca. 1917
20 × 30 inches
Museum of the City of New York

great botching of military preparations for the war with Spain, Root concluded that a closer administrative link was needed between the military command and civilian expertise, something akin to the German General Staff that smoothly guided tactical and supply operations in the Franco-Prussian War. American military power was a near obsession for President Roosevelt, and so when Pershing returned to the United States he found himself assigned with the cream of the Regular Army to the newly created General Staff.

One other aspect of the Army that Roosevelt wished to reform was the promotion system. He told Congress on December 7, 1903, that "the only people that are contented with a system of promotion by seniority are those who are contented with the triumph of mediocrity over excellence." Three years later Roosevelt would promote Pershing from captain to brigadier general, jumping him three grades and over the heads of 862 more senior officers. Meanwhile, Pershing's peregrinations continued. He had been sent to Tokyo as military attaché and then on to Manchuria as American observer during the Russo-Japanese War; and he had married the daughter of

a most influential man, the chairman of the Senate's Military Affairs Committee. Inevitably, Pershing's extraordinary advancement in rank raised invidious comment. The St. Louis *Post-Dispatch* attributed it to "social pull, service in Washington, good luck in an adventure of doubtful military value . . . and perhaps 'selection in marriage'." The president acidly responded that "to promote a man because he married a senator's daughter would be infamy; to refuse him promotion for the same reason would be equal infamy."

Pershing was sent back to the Philippines, this time as military governor of Moro Province. The southern islands were more or less pacified, but Americans still were subjected to sudden attack by militant and fierce Moros. When he was recalled from the Philippines in December, 1913, Pershing was commended for his successes by the governor general: "You have restored peace and disarmed the turbulent population, promoted civilization and education, and as rapidly as possible substituted civilian for military control of the districts."

In April of 1914, after months of confrontation with Mexico's new government—which America refused to recognize (Wilson called it "government by assassination")—the president ordered the seizure of Vera Cruz, the country's major customs port. General Pershing, who was now commanding the Presidio of San Francisco, was ordered to the border with two cavalry regiments in case additional military support was needed from the north. While on the border, where he would remain until February, 1917, the general first met Pancho Villa, as a figure of some political influence in northern Mexico. (In August, 1915, Pershing received the tragic news that his wife and three daughters had burned to death in the general's quarters at the Presidio; only his son had been spared. The bearer of this sad message reported that Pershing displayed no emotion and turned back to his work.)

Capping a series of incidents on both sides of the border, nineteen American citizens were abducted from a Mexican train in January, 1916, and murdered. On March 9, in the middle of the night, Pancho Villa crossed the border and burned the town of Columbus, New Mexico. As luck would have it, the 13th Cavalry was encamped there, so 215 *Villistas* never made it back across the border. Only seven American soldiers and eight civilians were killed. When news of the incursion reached Washington, D.C., the War Department telegraphed an immediate order to the commanding general of the Southern Department: "President has directed that an armed force be sent into Mexico with the sole object of capturing Villa

HERBERT ANDREW PAUS
United States Army Builds Men, ca. 1917
20 × 30 inches
Meehan Military Posters

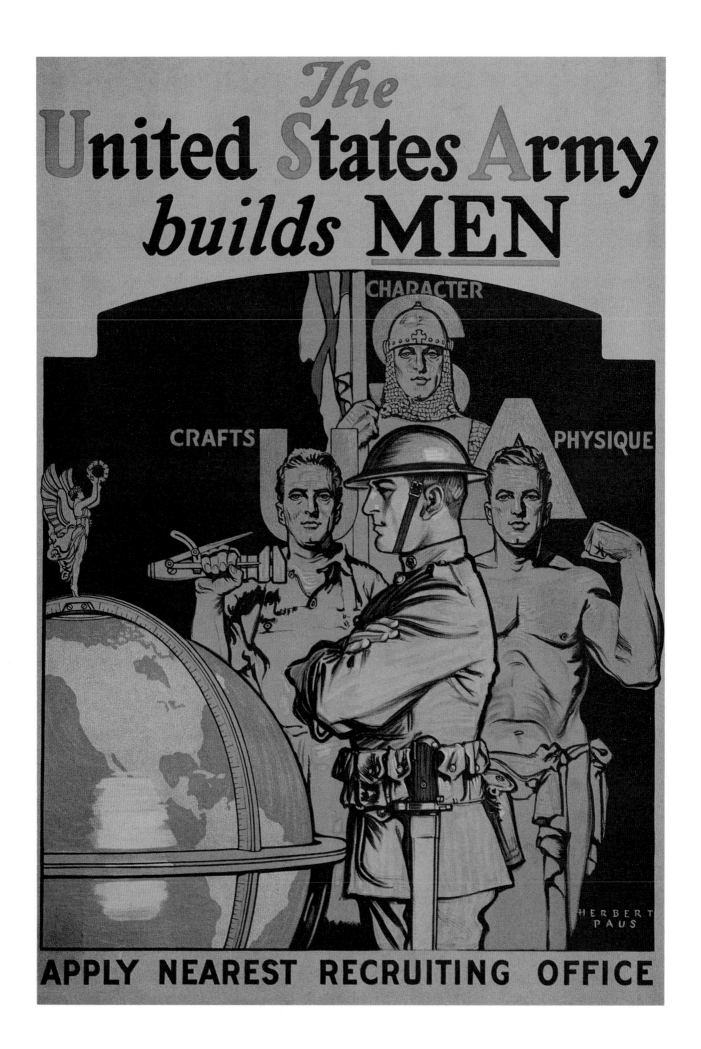

PRO PATRIA!

JOIN ARMY FOR PERIOD OF WAR.

and preventing any further raids by his bands, and with scrupulous regard for sovereignty of Mexico.'' Pershing was chosen to lead this expedition, and within a week of the Columbus raid his troops had crossed into Mexico.

As Pershing's force of almost ten thousand troopers pushed deeper and deeper into Mexico (ultimately four hundred miles), a concerned War Department moved the remaining regiments of the Regular Army to the border and mobilized the National Guards of Arizona, Texas, and New Mexico. Pershing's punitive mission was joined by a force completely new to American tacticians—the First Aero Squadron: ''Eight,'' as the general noted, ''of the thirteen antiquated tactical planes which constituted our all in aviation.'' Within a few weeks, six of the aircraft had crashed; while operable they were assigned to messenger service. One positive element of this ultimately futile expedition was that in the year just before their country went to war in Europe, almost two hundred thousand American soldiers received some measure of training in the field. The last troops returned across the American border on February 5, 1917.

WE'RE GOING OVER!

A month after President Wilson signed America's declaration of war against Germany, Pershing, now a major general, was ordered to Washington and given command of the American armies scheduled to be sent to Europe. Certain key aspects of the president's direct orders to Pershing would prove to be constant irritants to the Allied leaders:

> You are directed to cooperate with the forces of other countries employed against the enemy; but in so doing the underlying idea must be kept in view that the forces of the United States are a separate and distinct component of the combined forces the identity of which must be preserved. This fundamental rule is subject to such minor exceptions in particular circumstances as your judgment may approve. The decision as to when your command or any of its parts is ready for action is confided to you, and you will exercise full discretion in determining the manner of cooperation.

Within eighteen days of his arrival, Pershing had assembled an initial staff of 187. On May 28, 1917, he and his group embarked for Europe aboard the White Star liner *Baltic* in attempted secrecy, for in the first few months of renewed submarine warfare, U-boats had sunk scores of ships in Europe's war zone. Landing safely in Liverpool on June 8, Pershing spent four days in England before crossing to France on a Channel boat. On June 14, the day after he arrived, Pershing confided to his diary: ''Difficult to see how we are to meet the expectations of the French.''

Among those who had crossed into France with Pershing was Sergeant Eddie Rickenbacker, one of America's best-known racing drivers. Born in Columbus, Ohio, on October 8, 1890, of Swiss immigrant parents, Rickenbacker had ended his schooling at age twelve when his father was killed in a fight. To contribute to the family's support, he labored at several odd jobs, including one at a monument works that enabled him to carve a tombstone for his father. Another job was in an auto garage, where he taught himself to drive in customers' cars while the boss was not around. A whiz with engines, he soon landed a job road-testing automobiles for an early manufacturer. This mechanical facility eventually led him into auto racing, where Rickenbacker first made a name for himself as ''The Dutch Demon'' or ''Eddie the Big Teuton.'' He drove for the prestigious Due-

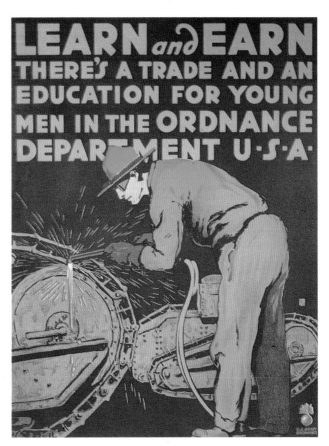

H. DEVITT WELSH
Pro Patria!, 1917
28 × 42 inches
Museum of the City of New York

CHARLES BUCKLES FALLS
Learn and Earn, ca. 1918
19 × 25 inches
George M. Dembo

senberg team in the first Indianapolis 500 in 1911 and accumulated numerous victories over the next few years, including lucrative first-place wins in 1914 and 1915 at the important Sioux City, Iowa, three-hundred-mile race. By the end of 1916 Rickenbacker had become the third-ranked racing driver in the country. While in California in 1916 for the Vanderbilt Cup Race he met airplane-maker Glenn Martin, who took him up for his very first flight. Rickenbacker later wrote: "With my rather intimate knowledge of automobiles and engines I had always felt certain that I should find it easy to fly."

Earlier in Rickenbacker's career, a racetrack publicity man got the bright idea of promoting Eddie as a champion driver from Germany named Baron von Rickenbacher (as his name was then spelled); needless to say, this stunt backfired when the European war got under way. Just before Christmas 1916, Rickenbacker went to England at the earlier invitation of the Sunbeam Motor Company to advise the management on building a racing team. Detained by the British at Liverpool as a German spy, the "Baron" was ultimately released through the intervention of Sunbeam executives but was still kept under surveillance. When America broke diplomatic relations with Germany in early February, 1917, Rickenbacker headed straight home. He had gone over on the same liner with two Lafayette Escadrille pilots returning from leave, and they had strongly urged him to join

their unit. Declining then to violate American neutrality, he subsequently had the idea of forming his own flying squadron of crack American racing drivers. In a February 18, 1917, interview with the *New York Times*, published under a two-column heading, FLYING CORPS OF DARING RACING DRIVERS PLANNED IF WAR COMES, Rickenbacker said, "If war is declared I will enlist at once for aviation work. . . . I expect to get up a body of not less than fifty of us who will volunteer." Former secretary of state William Jennings Bryan, who had once been chauffeured by Rickenbacker on a political trip to Columbus, Ohio, quipped in response that "every cab driver was a potential combat flyer." Rickenbacker took his idea directly to Brigadier General George O. Squier, head of the Signal Corps and its Aviation Section, but his plan was quickly turned down. When Rickenbacker tried later to enlist for flight training on his own, he once again was rebuffed—as too old and with too little education.

In late May, through the intervention of an army friend on Pershing's staff, Rickenbacker was offered the opportunity of going to France as a military staff driver. Though scheduled to race in Cincinnati on Memorial Day, Rickenbacker happily accepted the offer and immediately set off for the East Coast, where, he later reminisced, he "enlisted in the Signal Corps in New York and the next day sailed with General Pershing for the Front."

STALEMATE

In June of 1917, the war was at a standstill. Germany was in possession of large stretches of Belgium and France, and all Allied efforts to dislodge the invader had failed. France was very close to collapse. The vaunted spring offensive of General Robert Georges Nivelle had cost the French Army nearly two hundred thousand casualties and gained France absolutely nothing. Beleagured *poilus* in fifty-four combat divisions had mutinied, leading to twenty-three thousand courts-martial and the firing squad for an unfortunate fifty-five. Nivelle was summarily sacked, and General Henri-Philippe Pétain, the hero of Verdun, was put in command of French troops at the front, with the special mission of restoring the Army's morale.

At the end of June, the American First Division (which Pershing quickly formed from four old infantry regiments) landed in France, and on the Fourth of July it paraded up the Champs-Elysées singing "Onward, Christian Soldiers." Pershing laid a wreath on Lafayette's grave and said a few words, but not the oft-attributed "Lafayette, we are here!" Those words were spoken that day by Major Charles E. Stanton, the expeditionary force's paymaster.

Although the initial contingent of American combat

troops had been equipped and safely transported to Europe, the War Department then lapsed into chaos and dysfunction. The Army's assistant chief of staff intimated to Pershing that in terms of contingency plans "the pigeon hole was empty." "In other words," wrote Pershing, "the War Department was face to face with the question of sending an army to Europe and found that the General Staff had never considered such a thing. No one in authority had any definite idea how many men might be needed, how they should be organized and equipped, or where the tonnage to transport and supply them was to come from." Pershing's chief of staff, Major James G. Harbord, commented wryly in his diary

---

FRANK BRANGWYN
Back Him Up, ca. 1917
60 × 40 inches
George M. Dembo

JULES ABEL FAIVRE
The Liberation Loan, ca. 1918
47 × 31½ inches
George M. Dembo

BACK·HIM·UP **BUY WAR BONDS**

L'EMPRUNT DE LA LIBÉRATION

(published in 1925) on the War Department's failure to communicate, explaining how the French got around the Americans' problems:

> We say we have not yet heard from the War Department. They then cable their Embassy and they send down the Attaché to the War Department, and he finds out things, and wires his people, so that repeatedly we get news affecting us through the French War Office before we get it from our own War Department, and some things we get only through the French. No cable ever reached us about the sailing of our first convoy. Four transports sail tomorrow, according to the French, but we know nothing about them.

When Pershing cabled that "at least a million men" should be sent to France, the War Department ultimately responded that "twenty-one divisions, comprising about 420,000 men" were all that could be supplied within a year. One major problem was that America did not control enough ships to transport

LUCIEN JONAS
Courage Comrades, I'm Coming, ca. 1917
28 × 42 inches
George M. Dembo

the projected expeditionary force. Only the British had sufficient vessels (indeed, more than fifty percent of the American Army would travel on British ships), but they initially seemed unwilling to divert their ships to transporting American troops unless they were reinforcing British units. French as well as British leaders repeatedly argued for the integration of fresh American battalions directly into their own depleted ranks, but, of course, Pershing's orders—coupled, no doubt, with his own innate stubbornness—rejected this idea. The American general sought a battlefront for his "separate and distinct" army that would not position him in between his allies, which might "have made it difficult to avoid amalgamation and service under a foreign flag." He volunteered to take over the front between the Vosges Mountains and the Argonne Forest and act as the right wing to the French center and British left. His rationale was as follows:

> To the east the great fortified district east of Verdun and around Metz menaced central France, protected the most exposed portion of the German line of communications, that between Metz and Sedan, and covered the Briey iron region, from which the enemy obtained the greater part of the iron required for munitions and matériel. The coal fields east of Metz were also covered by these same defenses. A deep advance east of Metz, or the capture of the Briey region, by threatening the invasion of rich German territory in the Moselle Valley and the Saar Basin, thus curtailing her supply of coal or iron, would have a decisive effect in forcing a withdrawal of German troops from northern France.

Nevertheless, Pershing estimated that not until February, 1918—at the earliest—would the American Army be sufficiently mobilized, trained, and equipped to move into the line of battle. Outraged, the Allies claimed that their perilous situation demanded that arriving American units go directly into existing British and French armies at the front. French premier Georges Clemenceau analyzed the situation this way: "The fanatical determination of the great chiefs of the American Army to delay the arrival of the star-spangled banner on the battlefield . . . was costing us, and our Allies too, seas of blood. Their fierce super-patriotism refused to listen, and they wanted nothing less than a heaven-born strategical coup that should enable them to begin and end the war spectacularly with one stroke."

Pershing understandably did not wish to find himself a general without an army, but he also abhorred the idea of sending untrained American recruits to slaughter in the kind of battle then waged in the trenches. Rather than prolong a war of siege and attrition he vigorously called for "open warfare." In

ANONYMOUS
Keep Him Smiling, 1918
21 × 11 inches
Miscellaneous Man

GEORGE JOHN ILLIAN
Keep It Coming, ca. 1918
21 × 29 inches
George M. Dembo

JAMES MONTGOMERY FLAGG
The Road to France, ca. 1918
18½ × 24½ inches
George M. Dembo

phrases that could well have been uttered by French and German tacticians before 1914, Pershing admonished his training officers that "all instruction must contemplate the assumption of a vigorous offensive." Victory must be won "by driving the enemy out into the open and engaging him in a war of movement."

In preparation for fielding his army, Pershing turned his attention to establishing an ample and reliable supply line. To avoid adding to the burden on the Channel ports and the railroads of northern France, he chose to bring in American supplies through the Atlantic ports of Saint-Nazaire, La Pallice, Bordeaux, and Bassens. However, the European end of the supply line was to be a lesser problem than the American beginning. When troops began arriving without proper and adequate equipment (regulations still called for only four machine guns to a regiment—a figure that would be raised to 336 by Armistice), Pershing indignantly cabled the War Department: "Manner in which these regiments come to France does not indicate much improvement over conditions Spanish-American War." Indeed, there did appear to be some difficulty in securing the right equipment in the right quantity: 41 million pairs of hobnailed boots had been ordered for a projected military force of 4 million, as well as 965,000 saddles for 86,000 horses. It seemed that nothing was too good for our boys, and Pershing's supply line was soon swamped with items for which he found no pressing need. This irregular situation prompted the following cable to the War Department: "Recommend no further shipments to be made of following articles . . . bath bricks, book cases, bath tubs, cabinets for blanks, chairs except folding chairs, cuspidors, office desks, floor wax, hose except fire hose, step ladders, lawn mowers, refrigerators, safes except iron field safes, settees, sickles, stools, window shades, further stop orders will follow soon." Eventually a ten-man General Purchasing Board was set up in France, which handled procurement not only for the Army but the Red Cross and the Y.M.C.A. as well.

To be closer to projected operations, General Pershing transferred his headquarters on September 5, 1917, from Paris to the provincial city of Chaumont-en-Bassigny (thereafter known in official communications as "Somewhere in France"). As American troops arrived, most were handed over to the French 47th Chasseur Alpine Division (the "Blue Devils") for training in the foreign weapons and unfamiliar tactics of trench warfare. Once doughboy units reached a certain level of proficiency, they were moved into the front lines in quiet sectors for ten days' trench experience. On November 2, German troops, well aware of their presence, made a lightning raid on one of these units, capturing eleven Americans and killing three (who were memorialized in a Red Cross poster as "The First Three").

At the time American troops began landing in France, the Allies had a total of 185 divisions on the

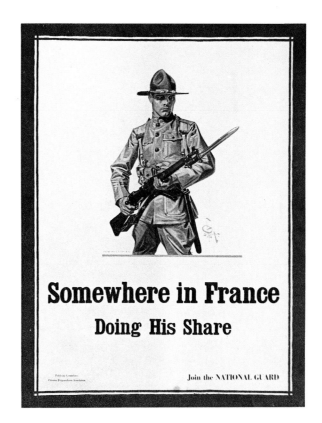

JOSEPH CHRISTIAN LEYENDECKER
Somewhere in France, 1918
19 × 25 inches
George M. Dembo

KIDDER
The First Three!, ca. 1917
20½ × 27½ inches
Meehan Military Posters

Western Front (115 French, 63 British, and 7 Belgian). Germany had countered them with 155 divisions, but upon the collapse of Imperial Russia 77 additional divisions were transferred westward. By the end of 1917, France and England already had suffered 5,800,000 casualties (to Germany's 3,349,000), and the Allies were desperate for fresh American manpower to replenish their losses. However, in the winter of 1917–18, Pershing had only four complete divisions in Europe, with only one scheduled to be combat-ready in the spring. Sir William Robertson, chief of the Imperial General Staff, summarized Allied feelings in a memorandum to the British War Cabinet: "America's power to help win the war—that is, to help us defeat the Germans in battle—is a very weak reed to lean upon."

As the Allies prepared for the next great phase of the conflict, the spring offensives of 1918, it became clear to the Supreme War Council that reliance on voluntary cooperation among the allied nations was no longer practical. Pershing was first among the leaders to agree that wars could not be successfully fought without unified command. However, it was not until January, 1918, that the three Allied field commanders first sat down together. Not too long afterward, on March 21, Germany opened her first spring offensive on a forty-mile front. Her plan was to separate the British Third and Fifth armies from the French center, drive them north out of Flanders, and capture ports on the Channel. The Germans won a salient fifty-five miles deep and forty-five miles wide, and subsequently launched a second offensive.

In late March, General Ferdinand Foch was named supreme commander of all Allied armies. As Pershing said in support, "each commander-in-chief is interested in his own army and cannot get the other commanders' point of view or grasp the problem as a whole. I am in favor of a supreme commander and believe that the success of the Allied cause depends upon it." Nevertheless, Pershing was pleased to see that Foch's role was precisely defined as "strategic direction of military operations," leaving tactical control in the hands of each nation's commander-in-chief. After all, Pershing had five divisions in France and forty-five more awaiting transport.

THE A.E.F. GOES OVER THE TOP

In a third offensive, this time against the French, Germany once again reached the banks of the Marne, capturing sixty-five thousand Frenchmen along the way. On the second day of the onslaught, May 27, 1918, the American Expeditionary Force went on the offensive for the very first time. Ordered to capture a strategic and heavily fortified village named Cantigny, the First Division handily accomplished its mission, but the Germans immediately counter-attacked in force. Pershing, anxious for success this first time out, ordered his troops to "hold on at all costs"—and they did.

On May 30, General Pétain strongly appealed for reinforcements on the Marne in the vicinity of Château-Thierry, where the Germans were attempting to force a crossing and threaten Paris, just fifty miles to the southwest. Although it meant once again splitting up the American Army, Pershing cabled the War Department about "the possibility of losing Paris" and responded to Pétain's desperate call by sending the Second and Third divisions. They advanced to the Marne through a retreating French Army that shouted repeatedly "*La guerre est finie.*" This led one doughboy to comment, "Here we are heading toward Metz while the French Army is moving on Paris, and we're both supposed to be fighting the same war." Ordered to prevent the Germans from crossing two main bridges on the Marne, the Third Division beat back every advance, while the Second Division replaced two decamping French divisions who should have been defending the highway to the capital.

Stymied at Château-Thierry, the Germans turned

ADOLPH TREIDLER
Another Notch, 1918
30 × 40 inches
Meehan Military Posters

toward Vaux and Belleau Wood, with the Americans moving between them and their ultimate goal. On June 4, the Germans once again attempted a breakthrough, but a United States Marine Corps brigade assigned to the Second Division held firm, going on the offensive itself two days later. In six more days the Marines had driven the Germans out of Belleau Wood, but at a cost of nearly ten thousand casualties (sixty-four percent of unit strength). Floyd Gibbons of the *Chicago Tribune*, who lost an eye covering the action at Belleau Wood, reported that he "never saw men charge to their death with finer spirit." At this point Americans were dying in action at the rate of twenty-five to thirty a day, but this would rise over the next few months to nearly two hundred. The newspapers at home were filled with somewhat overblown accounts of America's role in stopping the third German offensive (there were, after all, forty-three other Allied divisions engaged), but the doughboys and leathernecks had, indeed, exhibited a pugnacity not lately seen among the Allies. A fourth German offensive that opened toward Com-

HOWARD CHANDLER CHRISTY
If You Want to Fight, 1915
30 × 40 inches
Meehan Military Posters

JOSEPH CHRISTIAN LEYENDECKER
U.S. Marines, ca. 1917
18 × 24 inches
Meehan Military Posters

piègne on June 9 had been stopped by the French.

On July 15, General Erich Ludendorff sent fourteen assault divisions across the Marne, launching the fifth German offensive of 1918. Pétain was ready, and he brought this final offensive to a halt in just three days, with the help of the American Third Division (thereafter known as "The Rock of the Marne"), as well as Allied aircraft that bombed bridges behind the Germans and cut off their supplies and reinforcements.

General Foch, using the American First and Second divisions in the vanguard, set about retaking the railroad center at Soissons on July 18. Caught by surprise, the Germans retreated before the fierce American assault, and by July 21 the Second Division was six miles into new territory. The advance had been costly—five thousand casualties for the Second Division and seven thousand for the First—but at last the Germans were on the run, and American doughboys had made it happen. German chancellor Georg von Hertling wrote: "Even the most optimistic among us understood that all was lost, the history of the world was played out in those three days."

When Foch, as supreme commander, summoned a strategy session for July 24 to map out the rest of the war, Pershing already had decided to reclaim

JAMES MONTGOMERY FLAGG
Travel? Adventure?, ca. 1917
30 × 40 inches
Susan E. Meyer

JAMES MONTGOMERY FLAGG
Be a U.S. Marine!, ca. 1918
28 × 42 inches
Susan E. Meyer

BE A U.S. MARINE!

307 Evening Star Building, Washington, D. C.

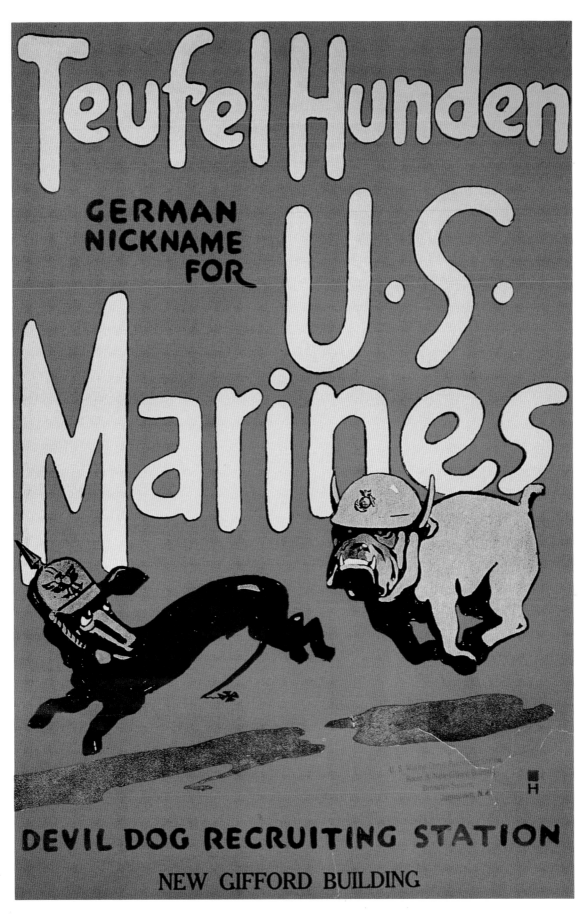

SIDNEY H. REISENBERG
Active Service on Land and Sea, ca. 1917
28 × 42 inches
Museum of the City of New York

H.
Teufel Hunden, ca. 1918
19 × 28 inches
Miscellaneous Man

his five divisions that were fighting under foreign flags. Bristling at Pershing's plan, British and French leaders argued that the Americans were not yet adequately equipped with heavy artillery and support units to fight independently. Pershing made a tour of supply-line components created to provision his army (which would consume seven hundred thousand tons of supplies a month) and cabled the War Department that facilities were sufficient "to provide for the needs of our expanded program." Then, on August 10, he unilaterally announced the formation of the independent First American Army; its mission was to reduce the Saint-Mihiel salient.

During the remainder of August, French, British, and American armies goaded the momentum of German withdrawal, forcing the enemy into fall-back positions where they fortified themselves for anticipated assaults in the autumn. On August 29, the French Army officially relinquished the Saint-Mihiel front to Pershing, who informed Allied generals he planned to storm the salient on September 12. By this time, British and French leaders were worried that a big American victory might popularly be construed as so instrumental in the defeat of Germany that their own roles might be diminished.

On August 30, Foch visited Pershing's headquarters with a new strategy to end the war—which incidentally called for the attachment of American divisions to French armies in another sector. Pershing was livid: "I can no longer agree to any plan which involves a dispersion of our units. . . . the American Army must be employed as a whole, either east of the Argonne or west of the Argonne." Foch was, of course, in strategic command of all Allied armies, but Pershing was adamant and a compromise had to be reached. The American Army could proceed with its Saint-Mihiel offensive, but on the condition that it must also participate in the much larger Meuse-Argonne campaign just two weeks later. Pershing saw his major problem, after reducing Saint-Mihiel, as moving six hundred thousand battle-weary troops and three thousand heavy guns the sixty miles to a new front, over exposed roads that could be traveled only at night.

Pershing's strategy for eliminating the Saint-Mihiel salient, a wedge through the front eighteen miles deep and thirty miles wide at its base, called for a double envelopment that would pincer through at the base. To protect the German rail center at Metz and nearby iron mines essential to her war industry, Germany had seized the Saint-Mihiel salient in September, 1914; since then the salient had gone unchallenged, and Germany was determined to keep it. Pershing was equally determined to take it over-

DOTKING
Give to the American Chocolate Fund, ca. 1918
21 × 27½ inches
George M. Dembo

whelmingly, for "anything short of complete success would undoubtedly be seized upon to our disadvantage by those of the Allies who opposed the policy of forming an American Army."

In addition to a growing American Army of nineteen divisions, Pershing faced the salient in command of four French divisions and an Air Service of nearly fifteen hundred planes, the largest force ever assembled under the American flag. Nearly half the air armada was made up of British or French aviators (and none of the planes was American); but the leader was an American, Colonel Billy Mitchell, who earlier had run afoul of Pershing because of his penchant for publicity. The old cavalryman felt that fliers were diverting too much credit away from the foot soldier, as is illustrated in this cable to Secretary of War Newton Baker: "Newspaper clipping from United States received here to effect that U.S. has thousands of fliers in Europe and that thousands of American aeroplanes are flying above the American forces in Europe today. As a matter of fact there is not today a single American-made plane in Europe. . . . Emphatically protest against newspaper publicity of this nature and urgently recommend drastic steps be taken to stop publication such articles." Mitchell had been chief of the Aviation Section

AUGUST HUTAF
Treat 'em Rough!, ca. 1918
28 × 41½ inches
Museum of the City of New York
The motto and the "Black Tom" mascot of the Tank Corps.

when it was part of the Signal Corps, but Pershing had cut him down a couple of notches by placing a reconstituted Army Air Service under the command of General Mason Patrick. When after a four-hour artillery barrage, the Saint-Mihiel attack began at 5:00 A.M. on September 12, the Air Service launched an assault on the German rear that did not stop for three days. A few weeks later, Pershing made Mitchell a brigadier general and put him in command of all American air units at the front.

AMERICA'S ACE OF ACES

Sometime earlier, Mitchell had personally chosen Eddie Rickenbacker to drive his twelve-cylinder Packard staff car—an opportunity the famous race driver welcomed mainly for a chance to hound the Aviation Section chief for a transfer into flying school. Rickenbacker was soon to be twenty-seven, two years over the cut-off age for aviation cadets, but with Mitchell's eventual intervention that disqualification was overlooked. Rickenbacker was commissioned in early August and on the twenty-fifth ordered to Primary Flying School at Tours. After seventeen days at school and twenty-five hours of flying time, he won his wings and a promotion to first lieutenant. He next went to Precision Training School at Issoudun, but because of his well-known skill with engines he was made the base engineering officer. Managing,

nevertheless, to get advanced flying lessons along with the students, Rickenbacker arranged to abandon his ground job and move on to air gunnery school at Cazeau. On March 6, 1918, he joined the 94th Aero Pursuit Squadron at Villeneuve. "It had taken me almost a year," he wrote, "to reach the Front as a combat pilot, but I was there." About then, Rickenbacker began to spell his name with a second "k"; an alert reporter noticed this and cabled his paper: "Eddie Rickenbacher has taken the Hun out of his name."

By the time Rickenbacker reached his squadron, Lafayette Escadrille ace Raoul Lufbery, now a U.S. Air Service major, had finally gotten free of his desk job at Issoudun, and, along with Escadrille colleague Captain James Norman Hall, was training the

K. WATKINS
The Victory Loan Flyers, 1919
20 × 30 inches
Meehan Military Posters

F. S. JR.
U.S. Naval Aviation, ca. 1920
30 × 40 inches
George M. Dembo

American pilots in combat tactics. Urging his students to be aggressive, Lufbery repeatedly said, "You can't shoot Huns in a hangar." The unit was moved up to the front near Toul when the 94th finally received its allotment of Nieuport 28 aircraft—planes the French had cast off for their habit of shedding wing-tops when being pulled out of a dive. At Toul, veteran French aviators from nearby airfields took pride in escorting the new American pilots on their maiden flights over enemy lines—until they learned to their horror that these fledglings were unarmed! Guns for the American Nieuports did not arrive until well into April.

Rickenbacker made his initial sortie over enemy lines with Major Lufbery, who had seventeen German kills to his credit, and Douglas Campbell, who was to become the first American Air Service ace. Fresh out of Harvard and ground-school training at Cornell, Campbell, in August, 1917, was among the earliest air cadets to arrive in France. Named adjutant of the American Flying School at Issoudun, Campbell enrolled himself in *advanced* flight training without ever once having flown. Within six weeks of first going aloft, he had downed his fifth enemy plane. Not too long afterward, Rickenbacker also became

an ace, and he recorded these thoughts in his diary: "The pleasure of shooting down another man was no more attractive to me than the chance of being shot down myself. The whole business of war was ugly to me. But the thought of pitting my experience and confidence against that of German aviators and beating them at their own boasted prowess in air combats had fascinated me."

On May 10, Raoul Lufbery had to jump out of a disabled and flaming plane at two hundred feet. Landing in a French lady's garden, he evidently had aimed for a nearby stream. She reported that he crashed through her fence, got up and appeared to bow, but was already dead. Rickenbacker led a flyover during the funeral and dropped flowers into the open grave from fifty feet up. Sometime later, he wrote that he could not "understand why we cannot have parachutes fitted on our airplanes to give the doomed pilot one possible means of escape. . . . For the past six months the German airmen had been saving their lives by airplane parachutes. A parachute is a very cheap contrivance compared to the cost of training an aviator."

On May 17, as he was pulling his Nieuport out of a dive in a dogfight, Rickenbacker heard the canvas

JOHN E. SHERIDAN
Wings, 1919
13½ × 21½ inches
George M. Dembo

CHARLES BUCKLES FALLS
For Our Aviators, ca. 1918
29¼ × 41 inches
Meehan Military Posters

top of his right wing rip off, which threw him into an uncontrollable spin. Eventually he mastered his craft's wild gyrations and was able to recross the front and crashland unhurt upon his own airfield. He reflected that "the aviator faces sudden death every time he sets foot in his machine, whether it be death from bullets and shells or from the possible collapse of his machine in mid-air." He commented later, "Our American pilots in France were compelled to venture out in Nieuports against far more experienced pilots in more modern machines. None of us in France could understand what prevented our great country from furnishing aircraft equal to the best in the world."

On June 27, the first four American fighter squadrons moved to the old French aerodome at Touquin in the Château-Thierry region. At this point, the 94th had seventeen pilots and twenty-four planes, which was approximately the strength of the other squadrons. In four weeks in the new sector, the Touquin group shot down thirty-eight Germans, but lost thirty-six American pilots, including Theodore Roosevelt's son Quentin, who went down on July 14. In an earlier incident, Roosevelt had become lost and joined the first formation he came upon, flying with it for fifteen minutes before realizing it was German. He opened fire on the plane just in front of him and streaked for home.

In mid-July Rickenbacker was hospitalized for a mastoid operation, which the doctors thought would end his career as a flier. Before the month was out he was flying again, with no apparent ill effects; however, on August 18 he was back in the hospital for another operation. When Rickenbacker returned to duty in mid-September, the 94th had moved to a new field near Verdun. Touquin had been so far from the steadily retreating front that the Americans had been forced to drop in on closer airfields to refuel before going behind the lines.

On September 15, Rickenbacker became the leading American ace—but not for long. In one twenty-minute period, ace "balloon-buster" Frank Luke had shot down two fighters, a photography plane, and two balloons; he had picked up fourteen victories in eight days! However, on the 29th, Luke failed to return from a mission and Rickenbacker once again had the distinction of being the living ace with the highest score. By now, he had been promoted to captain and made commander of the 94th, then known as the "Hat-in-the Ring" squadron because of its distinctive insignia. On the last day of October, Rickenbacker won two victories in the air, bringing his confirmed final total to twenty-six. His 94th Aero Pursuit Squadron had shot down sixty-nine Germans, the greatest number for any American unit, and it had lost only five pilots.

Just after the Armistice, Rickenbacker signed a book contract with the Frederick A. Stokes Company, and one of their editors, Laurence Driggs, stayed with him to assist in the writing. When the squadron was moved to Coblenz for occupation duty, the two took rooms in a hotel on the Rhine, where Driggs took down Rickenbacker's exciting story as he told it. By the middle of December the manuscript was complete, and the book was published the following year under the title *Fighting the Flying Circus*. In it Rickenbacker speculated on what the future held for ex-fighter pilots: "What sort of a new world will this be without the excitement of danger in it? . . . How can one enjoy life without this highly spiced sauce of danger? What else is left to living now that the zest and excitement of fighting airplanes is gone? Thoughts such as these held me entranced for the moment and were afterward recalled to illustrate how tightly strung were the nerves of these boys of twenty who had for continuous months been living on the very peaks of mental excitement."

When Rickenbacker returned to America in February, 1919, Secretary of War Baker was there to meet the ship. He called Rickenbacker "one of the real crusaders of America—one of the truest knights our country has ever known."

PINCHING OUT THE SAINT-MIHIEL SALIENT

With a great army threatening the apex and both flanks of their salient, the Germans began to withdraw even before the attack, and by noon on September 12, 1918, they were in full retreat, struggling to evacuate men and equipment before the envelopment. The Americans kept up their assault all through the night—many units reaching second-day objectives within hours—and by daylight on the thirteenth the pincers had closed on sixteen thousand German troops and 450 guns. Pershing kept pushing his field commanders forward for another day or so, but he was well aware that a large army had to be moved to the Argonne Front before September 26. His First Army had suffered seven thousand casualties in reducing the salient, but in

My Experiences in the World War Pershing recalled the "exultation in our minds that here, at last, after seventeen months of effort, an American Army was fighting under its own flag."

Allied leaders had long feared the war would drag on into the summer of 1919; but, with the Germans on the run, Foch called for a massive general offensive from the Meuse to the Channel to drive the Boche out of France in a matter of weeks. The joint effort

W. F. HOFFMAN
Join the Black-Toms, ca. 1918
19 × 25 inches
Miscellaneous Man

CLARENCE UNDERWOOD
Back Our Girls Over There, ca. 1918
21 × 28 inches
George M. Dembo

would consist of no less than 217 Allied divisions. The offensive would begin on September 26 with the American First Army and the French Fourth driving into the Argonne, the British First and Third going over the top toward Cambrai the next day, the Belgians and British Second in Flanders striking out on the twenty-eighth between the Lys and the Channel, and on the twenty-ninth the French First and British Fourth joining the move on Cambrai.

The Germans already had put out peace feelers, but their contingency plan was to fall back on their heavily fortified Hindenburg Line, which they believed they could hold indefinitely while their diplomats worked out advantageous peace terms. Before that happened, they would make a strong defense of the Argonne Forest, which the Allies had regarded as impregnable. Indeed, as Pershing reported, the region's natural defenses "were strengthened by every artificial means imaginable, such as fortified strong-points, dugouts, successive lines of trenches, and an unlimited number of concrete machine-gun emplacements. A dense network of wire entanglements covered every position. . . . It was small wonder that the enemy had rested for four years on this front without being seriously molested."

At 5:30 A.M. on the twenty-sixth, Pershing launched his assault against a narrow sector between the Meuse and the western edge of the German forest stronghold. After a four days' advance of about eight miles, the American Army's momentum was spent, and Pershing had to move fresh reserves into the line. For the next few weeks, American headway could only be described as slow but steady. The British, on the other hand, were having better success in the north, where they were driving into the outer defenses of the Hindenburg Line. The French, however, paced themselves on the general impetus of the offensive. British historian Basil Liddell Hart wittily described the French progression in *The Real War*. "In their skilful advance they usually kept a step in the rear of their allies on either flank. . . . If their commanders had been slow to learn how to economize life, they, and still more their men, had learnt it now." Nevertheless, French leaders hounded Pershing for more progress and even demanded his removal. It was during this period, however, that one American unit made too much progress and found itself surrounded by the Germans. This was Major Charles Whittlesey's famous "Lost Battalion," which, refusing to surrender, held out until rescued by advancing units. In one of the most publicized episodes of the war, the battalion was indeed "lost," for two-thirds of its men were killed.

A TURKEY SHOOT IN THE ARGONNE FOREST

Another legendary episode of the war took place in the Argonne in early October, an action incidentally instrumental in relieving the "Lost Battalion." Its hero was a lanky, red-haired, poorly educated corporal named Alvin Cullum York, who was not atypical of Pershing's civilian soldiers. Raised in a remote Tennessee mountain valley, York gave soldiering very little thought when he learned that his country was at war. "We never had any speakings in here," he said, "and I did not read the papers closely, and did not know the objects of the war. I did not feel I wanted to go." In addition, York was a Sunday-school teacher and choirleader, with a conviction that the biblical commandment "Thou shalt not kill" was reason enough for him not to go to war. A few years earlier, after a good bit of youthful hell-raising, he had given up "smoking, drinking, gambling, cussing, and brawling" and had joined the Church of Christ.

Join the Black Toms
(The Tanks)

TANK CORPS RECRUITING OFFICE
19 W. 44th STREET   NEW YORK

They Treat 'em Rough

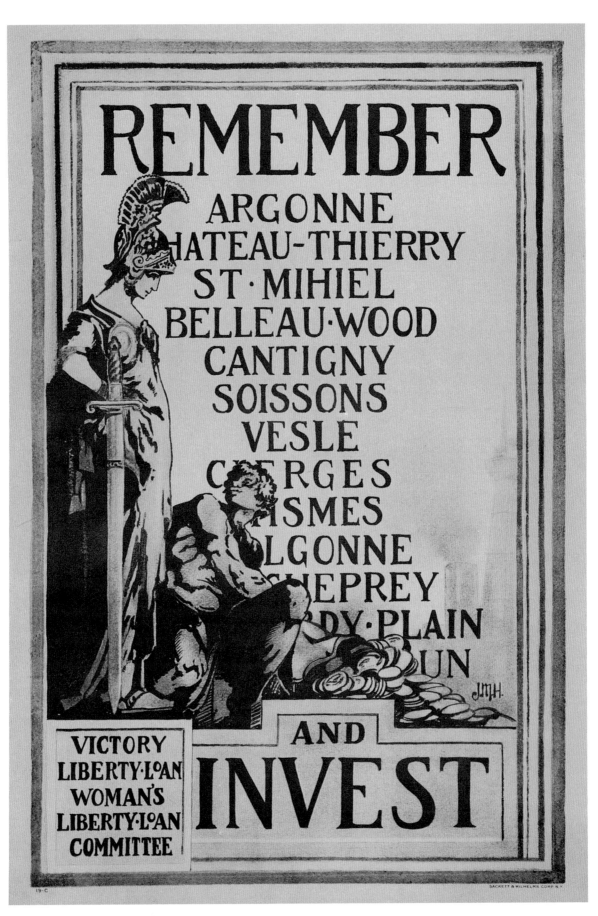

J.M.H.
Remember Argonne, ca. 1918
20 × 30 inches
Miscellaneous Man

York realized that as well as being a good Christian he must be a patriotic American, but he "always figured the two were sort of connected." However, when called to register for the draft, he asked for exemption from military service because of his religious beliefs. His appeal was rejected by the draft board, and on November 14, 1917, he was ordered to Camp Gordon, Georgia, for basic training. When he left the Valley of the Three Forks of the Wolf River, he took with him a blank memorandum book that he carefully titled "A History of places where I have been." York had lived all of his thirty years in the remote valley that once had been part of the short-lived State of Franklin, then of Kentucky, and finally of Tennessee. The nearest village was Pall Mall, not too far from the famous tree on which Daniel Boone carved the message that he "cilled a bar" there in 1760, but nearly fifty miles from the closest railroad. The York family home was a two-room log cabin expanded from a corncrib their pioneer ancestor Conrad Pile had built in the eighteenth century. York's father William worked as a blacksmith in the cave where "Old Coonrod" lived when he first settled the valley, and it was said of William "that he just about succeeded in making a hard living." Alvin was born on December 13, 1887, one of eleven children, and for most of his youth there was no school in the valley. Eventually he received the equivalent of a third-grade education, a few weeks at a time. His father died when Alvin was twenty-one, and he became the family's breadwinner, working at whatever he could from "can't see to can't see." When the war started, he was helping to build a highway, earning $1.65 a day—the most he had ever made.

York's "History" began with Camp Gordon: "I stayed there and done squads right and squads left until the first of February, 1918, and then I was sent to Company G, 328 Inf. 82nd Div." This was the "All-American" Division, formed of men from almost every state in the Union. York described his bunkmates as "a gang of the toughest and most hardboiled doughboys I ever heard of. . . . They could out-swear, out-drink, and out-cuss any other crowd of men I have ever knowed." York, however, could out-do them by far on the rifle range: "They missed everything but the sky." He was known as the best shot in the Cumberland Mountains, as his father had been before him. The shooting match had long been the ultimate test of manhood for hardscrabble mountainmen, and they prided themselves on mastering the old percussion-cap muzzle-loaders of their forebears. The most popular of the contests was the turkey shoot, where a wily old gobbler was tethered behind a big log so that just its head was showing. Not only was this target a bit small at forty yards' distance, but it also moved!

York was still troubled in his conscience about the possibility of having to kill another man; but, on a leave home before shipping overseas, he felt that

JOHN E. SHERIDAN
Write, Write, Write, ca. 1918
20 × 30 inches
Maurice Rickards

God had spoken to him. "I begun to understand that no matter what a man is forced to do, as long as he is right in his own soul, he remains a righteous man."

The 82nd Division was sent to France in mid-May of 1918 and immediately went into reserve with the British Army in the Somme, where the Germans had launched their second offensive of the spring. In June the division was shifted to the French Army near Tours, and in late summer it was among the divisions Pershing gathered in front of the Saint-Mihiel salient for a grand American assault on September 12. His Bible by his side throughout the fighting, Corporal York was confident that he would not be harmed, and, along with all units of the American First Army, he moved to the Argonne front after Saint-Mihiel for what was to be the last great drive of the war. His division was under fire for twenty-six days straight, the longest stretch for any American unit in that offensive.

On October 8, at 6:10 A.M., York's company was on the ridge of Hill 223, north of Châtel Chéhéry. The unit's orders were to take Hill 240, which was one of the three at the end of an open valley, beyond

E. M. ASHE
Lend the Way They Fight, ca. 1918
27½ × 41½ inches
Museum of the City of New York

which lay an important German supply line. Along the tops of these hills were German machine-gun nests with clear fields of fire across the valley floor the Americans had to traverse. The first wave of doughboys was pinned down immediately and almost annihilated. As York recorded: "I could see my pals getting picked off until it almost looked like there was none left." The only solution was to outflank the guns, and a detachment of sixteen men and a noncom was sent around to the left. Following an old trench system, they soon found themselves in the rear of Hill 240, where they stumbled onto the headquarters of the machine-gun battalion. Surprised while having breakfast, the Germans quickly surrendered. As the Americans rounded up their prisoners, alert gunners on the hill swung their weapons around. When the prisoners suddenly dropped to the ground, the gunners fired over their heads and immediately killed six doughboys and wounded three. Of the survivors, only York was caught out in the open. "There wasn't any tree for me, so I just sat in the mud and used my rifle, shooting at the machine gunners." Providentially, the German gunners were precisely forty yards away, the ideal distance for a turkey shoot, and, as the mountain marksman told it, "every time one of them raised his head, I just tetched him off." When York was charged by a squad of six or seven Germans from a nearby trench, he dropped them all before they had run ten yards, targeting the group from rear to front so they would not scatter at the sight of falling comrades. He then turned his attention back to the gunners on the hill, picking them off as they showed their heads. By this time, he had singlehandedly killed more than twenty Germans, while shouting repeatedly for them to surrender.

One of the prisoners pinned down in front of York was a major who had spent some time in America, and he offered to surrender the unit if the corporal would just stop killing his men. When the major blew his whistle, the machine-gun crews threw down their weapons and descended the slope. The seven surviving American privates got the prisoners lined up in a column of twos, and York warned the major he would shoot him if anyone tried anything funny. Having thus captured ninety veteran soldiers of the Prussian Guards, the eight Americans still had the daunting task of getting them back through enemy lines. York situated himself in the middle of the prisoners at the column's head and put the German major out in front, a Colt .45 automatic aimed at his back. As the column snaked through the woods it came upon other machine-gun nests, and the major got them all to surrender. When one German hesitated, York quickly shot him; he said he "hated to do it" but could not take any chances. After the determined corporal finally led his column into American lines, his flabbergasted commanding officer repeatedly lost count as he tallied the prisoners! When asked how he was able to bring off this feat, York said, "I am a witness to the fact that God did help me out of that hard battle, for the bushes were shot off all around me and I never got a scratch."

The official report of York's turkey shoot stated that "practically unassisted, he captured 132 Germans (three of whom were officers), took about 35 machine guns and killed no less than 25 of the enemy, later found by others on the scene of York's extraordinary exploit. The story has been carefully checked in every possible detail from Headquarters of this Division and is entirely substantiated."

Supreme Commander Marshal Foch personally decorated Sergeant York with the Croix de Guerre and professed his admiration: "What you did was the greatest thing accomplished by any private soldier of all of the armies of Europe." York also was awarded the French Legion of Honor, the Italian Croce di Guerra, and from his own country the Distinguished Service Cross and, ultimately, the Congressional Medal of Honor. When Sergeant York returned home in May, 1919, New York City gave him a ticker tape parade, and Tennessee made him an honorary colonel. He turned down all offers to capitalize on his fame, including seventy-five thousand dollars to appear in a movie and one thousand dollars a week to do the vaudeville circuit. The only thing of value he accepted was his home state's gift of four hundred acres of "bottom land" in the Valley of the Three Forks of the Wolf—land that his ancestor "Old Coonrod" had homesteaded in the early nineteenth century. He insisted that all other gifts be made to a fund that would build schools in the mountains.

WITH VICTORY IN THE AIR

By the middle of October, 1918, the increasingly effective American First Division had succeeded in piercing enemy defenses along the Aire River and had exposed the rear of German positions in the Argonne Forest. Victory was in the air. To keep America from laying too strong a claim to it, Clemenceau had once again taken up his campaign to unseat Pershing, arguing that the general's performance "was inferior to what was permissible to expect." Recognizing the French premier's motive as a "political gesture designed to minimize America's prestige at the peace conference," Pershing so informed his War Department superior. Secretary Baker tartly responded that "it would be a long time before any American commander would be removed by any European premier."

Clemenceau, along with other Allied leaders, was also determined to subvert the dedicated efforts of President Wilson to establish his Fourteen Points as the basis for any peace settlement. However, Prince

Max of Baden, who on October 3 was named the new German chancellor, had already sent an appeal to Wilson: "To avoid further bloodshed, the German Government requests the President to arrange the immediate conclusion of an armistice on land, by sea, and in the air." Wilson was slow to inform his allies of this development and carried on his own peace negotiations without the benefit of their consultation.

Well aware that Germany had asked for an armistice, Pershing had launched the second phase of his offensive on October 14. "There can be," he firmly stated, "no conclusion to this war until Germany is brought to her knees." Before the Argonne campaign was over, Pershing had thrown nearly 1.2 million doughboys into the front line, and many of them were fresh off the troopships. American losses totaling 117,000 were almost equal to the entire opposing force, and in some sectors the Germans were outnumbered nearly ten to one. From unrelenting Allied blows the Hindenburg Line was beginning to crack. At the end of October, in a clash with Prince Max over continued military resistance, General Ludendorff was forced to resign his command

and flee to neutral Sweden. His colleague Admiral Reinhard Scheer was not so easily intimidated and vowed to lead the High Seas Fleet out once more into the North Sea for a glorious showdown. At this suicidal prospect, thousands of German sailors mutinied, seizing their ships and murdering some of their officers. Armed insurrections broke out in the seaports of Hamburg and Bremen; in several industrial centers, councils of soldiers and workers were set up, based on the example of Russian soviets. Revolt spread rapidly throughout this demoralized and exhausted country, and the majority Social Democrats, vying with the Communists for leadership of the revolution, withdrew from the coalition in the Reichstag that supported the chancellorship of Prince Max.

In conducting preliminary peace negotiations with the beleaguered Prince Max, Wilson persuaded the German government to accept his Fourteen Points as well as the evacuation of all occupied territories before he would consider supporting an armistice. His patience came to an end when two passenger vessels were sunk on October 10 by German U-boats, with a combined loss of 820 civilians. Citing Germany's "illegal and inhuman" warfare, Wilson coldly informed the chancellor that henceforth specific terms for an armistice would be set unilaterally by the Allied military commanders. Germany bowed to the inevitable, and on October 23 the American president finally agreed to discuss the armistice proposal with his allies. Foch, Pétain, Haig, and Pershing met in Senlis on October 28, and the American general expressed his opposition to any "tendency toward leniency." Prepared to launch the final phase of his attack on November 1, Pershing said that "complete victory can only be obtained by continuing the war until we force unconditional surrender from Germany, but if the Allied Governments decide to grant an armistice, the terms should be so rigid that under no circumstances could Germany take up arms again."

Meanwhile, the Belgians and the British, having pierced the last outer shield of the Hindenburg Line, were advancing toward the Scheldt River on a broad front. The American First and Second armies were regrouping to thrust across the Meuse into northeastern Lorraine, where Germany was preparing a last line of defense as her cohorts—the Bulgarians, Turks, Hungarians, and Austrians—successively sued the Allies for armistice. With knowledge that Marshal Foch was prepared to meet with "properly accredited representatives," a German delegation led by Matthias Erzberger, secretary of state without portfolio, arrived on November 8 at a railway siding

CHARLES BUCKLES FALLS
You, Wireless Fans, ca. 1918
28 × 44 inches
Meehan Military Posters

ANONYMOUS
Crush the Prussian, 1918
28 × 42 inches
Museum of the City of New York

Crush the Prussian

BUY A BOND
3rd Liberty Loan

SIDE BY SIDE~
BRITANNIA!

JAMES MONTGOMERY FLAGG, 1918

Britain's Day Dec. 7th 1918

MASS MEETING

near Rethondes in the Forest of Compiègne. Received at 7:00 A.M. in a railway car that twenty-two years later would host a similar meeting under Hitler's auspices, the Germans were treated to a display of high truculence as Foch rejected all overtures suggesting that discussions or negotiations were about to take place. Ultimately Erzberger was forced to state that his purpose in coming was simply to ''hear'' the Allies' terms for an armistice, and he gasped as those terms were read: among them, that Belgium, France, Alsace-Lorraine, and the entire west bank of the Rhine were to be cleared of German armies within six days. The German statesman also heard that the Allies had no intention of lifting their naval blockade, a continuation of which, he pleaded, would surely plunge the German people into an abyss of hunger and want—and into the grips of Bolshevism. Winning concessions on some terms but no promised end to the blockade, Erzberger then asked for an immediate ceasefire to save men's lives on both sides of the front. Foch and his generals, having already settled on a later, more dramatic moment to declare an armistice, had time to kill.

Back in Germany, a provisional government was formed on the ninth of November when Emperor Wilhelm II was forced to abdicate, and Germany was proclaimed a republic. On the tenth, the former emperor reluctantly went into exile in neutral Holland, claiming sanctuary that could not be refused from a fellow knight of the Order of Saint John. At 5:00 A.M. on the following morning, Marshal Foch and the German Armistice Commission signed a document that set the ceasefire for six hours later, at the carefully chosen eleventh hour of the eleventh day of the eleventh month.

E. COURBOIN
One Last Effort, ca. 1918
31½ × 47½ inches
Meehan Military Posters

JAMES MONTGOMERY FLAGG
Side by Side Britannia!, 1918
20 × 30½ inches
Susan E. Meyer

"Über Alles"

You kept fit
and defeated the Hun
Now—
set a high standard
A
CLEAN
AMERICA
!
STAMP OUT VENEREAL DISEASES-
21294
THE H.C. MINER LITHO. CO. N.Y.

TAPS

It was not until dusk on Armistice Day that many battle-weary veterans could be persuaded that an end had finally come to what David Lloyd George called "the cruelest and most terrible war that has ever scourged mankind." Indeed, more human beings were slaughtered in the Great War than in all the wars of the previous two centuries combined—that many and half again more. Of the nearly sixty-five million young men mobilized by the belligerents, more than half—thirty-five million—became battle casualties, seven million of them permanently maimed and disabled. Almost nine million soldiers were killed, but also eight million civilians—not to mention the hundreds of thousands unaccounted for. France alone lost half her male population between the ages of twenty and thirty-two.

The war cost the nations involved a total of more than three hundred billion dollars, a quarter of that in property destroyed. For twenty-five months (from America's declaration of war until most of the boys were safely home), the United States spent in excess of one million dollars an hour on the war; during the final ten months the average daily expenditure reached forty-four million dollars. The aggregate cost to America was almost equal to the entire expense of governing the country from 1791 to 1914.

The United States of America sent an army of two million men to Europe, two-thirds of whom actually saw battle. Secretary of War Baker estimated that this was the largest army to cross a sea in the history of mankind, only the Persians who bridged and crossed the Hellespont with a million men more than two thousand years earlier came anywhere near. For two hundred days straight the American Army was in combat somewhere along the Western Front, taking part in thirteen major operations. The country suffered 256,000 battle casualties and lost a total of 125,500 men. Of that number, 50,280 were killed on the battlefield or died from wounds, an equal number died from disease (most from the influenza epidemic), and the rest were victims of accidents both in France and at home. Nearly five thousand Americans were taken prisoner. More than three hundred thousand men were said to have evaded the draft or deserted, some eleven thousand having gone A.W.O.L from rear units to get themselves *into* the fighting.

The cost of the Great War was very great, but President Wilson assured the country that "everything for which America fought has been accomplished." He went on to say that "it will now be our fortunate duty to assist by example, by sober, friendly counsel, and by material aid in the establishment of just democracy throughout the world." In Belgium and northern France, the American Relief Administration was continuing to feed ten million unfortunate people.

ANONYMOUS
The Past Is Behind Us, ca. 1919
12 × 19 inches
Meehan Military Posters

ERNEST FUHR
You Kept Fit, ca. 1919
30 × 40 inches
State Historical Society of Iowa

After the Welcome Home –
a JOB!

U.S. EMPLOYMENT SERVICE *Dep't of Labor*

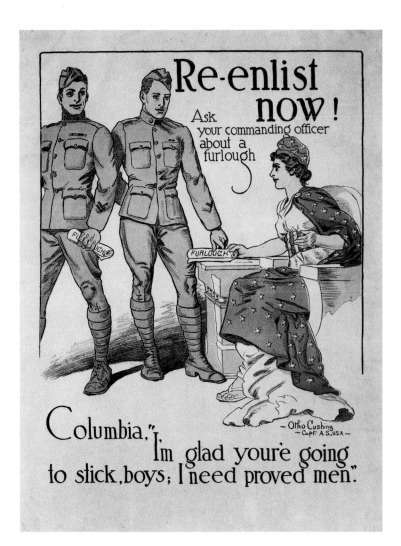

E. M. ASHE
After the Welcome Home,
ca. 1919
28 × 41½ inches
Museum of the City of
New York

OTHO CUSHING
Re-enlist Now!, ca. 1919
11 × 14 inches
University of Texas at Austin

GORDON GRANT
Jobs for Fighters, ca. 1919
15 × 25 inches
University of Texas at Austin

GORDON GRANT
Forget It, Son, ca. 1919
14 × 11 inches
University of Texas at Austin

ERNEST HAMLIN BAKER
Let's Stick Together, ca. 1919
28 × 41 inches
George M. Dembo

Following the Armistice, the Paris edition of the *Chicago Tribune* ran a banner every day: GET THE BOYS HOME TOOT SWEET. That was, indeed, America's aim, but the British, who transported more than half the American Army to Europe, were now in need of their ships to return thousands of colonial troops to Canada, Australia, and South Africa. To remedy this lack of transport, America quickly converted cargo ships into troop carriers and called on the Navy to ferry doughboys home in cruisers and battleships. Although this repatriation extended into the summer of 1919 (340,000 troops returned in June, the peak month), the American Army actually went home faster than it was taken over.

General Pershing did not leave Europe until September 8, 1919, aboard the *Leviathan* (the former German liner *Vaterland*), for he still had to oversee America's part in the occupation of the Rhineland. "Succeed in this and little note will be taken and few praises will be sung," he counseled the occupation force. "Fail, and the light of your glorious achievements of the past will sadly be dimmed."

Allied troops moved into position along the Rhine River in mid-December, 1918, guarding the important bridgeheads at Coblenz, Mainz, and Cologne from any resurgence of German militarism. American troops would not withdraw from the Coblenz district until 1923; the British and French would occupy their sectors until 1930.

The treaty of peace was signed at Versailles on June 28, 1919, by twenty-eight Allied and Associated Powers and Germany. President Wilson succeeded in incorporating the covenant of a new League of Nations into the treaty, and this represented the last of his Fourteen Points. For him the League was not only the fulfillment of a long-held dream of establishing an international forum for maintaining peace but a way of eventually rectifying all the inequities he saw created by the Versailles treaty.

Wilson submitted the treaty to a Republican-dominated Senate for ratification on July 10, and—with some inkling of its fate—cautioned recalcitrant senators: "Dare we reject it and break the heart of the world?" But he had made political mistakes that inevitably alienated the very people whose support he now needed. Most notably, he had failed to name to the Peace Commission anyone who truly represented either the Republican party or the U.S. Senate. As bipartisan attempts were made at amending the document, to give it a chance of winning two-thirds approval for ratification, Wilson turned unyielding against any change. The senators objected to numerous provisions in the treaty, but especially to Article X, which obligated a signatory to "preserve as against external aggression the territorial integrity and existing political independence" of any other signer. Aware that he was losing his battle in the Foreign Relations Committee, Wilson went directly to the people, traveling 8,000 miles and making more than thirty-six prepared speeches and numerous talks in less than a month. In late September, while still on the road, he suffered a stroke that left him not only incapable of continuing his fight for the League of Nations but of fulfilling most of his presidential duties. The legislators, still leery of foreign entanglements, rejected the peace treaty outright on November 19, 1919, and again in March of the following year.

The Versailles Treaty was never ratified by the Senate, America never became a member of the League of Nations, and Wilson died in 1924, "as much a victim of the war," said David Lloyd George, "as any soldier who died in the trenches." Less than fifteen years later, the Great War—the war to end all wars—became just the *first* world war.

GEORGE CARLSON
Say! Young Fellow, ca. 1919
19 × 24¾ inches
Maurice Rickards

ACKNOWLEDGMENTS

First, I would like to thank Albert K. Baragwanath for guiding me to the World War I poster collection in his care at the Museum of the City of New York. It was the opportunity to carefully examine more than six hundred of these dramatic works of art that initially stimulated my appreciation for them. Joseph Veach Noble, then director of the museum, encouraged me to undertake this study and granted permission for the photography. George Dembo of Gallery 9 came to my aid early by lending books and catalogs pertaining to these posters and through his good advice. George Theophiles of Miscellaneous Man was extremely helpful and deserves the gratitude of all World War I poster collectors for his pioneer work on the subject. When it became time to illustrate this volume, both Georges generously came forth with posters to add to my collection or with photographs and transparencies, as did Mary Ellen Meehan of Meehan Military Posters. Walt Reed of Illustration House provided several good posters, and Delinda Buie of the University of Louisville was helpful in sending lists of posters in her care. Kathleen Hjerter at the Humanities Research Center of the University of Texas most hospitably guided me through that extensive collection. Mary Bennett of the State Historical Society of Iowa was very cooperative in supplying several unusual posters, as was Terry Shargel of Posters Please in New York. Merrill Berman kindly lent me transparencies, and Arlen Ettinger of Guernsey's permitted me to borrow a number of posters to photograph. Susan Meyer graciously furnished transparencies of posters in her collection, and Bill Brennan entrusted me with his Liberty Loan buttons for photographing. Maurice Rickards, the first writer since the period to study the posters of World War I, gave excellent advice on shaping the manuscript, as well as photographs and transparencies of posters in his archive. George Roos, Eric Nelson, and Frank Yoshikane expertly did most of the photography for reproduction.

Mark Magowan good-naturedly commented on early versions of the manuscript, in the random order it was written. John Holland helped immeasurably in cutting and polishing the prose as the text neared completion, and Jamshid Hakim provided invaluable details on the influenza pandemic of 1918 from the medical literature. My editor Alan Axelrod was a tower of strength in the final days of putting the book together and placing the illustrations. Robin James expertly shepherded the manuscript through copyediting and typesetting, and Danielle Sacripante was especially diligent in preparing the mechanicals. Hope Koturo skillfully and patiently saw the book through its complex production stages. Nai Chang is responsible for the handsome design and cheerfully agreed to last-minute rearrangements. My wife Brenda repeatedly and lovingly put up with the excuse that ''once the book is finished'' things would get done around the house. To all these very generous friends and colleagues, I owe hearty thanks.

JAMES MONTGOMERY FLAGG
Hold On To Uncle Sam's Insurance, ca. 1919
20 × 30 inches
Susan E. Meyer

BIBLIOGRAPHY

A work of this nature is necessarily a retelling, and I have relied upon the work of others in shaping my own version of this period's history. Many of the key figures, such as Pershing, Creel, Rickenbacker, and Hoover, wrote their own memoirs; others, such as Roosevelt, Gibson, Seeger, York, and Andrew, told their stories in numerous articles and interviews. As much as possible I based my narrative on such first-person sources and let the participants tell this story in direct quotation. Many of the writings, public statements, translations, and statistics come from a seven-volume compilation of war-related documents that was issued by the American Legion in 1923. When I could find the right comments from people who had lived through the First World War, I refrained from making my own summaries for the reader.

For certain episodes, however, I have relied rather heavily on comprehensive studies done by others, whose works are cited in the bibliography. For background details on the sinking of the *Lusitania* I consulted Colin Simpson; for the story of the Lafayette Escadrille, Herbert Molloy Mason, Jr.; for Henry Ford's Peace Ship, Barbara Kraft; for the Field Service of the American Ambulance, Andrew Gray; for the Red Cross, Henry P. Davison; for the Liberty Loans, Labert St. Clair; and for the story of Sergeant York, Samuel K. Cowan. However, as the bibliography will show, I was also able to call upon firsthand accounts to amplify or enhance these episodes.

For a general coverage of the war, I followed S.L.A. Marshall, but details on specific events come from numerous reference works and firsthand accounts. I am especially indebted to David M. Kennedy for his thoroughly documented study of home-front America. The Brooklyn Public Library, which was the source of many publications cited, is to be praised for preserving so much material from the period.

Adams, James Truslow. *The March of Democracy.* Vol. 2, *From Civil War to World Power.* New York: Charles Scribner's Sons, 1933.

Adamson, Hans Christian. *Eddie Rickenbacker.* New York: The Macmillan Company, 1946.

Addams, Jane. *Peace and Bread in Time of War.* New York: The Macmillan Company, 1922.

Ades, Dawn, et al. *The 20th-Century Poster: Design of the Avant-Garde.* New York: Abbeville Press, Inc., 1984.

Allyn, Nancy E.H. *Broadsides and Posters from the National Archives.* Washington, D.C.: National Archives and Records Service, 1986.

Andrew, Abram Piatt, Stephen Galatti, et al. *Friends of France: The Field Service of the American Ambulance.* Boston: Houghton Mifflin Company, 1916.

Baker, Newton Diehl. *Why We Went to War.* New York: Harper and Brothers, 1936.

Baker, Ray Stannard, and William E. Dodd, eds. *The Public Papers of Woodrow Wilson.* 6 vols. New York: Harper and Brothers, 1925–27.

Barnicoat, John. *A Concise History of Posters.* New York: Oxford University Press, 1972.

Baruch, Bernard Mannes. *My Own Story.* New York: Holt, Rinehart, and Winston, 1957.

Bowen, Ezra. *Knights of the Air.* Epic of Flight series. New York: Time-Life, 1980.

Brandt, Nat. "Sergeant York." *American Heritage* vol. 32. (August/September 1981): pp. 56–64.

Brown, Malcolm, and Shirley Seaton. *Christmas Truce: The Western Front, December 1914.* New York: Hippocrene Books, 1984.

Bryan, C.D.B. *The National Air and Space Museum.* New York: Harry N. Abrams, Inc., 1979.

Clark, Alan. *Aces High: The War in the Air Over the Western Front, 1914–1918.* London: Weidenfeld and Nicolson, 1973.

Clark, Kenneth. *The Best of Aubrey Beardsley.* New York: Doubleday and Company, Inc., 1978.

Cochran, Thomas C., and Wayne Andrews, eds. *Concise Dictionary of American History.* New York: Charles Scribner's Sons, 1962.

Constantine, Mildred, and Alan M. Fern. *Word and Image.* New York: The Museum of Modern Art, 1968.

Cowan, Samuel Kinkade. *Sergeant York and His People.* New York: Funk and Wagnalls Company, 1922.

Creel, George. *How We Advertised America.* New York: Harper and Brothers, 1920.

Crowell, Benedict, and Robert Forrest Wilson. *The Giant Hand: Our Mobilization and Control of Industry and Natural Resources, 1917–1918.* New

Haven: Yale University Press, 1921.

Cummings, E. E. *The Enormous Room.* New York: Modern Library, 1934.

Darracott, Joseph. *The First World War in Posters.* New York: Dover Publications, Inc., 1974.

Darracott, Joseph, and Belinda Loftus. *First World War Posters.* London: Imperial War Museum, 1972.

Davidson, Margaret E. "Homefront: Hamburg, Iowa." *The Palimpsest* vol. 60. (July/August 1979): pp. 116–20.

Davison, Henry P. *The American Red Cross in the Great War.* New York: The Macmillan Company, 1919.

Dawson, Conningsby. *The Glory of the Trenches.* New York: Lane, 1918.

Dembo, George M. "The Statue of Liberty in Posters: Creation of an Amerian Icon." *P.S.: The Quarterly Journal of the Poster Society,* Winter 1985/1986, pp. 18–21.

Derr, Nancy. "The Babel Proclamation." *The Palimpsest* vol. 60. (July/August 1979): pp. 98–115.

Downey, Fairfax. *Portrait of an Era as Drawn by C.D. Gibson.* New York: Charles Scribner's Sons, 1936.

Dreisziger, N.F.D., ed. *Mobilization for Total War.* Waterloo, Canada: Wilfrid Laurier University Press, 1981.

Empey, Arthur Guy. *"Over the Top" by an American Soldier Who Went.* New York: Putnam's, 1917.

Farr, Finis. *Rickenbacker's Luck: An American Life.* Boston: Houghton

Mifflin Company, 1979.

Gallatin, Albert Eugene. *Art and the Great War.* New York: E.P. Dutton and Company, 1919.

Gallo, Max. *The Poster in History.* New York: American Heritage Publishing Company, Inc., 1974.

Garraty, John A., and Peter Gay. *The Columbia History of the World.* New York: Harper & Row, Publishers, 1972.

Genthe, Charles V. *American War Narratives, 1917–1918.* New York: David Lewis, 1969.

Gilbert, Cass, et al. *Victory Dinner and Dance of the Division of Pictorial Publicity.* New York: Division of Pictorial Publicity, 1919.

Gilbo, Patrick F. *The American Red Cross.* New York: Harper & Row, Publishers, 1981.

Graves, Robert. *Good-bye to All That.* Garden City, N.Y.: Doubleday and Company, Inc., 1957.

Gray, Andrew. "American Field Service." *American Heritage* vol. 26. (December 1974): pp. 58–63.

Gregory, Ross. *The Origins of American Intervention in the First World War.* New York: W.W. Norton & Company, Inc., 1971.

Griffiths, William R. *The Great War.* West Point Military History Series. Wayne, N.J.: Avery Publishing Group, Inc., 1986.

Guest, Edgar Albert. *Collected Verse of Edgar A. Guest.* Chicago: Contemporary Books, 1934.

Hall, James Norman, C.B. Nordhoff, and E.G. Hamilton. *The Lafayette Flying Corps.* Boston: Houghton Mifflin Company, 1920.

Harbord, James G. *The American Army in France, 1917–1919.* Boston: Little Brown, 1936.

Hershey, Burnet. *The Odyssey of Henry Ford and the Great Peace Ship.* New York: Taplinger Publishing Company. 1967.

Hoover, Herbert Clark. *The Memoirs of Herbert Hoover: Years of Adventure, 1874–1920.* New York: The Macmillan Company, 1951.

Hopkins, Joseph G.E., ed. *Concise Dictionary of American Biography.* New York: Charles Scribner's Sons, 1977.

Horne, Charles F., and Walter F. Austin, eds. *Source Records of the Great War.* 7 vols. Washington, D.C.: National Alumni/The American Legion, 1923.

House, Edward Mandell. *The Intimate Papers of Colonel House Arranged as a Narrative by Charles Seymour.* 4 vols. Boston: Houghton Mifflin Company, 1926–28.

Hoyt, Edwin P. "Predator Beyond all Rules." *Military History,* February 1985, pp. 34–41.

Ions, Edmund. *Woodrow Wilson: The Politics of Peace and War.* New York: American Heritage Press, 1977.

Kiehl, David W., et al. *American Art Posters of the 1890s.* New York: The Metropolitan Museum of Art, 1987.

Kennedy, David M. *Over Here: The First World War and American Society.* New York: Oxford University Press, 1980.

Kloster, Donald E., and Edward C. Ezell. "American Posters and the First World War." *AB Bookman's Weekly* vol. 79. (June 29, 1987): pp. 2879–84.

Kraft, Barbara S. *The Peace Ship: Henry Ford's Pacifist Adventure in the First World War.* New York: The Macmillan Company, 1978.

Langer, William L. *Gas and Flame in World War I.* 1919. Reprint. New York: Alfred A. Knopf, 1965.

Liddell Hart, Basil Henry. *The Real War, 1914–1918.* Boston: Little Brown, 1930.

Lord, Walter. *The Good Years: From 1900 to the First World War.* New York: Harper and Brothers, 1960.

Ludwig, Coy. *Maxfield Parrish.* New York: Watson-Guptill Publications, 1973.

Lyons, Eugene. *Herbert Hoover: A Biography.* Garden City, N.Y.: Doubleday and Company, Inc., 1948.

McAdoo, William Gibbs. *Crowded Years.* Boston: Houghton Mifflin Company, 1931.

Marshall, S.L.A. *The American Heritage History of World War I.* New York: American Heritage Publishing Company, Inc., 1964.

Mason, Herbert Molloy, Jr. *The Lafayette Escadrille.* New York: Random House, Inc., 1964.

Meyer, Susan E. *America's Great Illustrators.* New York: Harry N. Abrams, Inc., 1978.

———. *James Montgomery Flagg.* New York: Watson-Guptill Publications, 1974.

Mock, James R., and Cedric Larson. *Words That Won the War: The Story of the Committee on Public Information, 1917–1919.* Princeton, N.J.: Princeton University Press, 1939.

Morison, Samuel Eliot. *The Oxford History of the American People.* New York: Oxford University Press, 1965.

Morris, Richard B., ed. *Encyclopedia of American History.* New York: Harper and Brothers, 1961.

O'Connor, Richard. *Black Jack Pershing.* New York: Doubleday and Company, Inc., 1961.

Palmer, Frederick. *Newton D. Baker: America at War.* 2 vols. New York: Dodd, Mead, 1931.

Parkinson, Roger. *Origins of World War One.* New York: Putnam, 1970.

Pennell, Joseph. *Joseph Pennell's Liberty-Loan Poster: A Textbook for Artists and Amateurs, Governments and Teachers and Printers.* Philadelphia: J.B. Lippincott, 1918.

Pershing, John Joseph. *My Experiences in the World War.* 2 vols. New York: Frederick A. Stokes, 1931.

Phillips, Charles. "Images of War." *The Palimpsest* vol. 59. (November/December 1978): pp. 176–81.

Pitz, Henry C. *200 Years of American Illustration.* New York: Random House, Inc., 1977.

Reed, Walt, and Roger Reed. *The Illustrator in America, 1880–1980.* New York: Madison Square Press, Inc., 1984.

Rhodes, Richard. *The Making of the Atomic Bomb.* New York: Simon and Schuster, 1986.

Rickards, Maurice. *Posters of the First World War.* New York: Walker & Company, 1968.

———. *The Rise and Fall of the Poster.* New York: McGraw-Hill Book Company, 1971.

Rickards, Maurice, and Michael Moody. *The First World War: Ephemera, Mementoes, and Documents.* London: Jupiter Books, 1975.

Rickenbacker, Edward V. *Fighting the Flying Circus.* New York: Frederick A. Stokes, 1919.

St. Clair, Labert. *The Story of the Liberty Loans.* Washington, D.C.: James William Bryan Press, 1919.

Schau, Michael. *J. C. Leyendecker.* New York: Watson-Guptill Publications, 1974.

Schnessel, S. Michael. *Jessie Willcox Smith.* New York: Thomas Y. Crowell, 1977.

Seeger, Alan. *Poems.* New York: Charles Scribner's Sons, 1917.

Shadwell, Wendy. "The Statue of Liberty: A Century in the Graphic Arts." *Imprint* vol. 10. (Spring 1985): pp. 20–27.

Simpson, Colin. *The Lusitania.* Boston: Little Brown, 1973.

Splete, Allen P., and Marilyn D. Splete. *Frederic Remington: Selected Letters.* New York: Abbeville Press, Inc., 1988.

Stacey, Robert. *The Canadian Poster Book: 100 Years of the Poster in Canada.* Toronto: Methuen Publications, 1979.

Steichen, Edward. *A Life in Photography.* Garden City, N.Y.: Doubleday and Company, Inc., 1963.

Taylor, A.J.P. *The First World War.* New York: Capricorn Books, 1972.

———. *The Last of Old Europe.* New York: Quadrangle, 1976.

Thayer, William Roscoe. *Theodore Roosevelt: An Intimate Biography.* Boston: Houghton Mifflin Company, 1919.

Theofiles, George. *American Posters of World War I.* New York: Dafran House Publishers, Inc., 1973.

Tuchman, Barbara W. *The Guns of August.* New York: The Macmillan Company, 1962.

———. *The Proud Tower: A Portrait of the World Before the War, 1890–1914.* New York: The Macmillan Company, 1966.

———. *The Zimmermann Telegram.* New York: Viking Press, 1958.

Vaughn, Stephen. *Holding Fast the Inner Lines: Democracy, Nationalism and the Committee on Public Information.* Chapel Hill, N.C.: University of North Carolina Press, 1980.

Weill, Alain. *The Poster: A Worldwide Survey and History.* Boston: G.K. Hall & Co., 1985.

INDEX